FINGERPRINT

The Beauty of Numbers in Scripture and Creation

COMPACT EDITION

David J Lambourn

Copyright © 2023 David J Lambourn

All rights reserved.

ISBN: 9798391468004

DEDICATION

to Brian Lambourn

CONTENTS

Introduction   *1*

1   One: The Number of Identity   6

2   Two: The Number of Relationship   33

3   Three: The Number of Fulfilment   67

4   Four: The Number of Life   91

5   Five: The Number of Order   121

6   Six: The Number of Dominion   146

7   Seven: The Number of Perfection   166

8   Infinity and Beyond   196

Endnotes   *231*

Picture Acknowledgements   *233*

ACKNOWLEDGMENTS

I would like to acknowledge with profound thanks the constant support of my family, friends and Hope Community Church. Without them this volume would not have been possible.

Introduction

> 'Consider the lilies of the field, how they grow: they neither toil nor spin, yet I tell you, even Solomon in all his glory was not arrayed like one of these.' (Matt. 6:28-29)

This famous verse, in the heart of the Sermon on the Mount, gives us a breathtaking glimpse not only of the boundless provision that God has for each one of us, but also of the incredible pride and pleasure he takes in the natural world. In this verse Jesus is inviting us to step back and contemplate the intricate but fragile beauty that we see in a flower and reflect on the amazing extent of God's bountiful goodness towards us. It is one of a great many instances throughout the Bible where plants are used to teach us vital spiritual truths.

In considering lilies, then, or other flowers, we might appreciate not only their beautiful colours and scents but also the amazing ways in which God has structured them. A lily has three petals, for instance, a buttercup has five, a delphinium has eight, ragwort, thirteen, an aster, twenty-one, a daisy, thirty-four, and a Michaelmas daisy, eighty-nine. These figures are not accidental or mere whims of nature, but correspond to a sequence of numbers called the Fibonacci series, in which each number in the series is created by adding the two previous ones together. Thus 1+1 = 2, 2+1 = 3, 3+2 = 5, 5+3 = 8, producing the series 1, 1, 2, 3, 5, 8, 13, 21, 34, 55, 89, 144, and so on. The proportions between these numbers appear to be written across large swathes of the natural world and many similar intricate mathematical structures seem to be hard-wired into the design of the entire created realm, from the tiniest atom to the largest galaxy.

If numbers and patterns are inscribed throughout the universe, we should not be taken aback to find them appearing in scripture in highly significant ways. For a book that has been apparently 'randomly' put together by forty different authors, working in different cultures at different periods of history, the Bible exhibits extraordinarily high levels of organisation. Indeed, God's word contains the DNA of the Trinity embedded within it at every level.

For some, this may come as a surprise. We might expect a preoccupation with numbers to be a symptom of the modern world. Instead, we are talking about an era without calculators, digital timers, spreadsheets, sales targets, computers, or the priesthood of number-crunching economists, modellers and forecasters that supervises our lives today. Scripture, however, opens the way up into its own highly ordered world, once we begin to explore in depth.

FINGERPRINT

Above and below: The petals of many flowers follow the proportions laid down by the Fibonacci series, creating strikingly beautiful arrays to the human eye. We seem to be hard-wired in our brain to respond emotionally to such mathematical designs, reflecting the image of our Creator.

Indeed, everything in the Bible suggests that God is passionate about design, numbers and proportions, and we should be as well. At one level this was to be a simple, everyday matter. The Levites in the temple were to be concerned with 'all measures of quantity or size' (1 Chron. 23:29) and the Israelites to be faithful in 'measures of length or weight or quantity' (Lev. 19:35). We are reminded that unequal weights and unequal measures are an 'abomination' to the LORD (Prov. 20:10).

At the same time, something bigger is being expressed in this concern for exact proportion and balance. This is particularly evident in the precision with which God spells out the dimensions for the tabernacle, where his glory was to dwell. He tells Moses after describing the fittings to '*see to it* that you make them *according to the blueprint* for them that you were shown on the mountain' (Ex. 25:40 CEV). Likewise, when David begins to contemplate the temple which was to follow, he says that 'all this … I have in writing as a result of the LORD's hand on me, and he enabled me to understand *all the details of the plan*' (1 Chron. 28:19 NIV). And before the angel shows Ezekiel the detailed measurements for a future temple, he is told, '*set your heart* upon all that I shall show you', and, 'declare *all that you see* to the house of Israel' (Ezek. 40:4). The importance of these outlines goes beyond mere aesthetic beauty. As the writer to the Hebrews suggests, they were seeking to make an earthly copy of a heavenly original (Heb. 8:5; 9:23-4).

This attempt to reflect higher cosmic realities runs as a thread throughout scripture. Some four thousand years ago, Abraham was told to cast his eyes upwards and count the stars (a seemingly impossible task). The naked eye can at most distinguish a few thousand of these. Yet Abraham is later told that their number is comparable to the number of grains of sand on the seashore, a potentially staggering quantity that runs into countless trillions (Gen. 15:5; 22:17). Only today, with the advent of modern telescopes, have we grasped the astonishing accuracy of this comparison. God knows the total because he actually counts and labels the stars individually (Ps. 147:4; Is. 40:26)!

As we look around us each day, the structure of the universe advertises exuberantly the artistry and wisdom of its Maker. We are reminded of this repeatedly in the Psalms:

> The heavens declare the glory of God;
> the skies proclaim the work of his hands.
> Day after day they pour forth speech;
> night after night they reveal knowledge.
> (Ps 19:1-2 NIV)

The earth, likewise, reveals the same precision engineering. God asks Job,

> "Where were you when I laid the foundation of the earth?
> Tell me, if you have understanding.
> Who determined its measurements—
> surely you know!
> Or who stretched the line upon it?"
> (Job 38:4-5)

This amazing sense of structure is also apparent in other spheres as well. One remarkable example is the realm of music. We have already mentioned the Fibonacci series (1, 1, 2, 3, 5, 8, 13 and so on) which governs so many things in creation

Music of the Spheres

The Greek mathematician and philosopher Pythagoras, observing that the proportions between musical notes were similar to those between planetary orbits, concluded that each heavenly body must 'sing' its own note: the so-called 'music of the spheres' (an idea later revived by the Christian astronomer Johannes Kepler).

In recent times, this idea has taken on a new lease of life. Astronomers working at Cambridge University discovered in 2003 that the black hole in the centre of the Perseus cluster, 250 million light years away, was emitting a B flat, 57 octaves below middle C or one million, billion times lower than the lowest sound that the human ear can hear. The lowest sounds our ears can detect have a frequency of one twentieth of a second. The Perseus black hole's sound waves, by contrast, are thought to have a frequency of 10 million years!

Praise him, sun and moon, praise him, all you shining stars! (Ps.148:3)

---

from the proportions of the Ark of the Covenant and the altar in the Tabernacle to the movement and spacing between the planets of the solar system (Venus, for example, goes round the sun 13 times for every 8 orbits of the earth). This same series also appears to govern the numerical relationships between the different notes that make up a chord, the basic unit of musical harmony, as the following diagram shows:

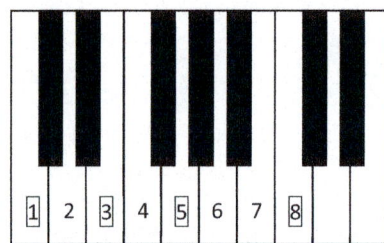

Given that the true and only final purpose of music is to declare God's glory and to offer him worship and praise (Rev. 14:2-3), there is a sense, therefore, in which it seems to encode God's order within the realm of sound. Other significant musical numbers such as 3 (the number of notes in a triad), 7 (the number of notes in a major scale) and 12 (the number of notes in a chromatic scale) all have critical importance in the Bible.

As with chords and melodies, so also shapes and numbers can have different characters and personalities of their own. So much so, indeed, that Revelation talks about 'those who had conquered the beast and its image and *the number of its name*' (15:2). The idea of conquering a *number* might seem extraordinary to us, but it is essential to understanding the drama of Revelation. Not only can numbers reflect different aspects of God's nature and being, but they can also imply rebellion against him.

That numbers can take a real slice in the action can be deduced from the fact that the Hebrew verb *saphar* ('to count') can also mean to 'tell', 'declare' or 'recount': it is the root for the related words for 'scribe', 'letter' and 'book'. In other words, rather than being uninvolved bystanders, numbers can be central protagonists in the plot. And if they reveal particular qualities in God, they can also have a direct application in our own lives.

The author of the laws of mathematics and physics is the same God who has designed you and me to live in a personal relationship with him. The universe is intricately constructed like a vast living organism, and this complex detail also appears in the Bible in a multitude of forms, much of it relevant directly to our relationship with the one who made us. Exploring these patterns gives us not only a fuller appreciation of our wonderfully meticulous Creator, but also affords an opportunity to bring deeper levels of his order and balance into our own lives.

Within this framework it is important to notice that Biblical numbers are dynamic, not static in nature: each number contains the blueprint of the next number within the series inside itself. Thus, as we shall see, 'one' when applied to God already carries the implication of 'two', while 'two' carries the basis of 'three', and so on. Expressions such as 'when **two** or **three** are gathered in my name' (Matt. 18:20) are very common in scripture. Numbers are as much about 'becoming' as they are about 'being', and each one in turn represents a different level of completeness.

We do, of course, have to recognise the limitation of any investigation into numerical patterns or geometric shapes. Some would prefer to steer clear of any such discussion because of its associations with occult practices and the New Age. Many would be concerned that it distracts from the plain message of scripture and places too much focus on matters of peripheral importance.

But to dismiss such things out of hand is to miss some priceless treasures. Look at a snowflake under a microscope and you will see something completely new about it that the unaided natural eye will never perceive. It is God who 'reveals deep and hidden things' and 'knows what is in the darkness' (Dan. 2:22), and it is he who has commissioned us to hunt diligently for such hidden secrets. Job expresses this beautifully when he declares:

> "Man puts his hand to the flinty rock
> and overturns mountains by the roots.
> He cuts out channels in the rocks,
> and his eye sees every precious thing.
> He dams up the streams so that they do not trickle,
> and the thing that is hidden he brings out to light."
> (Job 28:9-11)

At the same time, we should not become so preoccupied with numbers that we miss the beauty of the story itself. There are no hidden subtexts that run contrary to the words and sentences that we can read on the surface of scripture. Certainly, there are remarkable patterns that can be unearthed at a deeper level: many remarkable discoveries have been made, for example, by calculating the numerical values of words or by studying skip sequences between letters in the Hebrew text. But there is always a danger in trying to fit God into an algorithm or a scheme. Like

> So Moses numbered them according to the word of the LORD, just as he had been commanded.
> (Numbers 3.16 NASB)

a quantum particle, every time that we try to pin him down, he eludes us. And yet the plain message of the gospel which is essential for each one of us is so simple that even a child can understand it.

In this sense, while numbers provide a useful tool for understanding God's purposes, they can never go beyond that: there is a measure of unpredictability in scripture, just as there is in nature, and there are always exceptions which refuse to be nailed down by human reasoning, or our desire to find regular patterns. In the end, God is beyond number and design just as he is beyond time and space, and we need a degree of humility in the face of that.

For this reason, I would ask the reader the weigh the evidence presented here very carefully. Some of the examples quoted, for instance with regard to chapter and verse numbers (which were not added until centuries after the Bible had been completed) might be criticised as falling into the category of 'felicitous coincidences' with no ultimate significance. However, I would point out in their defence that, in God's providence and foresight, so-called 'coincidences' have a habit of arranging themselves in such a persistent array that they end up looking rather deliberate and pre-planned. God knows the end from the beginning, and sometimes likes to leave us intrigued.

> "But even the hairs of your head are all numbered."
> (Matthew 10.30)

Whatever the potential pitfalls, it is my hope that every reader would be able to take something away from this book that will enrich their understanding of God and the extraordinary handbook that he has given us (quotations from which are taken, unless otherwise indicated, from the English Standard Version). As we embark on this adventure of discovery, let us open our hearts to the one who has a specific purpose and plan for each one of us, for whom no detail is trivial or unimportant, and who is longing to reveal more of himself to us each day.

Chapter One

One

The Number of Identity

1. There is **one** God

The most famous verse in Judaism is the so-called *Shema* ('Hear O Israel: The LORD our God, the LORD is **one**', Deuteronomy 6:4). In synagogue services orthodox Jews take utmost care in pronouncing each syllable (particularly the word '*one*') and cover their eyes with their hand while doing so. It is the first Bible verse that a Jewish child has to learn and, traditionally, the last words that are spoken before death.

The Bible consistently affirms, throughout Old and New Testaments, that there is only **one** true God, the creator of the entire universe (Gen. 1:1; Acts 17:24). All other beings that we might consider as God are futile projections of our own mind. The entire universe belongs to him (Deut. 10:14), and he fills it (Jer. 23:24) and controls it (Eph. 1:11), even down to the level of apparently 'random' events (Prov. 16:33). His greatness is unsearchable (Ps. 145:3) and therefore our human minds can only capture the most fleeting glimpse of his glory and power (Is. 55:8-9). He is unlimited by spatial dimensions (John 4:24) to the extent that even the entire universe cannot contain him (1 Kings 8:27).

As a unique and transcendent being, God cannot be exactly compared with anything else. Therefore, in revealing himself to Israel, God defines **himself by himself**. We discover this in the conversation he has with Moses from the midst of a burning bush on Mount Sinai, when he commissions him to lead Israel out of servitude in Egypt:

> ಸಿಲ್ಸ
>
> But Moses said to God, "Who am I that I should go to Pharaoh and bring the children of Israel out of Egypt? ... If I come to the people of Israel and say to them, 'The God of your fathers has sent me to you,' and they ask me, 'What is his name?' what shall I say to them?" (Ex. 3:11,13)
>
>

Here, now is God's reply:

> ❧☙
>
> 'God said to Moses, "I AM WHO I AM." And he said, "Say this to the people of Israel:
> 'I AM has sent me to you.'" (Ex. 3:14)
>
> ❧☙

Notice here that God's revelation of his own nature as '**I am who I am**' comes shortly after Moses' question '*Who am I?*' The way we see ourselves today can perhaps be summed up by the famous declaration of René Descartes in 1637, 'I think, therefore I am'. We define ourselves in terms of ourselves.

However, the Biblical answer is the complete opposite of this. It is, rather, 'I think because **he is**.'

Our consciousness is ultimately dependent on his being, and therefore if we are to discover our true identity, we need to recognise that it springs out of his. We are created in the image of God, and therefore it is he who defines us, not we who define ourselves. He is the source of all identity and all purpose.

The words '**I am who I am**' spawn a whole network of possible associations which we might lay out as follows:

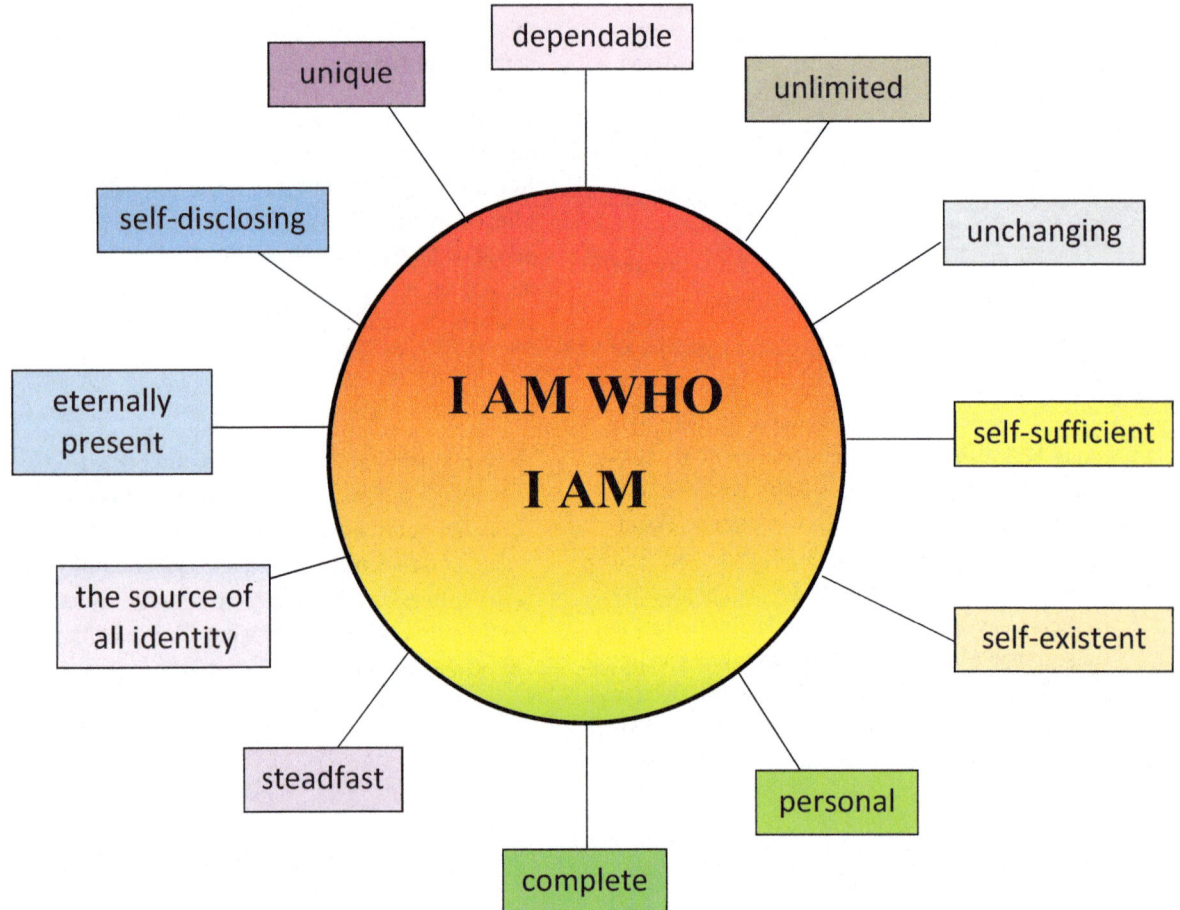

Because our identity is bound up inextricably with that of God himself, many of the qualities shown in the diagram can impact our own lives in a powerful way. As with Moses, God is actively seeking a relationship with each one of us and can offer us all the purpose, meaning and direction that we currently lack. He longs for godly offspring (Mal. 2:10; John 1:12) who can know him as Father (Jer. 3:19). Many of us are insecure in our identities and ultimately we can only find our security in the one who is completely secure in his. We find our completeness in him.

It is essential, therefore, to understand our individual purpose in life. We have been made in God's image (Gen. 1:26), created to be his representatives on earth (Ps. 115:16). We are therefore called to be like him in every way (Lev. 19:2; Matt. 5:48; Luke 6:36). We need to see what the Father is doing and copy (John 5:19). He is on our side (Ps. 56:9; Rom. 8:31); he has wonderful plans for our lives (Jer. 29:11-12) and his righteousness lifts us up (Ps. 89:16). A deficient view of God stunts the way we the way we see ourselves and how we live our lives.

2. There is **one** set of laws governing the universe

Because there is **one** God, it is natural that he should establish **one** fundamental principle to govern the whole universe. Rather than one rule for 'up there' and another for 'down here', he intended the whole creation to work harmoniously within a fixed set of laws. This comes across clearly in the book of Job:

> 'Do you know the ordinances of the heavens?
> Can you establish their rule on the earth?'
> (Job 38:33)

Likewise the Psalms show us how God's order reflects his constancy and dependability:

> Forever, O LORD, your word
> is firmly fixed in the heavens.
> Your faithfulness endures to all generations;
> you have established the earth,
> and it stands fast. (Ps. 119:89-90)

In Proverbs we see the idea developed further. Here a single principle of order, described as God's 'wisdom', is portrayed as a living personality, penetrating every aspect of creation and every field of human endeavour. These characteristics are particularly apparent in Chapter 8, where they spread out into a variety of different realms, as the diagram on the next page shows (quotations taken from the original edition of the New International Version):

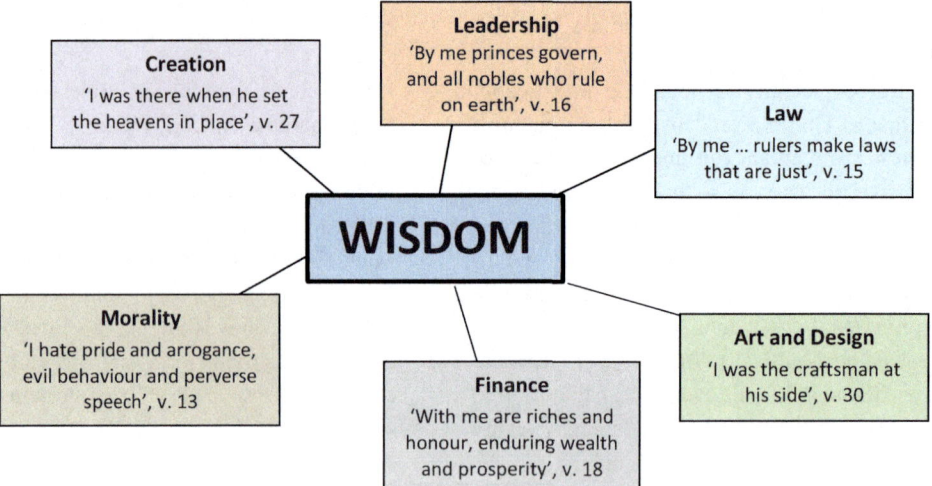

Elsewhere we see how this same principle of 'wisdom' underlies all aspects of human creativity. In Exodus 31, for instance, God tells Moses,

> ℰ☙
>
> See I have chosen Bezalel ... and I have filled him with the Spirit of God, with **wisdom**, with understanding, with knowledge and with all kinds of skills – to make artistic designs for work in gold, silver and bronze, to cut and set stones, to work in wood, and to engage in all kinds of crafts. (v. 2-5 NIV)
>
> ℰ☙

This gift of God seems to work at every level: the same Hebrew word is used for the women who spin goat's hair for the tabernacle (Ex. 35:26) right up to Daniel gaining 'learning and skill in all literature and **wisdom**' at the highest level in Babylon (Dan. 1:17). In other words, it runs consistently from kitchen up to university.

Put another way, everyday human activity reflects a much larger set of laws ordering the whole of reality. Every gift given to us reveals the one God who has set these universal decrees in place.

But God does not merely establish these laws and then retreat from the scene. Rather, he seeks a direct relationship with each one of us which far outstrips in importance the vastness of the created order around us. This is apparent, for example, if we look at God's covenant promises to Israel in Jeremiah:

> ℰ☙
>
> Thus says the LORD,
> who gives the sun for light by day
> and the fixed order of the moon and the stars for light by night,
> who stirs up the sea so that its waves roar—
> the LORD of hosts is his name:
> "If this fixed order departs
> from before me, declares the Lord,
> then shall the offspring of Israel cease
> from being a nation before me for ever." ...
> "If the heavens above can be measured,
> and the foundations of the earth below can be explored,
> then I will cast off all the offspring of Israel
> for all that they have done,
> declares the LORD." (Jer. 31:35-37)
>
>

Nothing could be more reassuring to Israel, and by extension to all God's people. However much we go off track, God has underwritten his promises to us with nothing less than the laws of physics themselves!

There is an extraordinary link, therefore, between ourselves and objects on the very largest or the very smallest scale. We are all governed by **one** fundamental principle of order, which connects everything together within a vast, divinely woven tapestry. As we noticed in the introduction, God tells Abraham to compare his offspring both to the number of stars in the sky at one level of magnitude, or to the number of grains of sand on the seashore at the opposite end of the scale.

This clearly points to a common factor connecting the very large to the very small. But what might this be?

One of the climactic moments in scripture is John's jaw-dropping vision of the throne room in heaven, in which God sits in incomparable splendour, surrounded by four angelic creatures, seven spirits (either archangels, or, more likely, a sevenfold manifestation of the Holy Spirit) and twenty-four other thrones on which elders are seated. Around him a fully circular rainbow radiates out from the throne (a rare sight on earth, normally only visible from aircraft). This might be pictured very crudely in the diagram below:

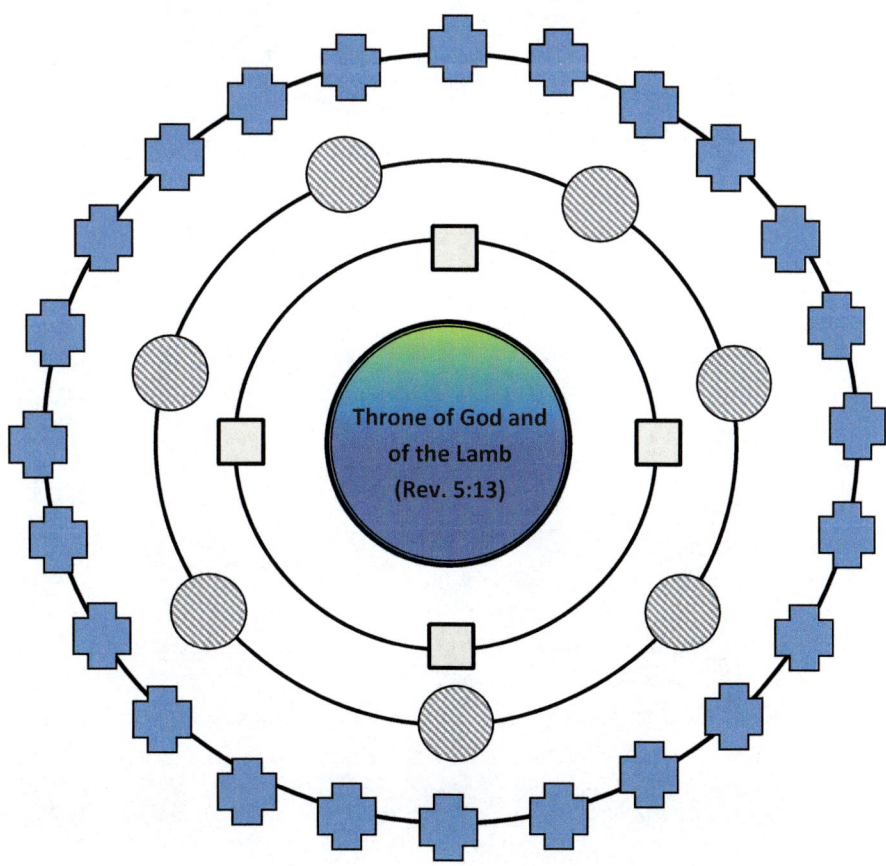

Above: A circular rainbow photographed in Thailand
Below: A picture of the Victoria Falls taken in January 2013

It is striking that both the rainbow and the worshippers around the throne appear to be arranged in concentric circles. When Ezekiel has a vision of the heavenly throne and the four living creatures in the Old Testament, he is also struck by the sight of such interlocking rings (or 'a wheel within a wheel', Ezek. 1:16), while Daniel also sees fiery wheels (Dan. 7:9).

Given that this is the control room for the entire cosmos, it would not be totally surprising to see this same pattern repeated at every level of existence, from the smallest to the largest. Consider, for example, the atom, the fundamental building block of the universe, where we see electrons orbiting around a nucleus of protons and neutrons:

At a different level of scale, we can marvel at the wonders of the solar system, where every planet is assigned its own position and orbit around a central hub:

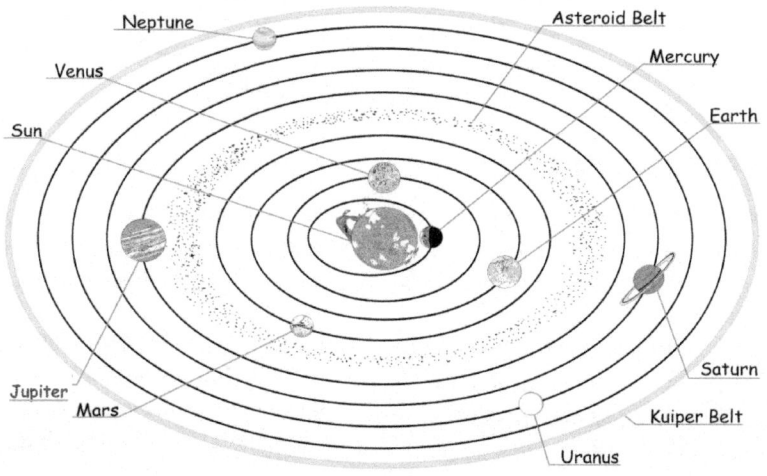

It is also possible to see the same patterns embedded within the Bible. There is also a striking interpretation of scripture by R. A. McGough,[1] for example, which also sees it arranged as a series of concentric rings corresponding with the 22 letters of the Hebrew alphabet:

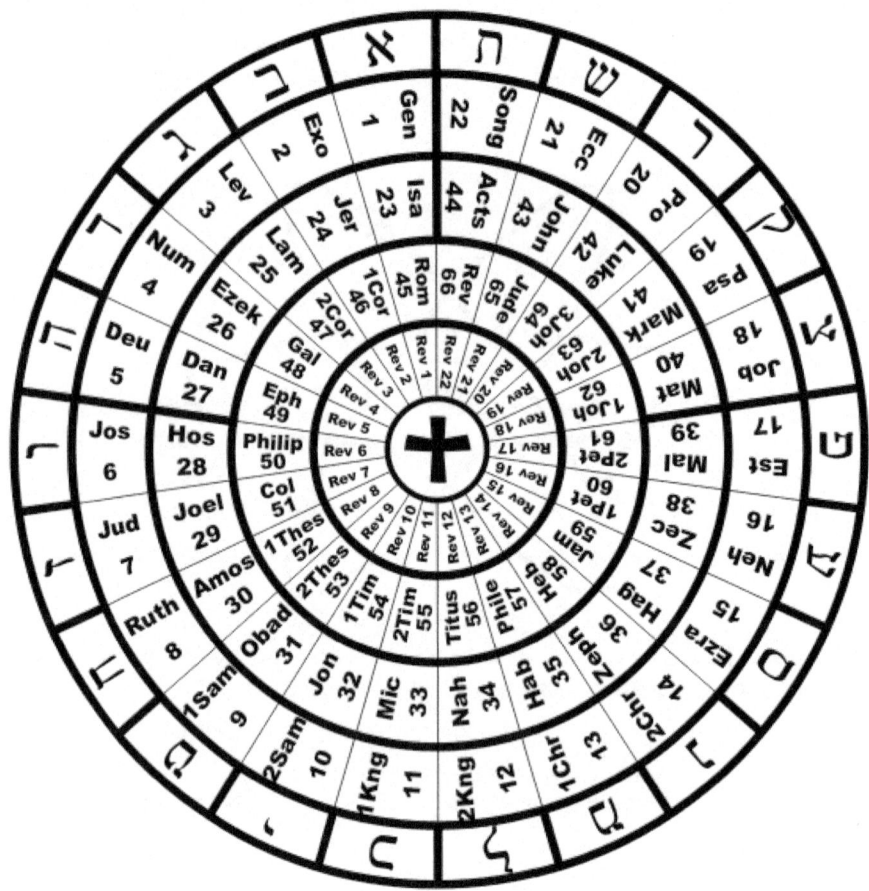

Given the possibility of seeing God's Word arranged in this manner, we might remember that a prominent feature of the Revelation account is the opening of a scroll, which determines the outworking of the end of human history. A scroll by its nature is a piece of parchment wrapped in a spiral. The structure of Revelation is itself unusual as it seems to spiral outwards from a central hub in a series of ever-increasing circles, pointing, maybe, to a larger heavenly pattern. It is from a different kind of spiral, a whirlwind, that God reveals himself to Job (Job 38:1).

Spiral formations are prominent at every level of creation from galaxies containing billions of stars down to the structure of DNA. It is the logic of a particular kind of spiral which determines why the number of petals on many plants follow the Fibonacci series, as we saw in the introduction.

ONE: THE NUMBER OF IDENTITY

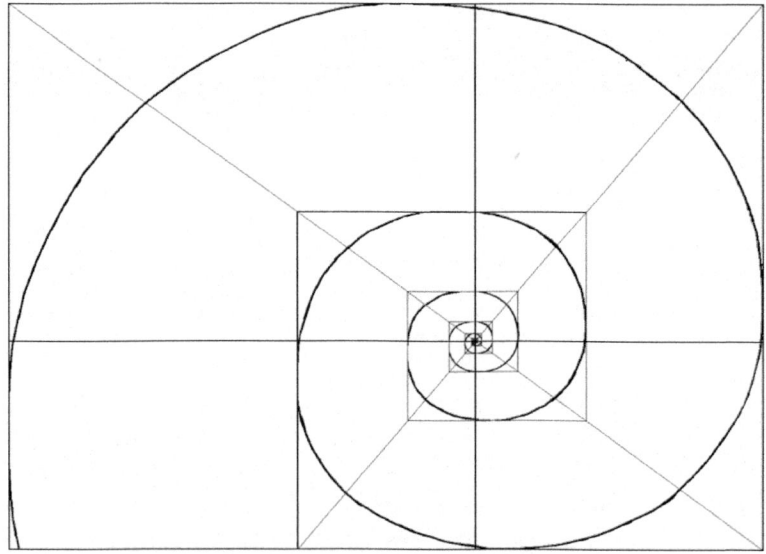

If we compare the structure of a natural object such as a nautilus shell, we will see a very close similarity:

Many great works of art can also be shown to have followed these proportions: they seem to be deeply embedded in the human spirit.

If one thing stands out above all in these examples, it is that God has arranged things in hierarchies that fan out from a central hub. The very word 'hierarchy' is striking in that it literally means 'the rule of priests' (the 24 elders around the throne in Revelation 6 correspond to the 24 priestly orders described in 1 Chronicles 24). We can see such hierarchies spanning every aspect of existence from the realm of subatomic particles, up through the structure of living things, to the black hole in the centre of the Milky Way. There is a nucleus at the core of every system, and that nucleus is a representation of God himself.

Above: The Glory Window in the Chapel of Thanks-Giving in Dallas, Texas, designed by Gabriel Loire and inspired by the structure of the nautilus shell.
Below: Spiral Galaxy NGC 1232, taken by the European Southern Observatory in September 1998.

Music and the Divine Order

As we saw earlier, one area in which God's creation principles seem to be fully expressed is the realm of music. When we hear a musical note we are not hearing a single tone but a whole spectrum of tones projected out from the original, which influence the quality and nature of the sound. This is because each note generates a reflection of itself in its own image, producing a kind of 'family tree'. The result is a gradually unfolding spiral, like ripples spreading out on a pond, which is called the 'overtone series', with the number of tones doubling at each octave:

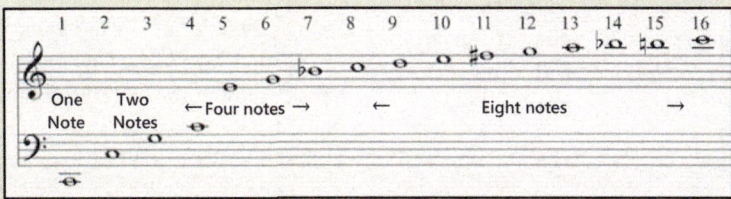

In this case the second note in the series vibrates at twice the frequency of the second, the third at three times its original frequency, and so on, such that all the notes are related by simple geometric ratios:

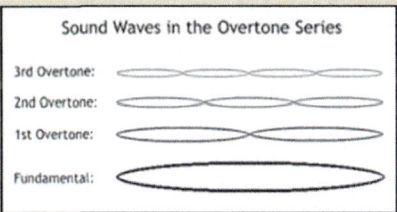

Before the invention of valves in the nineteenth century, certain instruments (such as the trumpet) were limited to playing only this or a related series of notes by using different levels of air pressure (which is why there are only five notes in certain trumpet fanfares, such as 'The Last Post').

Yet in the Bible it is the trumpet which of all instruments plays a key role, as a symbol of God's rulership and dominion. It is the sound of the trumpet that is used to gather Israel in the wilderness, to summon Moses up Mount Sinai, to proclaim the Year of Jubilee, to cause the walls of Jericho to collapse, and to warn of impending disaster. In the New Testament it is the trumpet that will announce when Jesus returns, and the inauguration of God's kingdom on earth.

Moreover, just as everything in the universe finds its value and significance in its relationship to God, so in a piece of music the function of each note is defined by its relationship to the fundamental or 'tonic', which acts as a nucleus around which everything else revolves. It is where a piece normally begins, where it ends, and everything in the piece is determined in relation to it.

This is what is meant by the 'key' of a musical composition. A piece, for example, is said to be 'in C' if it starts on C, finishes on C and every event and deviation in the piece is measured relative to that foundational note. It permeates and pervades every aspect of the piece.

There is a beautiful parallel here when the believer is said to be 'in Christ'. It means that we are bound up with him and live our whole lives in relationship to him. He is our beginning and our end, the ground and purpose of our being. He is the 'key' in which the whole of our lives find meaning.

*Then the seventh angel blew his **trumpet**, and there were loud voices in heaven, saying, "The kingdom of the world has become the kingdom of our Lord and of his Christ, and he shall reign for ever and ever." (Rev. 11:15)*

To view this in more personal terms, we might say that God has arranged objects and elements into families. The highest revelation of God in scripture is as 'Father', from whom 'every family in heaven and on earth is named' (Eph. 3:15).

Every aspect of human culture and society around us seems to reflect these regular 'family' structures, as is apparent in the realm of music (see the box on the previous page). But they act as mirrors for much wider physical laws of nature.

One example can be seen in the way living cells divide. From progressive division of the nucleus of an embryonic stem cell into 2, 4, 8, 16 and so on an entire organism can be generated, each part gradually specialising into its own unique and individual functions.

This provides a helpful model for the growth and development of the church. Paul, for example, uses this picture in his letter to Corinth to show how each believer performs a unique and essential function within the **one** body. The Spirit of God becomes the means wellspring through which the life, fellowship and activity of the church is constantly nurtured and enhanced:

To each is given the manifestation of the Spirit for the common good. For
- to one is given through the Spirit the utterance of wisdom,
- to another the utterance of knowledge according to the same Spirit,
- to another faith by the same Spirit,
- to another gifts of healing by the one Spirit,
- to another the working of miracles,
- to another prophecy,
- to another the ability to distinguish between spirits,
- to another various kinds of tongues,
- to another the interpretation of tongues.

All these are empowered by one and the same Spirit, who apportions to each one individually as he wills. ... As it is, there are many parts, yet **one** body. (1 Cor. 12:7-11, 20)

In short, we can see that everything in the universe is arranged in hierarchies, from the smallest to the largest, through the wisdom of the **one** God, in whom 'we live and move and have our being' (Acts 17:28).

3. There is **one** Mediator between God and mankind

So far we have seen how God has expressed himself through universal laws and structures which spring from deep within his nature. We have also noticed that the Old Testament principle of 'Wisdom' which lies behind these is portrayed as a living personality in Proverbs.

In the New Testament this idea takes a quantum leap forward. The 'Wisdom' or 'Word' of God is revealed not merely as an aspect of God but as having a real personality and will of its own, sharing God's own nature and yet standing alongside him. John opens his gospel with these extraordinary words:

In the beginning was the Word, and the Word was *with* God, and the Word *was* God. He was with God in the beginning. Through him all things were made; without him nothing was made that has been made. (John 1:1-3 NIV)

Wrestling with similar ideas, Paul talks of 'the image of the invisible God' in whom 'all things hold together' (Col. 1:15-17) and the writer to the Hebrews writes similarly about 'the radiance of the glory of God and the exact imprint of his nature' who 'upholds the universe' (Heb. 1:3).

John goes on to tell us that no-one has ever seen God, but that the Word has revealed him (1:14). He also makes a breathtaking statement that goes far beyond anything in the Old Testament:

> And the Word **became flesh** and dwelt among us, and we have seen his glory, glory as of the only Son from the Father, full of grace and truth. (John 1:14)

In other words, he is describing the life of the most remarkable person that has ever lived on earth: Jesus of Nazareth. God's Word had appeared on earth as a tiny, helpless baby, as foretold seven hundred years earlier by Isaiah:

> For to us a child is born,
> to us a son is given ...
> and his name shall be called
> Wonderful Counsellor, Mighty God,
> Everlasting Father, Prince of Peace. (Is. 9:6)

His miraculous birth demonstrates that he was in a real sense both fully man and fully God, expressed in part by the mysterious title, 'Son of God', and also by the name 'Emmanuel', given before his birth, which means 'God with us'.

Jesus later himself claimed that 'Whoever has seen me has seen the Father' (John 14:9).

We can, then, talk both about 'God the Father' and 'God the Son' (John 1:18 NRSV; 2 John 9), completely bound together in glory for the whole of eternity. Both are included in the statement 'The LORD our God, the LORD is **one**', since the Hebrew word used here for **one**, *echad*, can embrace difference and variety. (One of its earliest uses in the Bible, for instance, is to describe Adam and Eve as '**one** flesh' in Genesis 2:24).

Thus John can say in the same breath both that 'the Word was *with* God' and yet 'the Word *was* God' without contradiction. Jesus was able to make the shocking statement that 'I and the Father are **one**' (John 10.30) without caving in on the principle of God's uniqueness. Likewise Paul, born and bred a Jew, can write:

> For us there is but **one** God, the Father, from whom all things came and for whom we live; and there is but **one** Lord, Jesus Christ, through whom all things came and through whom we live. (1 Cor. 8:6 NIV)

As a result, virtually everything that the Bible says about God the Father is also true of God the Son. For example, we see Jesus repeatedly using the exclusive title that God the Father used in the book of Exodus. When he walks on the water, he literally says, '**I am**; don't be afraid' (John 6:20). When asked how he knows Abraham, he replies, 'Before Abraham was, **I am**' (John 8:58). When asked by the motley crew of guards whether he is Jesus of Nazareth and he replies with the emphatic, '**I am**', they all fall backwards (John 18:5-6).

But why would God, the creator of countless trillions of galaxies, choose to appear in human form? What is the reason Jesus had to come?

To answer this question we need to step back a little. We have already touched on the nature of God, whose essence of unfathomable power and dazzling glory is expressed in infinite love and grace, and whose innermost being embraces both an explosive vitality and yet a profound stillness. Constantly self-giving and self-emptying, the overflowing life of God actively sustains every living thing (Ps. 104:29-30).

There is, however, a competing principle against this dynamic oneness which the Bible calls 'sin'. It acts like of a cancer, ultimately destroying life: a competing 'me' against the all-inclusive 'I am' of Father and Son. With an insatiable appetite, it draws everything towards itself and allows nothing to escape. Ultimately it is a denial of everything that God stands for.

God is absolutely holy. He cannot look upon sin. Nor could we survive for a moment in his presence unless the sin in our lives is dealt with. Just **one** speck of sin is enough to cut us off from him forever (Is. 59:2; James 2:10). And yet we are all absolutely riddled with it, from head to toe:

Despite this, as we have said already, God longs for us to be reconciled with him. Just as he has set up universal laws, he has also set up a universal means by which we may approach him. The only way to override the problem of sin was for him to step into the created order himself and fix it from inside. Since 'no one can redeem the life of another or give to God a ransom for them' (Ps. 49:7 NIV) it is he alone who had to come and do the work himself (Ps. 49:15; Is. 59:16).

The Lamb of God

Before Jesus came to the earth a temporary means for forgiveness was established. The sinner laid his hands on an innocent lamb or goat which was then slaughtered in his place. By this act he was identifying himself with the slaughtered animal whose death cancelled out the sin. This, however, was a repeated action which never dealt with the root of the problem.

However, when John the Baptist first saw Jesus he said, "Behold, the Lamb of God, who takes away the sin of the world!" (John 1:29). By laying our burdens on Jesus, we identify ourselves with this divine Lamb whose death cancels out our sin once and for all, and destroys it at its source.

And when he had taken the scroll, the four living creatures and the twenty-four elders fell down before the Lamb…And they sang a new song, saying,

"Worthy are you to take the scroll and to open its seals,
  for you were slain, and by your blood you ransomed people for God from every tribe and language and people and nation …
  and they shall reign on the earth."   (Rev. 5:8-10)

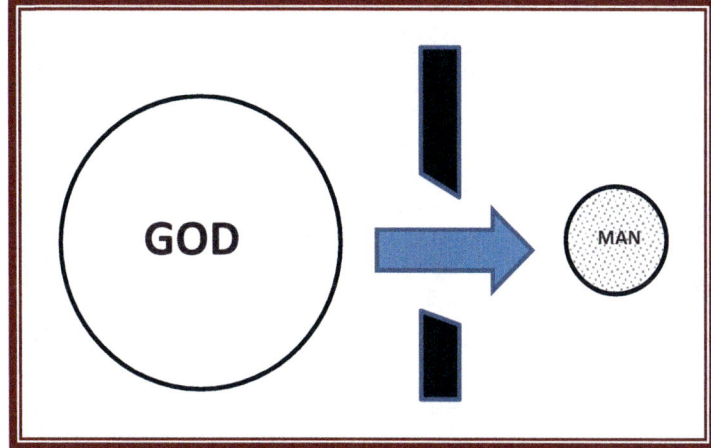

For this reason, Jesus says that 'if you do not believe that **I AM**, you will die in your sins' (John 8:24 NAB). In other words, his unique nature as both fully God and fully man provides the **only** possible means for us to be put right with God. As he later reminds us,

> "I am the way, and the truth, and the life. **No one** comes to the Father except through me. (John 14:6)

Peter likewise declares:

> "And there is salvation in no one else, for there is **no other name** under heaven given among men by which we must be saved." (Acts 4:12)

Jesus' death on the cross provides the **one** means by which the consequences of our sin can be dealt with. Just as God has written other immutable laws into the universe, the 'law of sin and death' determines that the death of an innocent victim is the only way to atone for the effects of sin. The curse of sin which cuts us off from the Father had to be transferred onto Jesus for us to be free of it, and the only means to achieve this was through his offering of himself for us. He died in our place as our substitute.

Recycling God's way:

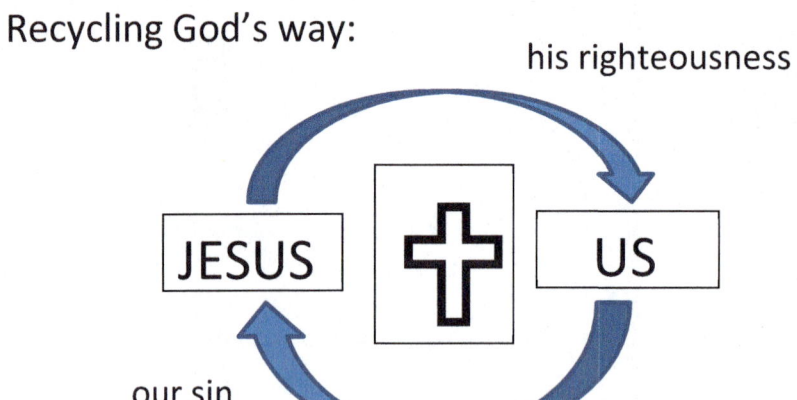

The death of Jesus was thus God's single and final answer to sin. As the writer to the Hebrews puts it:

> ෴
>
> ... he has appeared **once** for all at the end of the ages to put away sin by the sacrifice of himself. And just as it is appointed for man to die **once**, and after that comes judgement, so Christ, having been offered **once** to bear the sins of many, will appear a second time, not to deal with sin but to save those who are eagerly waiting for him. (Heb. 9:26-28)
>
> ෴

This is why Paul can write,

> "For there is **one** God, and there is **one** mediator between God and men, the man Christ Jesus, who gave himself as a ransom for all. (1 Tim. 2:5-6)

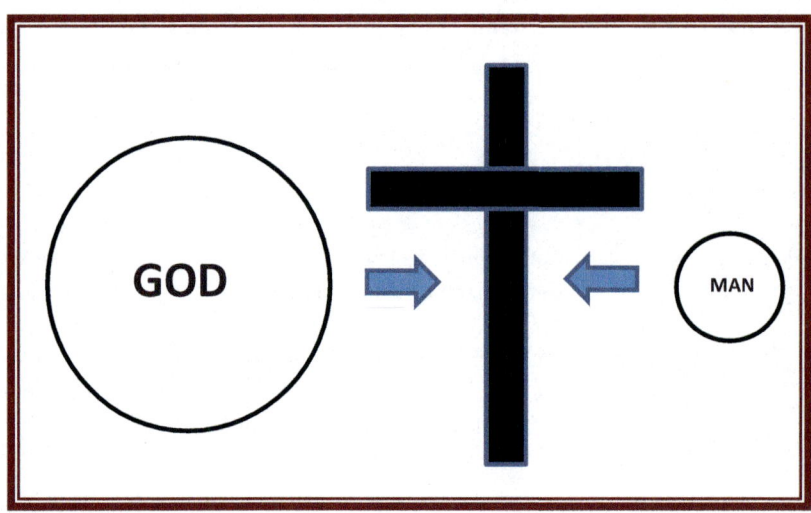

4. We are **one** with Jesus through his death

In order to completely identify with the human condition, Jesus had to be made like us in every conceivable way (all Bible quotations on this page from the New International Version) :

> ℘
>
> Since the children have flesh and blood, he too *shared in their humanity* so that by his death he might break the power of him who holds the power of death – that is, the devil – and free those who all their lives were held in slavery by their fear of death ... For this reason he had to be made like them, *fully human in every way*... that he might make atonement for the sins of the people. (Heb. 2:14-15, 17)
>
> ℘

> ℘
>
> For we do not have a high priest who is unable to feel sympathy for our weaknesses, but we have one who has been *tempted in every way, just as we are* – yet he did not sin. (Heb. 4:15)
>
> ℘

This action, however, came at an almost unimaginable cost, as Paul makes clear in his letter to the Philippians:

> ℘
>
> Christ Jesus ... who, being in very nature God,
> did not consider equality with God
> something to be used to his own advantage;
> rather, he made himself nothing
> by taking the very nature of a servant,
> *being made in human likeness.*
> And being *found in appearance as a man*,
> he humbled himself
> by becoming obedient to death –
> even death on a cross! (Phil. 2:5-8)
>
> ℘

The extent of that obedience goes almost beyond description. Worse still than the terrible human agony of crucifixion was the weight of the world's sin pressing down onto Jesus on the cross. In one instant of time, it seems that the Father turned his face away, and Jesus cried out in agony, 'My God, my God, why have you forsaken me?' (Matt 27:46), the only prayer where he did *not* address God as 'Father'. For a split second that may have seemed like an eternity, the Godhead itself was torn in two.

We have already seen how each atom in the universe seems to be modelled on the throne room of God. Knowing the extraordinary power that is released by splitting that single atom, the thought of the very foundations of the universe breaking open for each one of us should take our breath away. It is something that should cause us to remain in a constant state of praise and thanksgiving.

This is why the cross is at the absolute centre of the Christian faith. It is the meeting-point between heaven and earth, between a holy God and sinful humanity, between past and future, where our identity is changed once and for all.

At the cross a transference or exchange takes place. We are no longer 'dead in our sins and transgressions'. All our sin and rebellion is put onto Jesus. At the same time, all his righteousness and holiness is put onto us. As Paul puts it, 'For our sake he made him to be sin who knew no sin, so that in him we might become the righteousness of God' (2 Cor. 5:21).

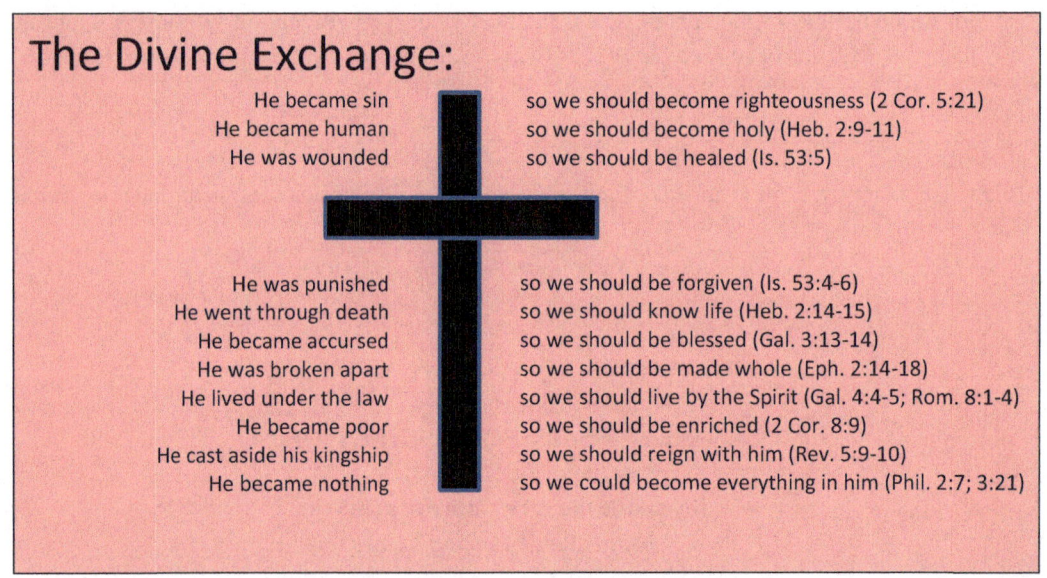

The Divine Exchange:

He became sin	so we should become righteousness (2 Cor. 5:21)
He became human	so we should become holy (Heb. 2:9-11)
He was wounded	so we should be healed (Is. 53:5)
He was punished	so we should be forgiven (Is. 53:4-6)
He went through death	so we should know life (Heb. 2:14-15)
He became accursed	so we should be blessed (Gal. 3:13-14)
He was broken apart	so we should be made whole (Eph. 2:14-18)
He lived under the law	so we should live by the Spirit (Gal. 4:4-5; Rom. 8:1-4)
He became poor	so we should be enriched (2 Cor. 8:9)
He cast aside his kingship	so we should reign with him (Rev. 5:9-10)
He became nothing	so we could become everything in him (Phil. 2:7; 3:21)

At the same time, our identity changes: we are placed 'into' Christ. Because Jesus has fully identified himself with us, we are now in turn fully identified with him. We are now indissolubly joined to him as **one.**

> **The Priestly Garment**
>
> In the Old Testament, the High Priestly garment called the *ephod* bore the names of the children of Israel (Ex. 28:6-12). By wearing it, the High Priest carried them into God's presence (verse 29). In the same way, Christ clothed himself with human flesh in coming to earth as a man (Heb. 10:5), so that he could carry us back into the presence of God (Heb. 9:24). 'He is able to save to the uttermost those who draw near to God through him, since he always lives to make intercession for them' (Heb. 7:25).
>
> In this sense, it might be said that when Jesus was transfigured at the top of the mountain, it was *us* who were transfigured: his garments (our humanity) became dazzling white (Mark 9:2-3). This is how all redeemed humanity will appear in God's presence one day (Rev. 7:9; 19:8).
>
> *All of us are looking with unveiled faces at the glory of the Lord as if we were looking in a mirror. We are being transformed into that same image from one degree of glory to the next degree of glory. This comes from the Lord, who is the Spirit.* (2 Cor. 3:18 CEB)

This has several radical implications. Firstly, **it affects the way that God looks at us**: Just as when Isaac looked on Jacob wearing Esau's clothes and saw Esau, so when God turns his gaze upon us, identified with Christ through his sacrifice, he sees Jesus. This is part of what Paul means when he tells us to 'clothe yourselves with the Lord Jesus Christ' (Rom. 13:14 NIV).

Put another way, the father places his *own* cloak on the prodigal son when he returns home (Luke 15:22). We become wrapped in God's own identity:

> I will greatly rejoice in the LORD;
> my soul shall exult in my God,
> for *he has clothed me with the garments of salvation*;
> *he has covered me with the robe of righteousness*,
> as a bridegroom decks himself like a priest with a beautiful headdress,
> and as a bride adorns herself with her jewels. (Is. 61:10)

Secondly, **it affects the way that *we* look at ourselves**:

> I have been crucified with Christ. *It is no longer I who live*, but Christ who lives in me. And the life I now live in the flesh I live by faith in the Son of God, who loved me and gave himself for me. (Gal. 2:20)

In Christ we are no longer living for ourselves. We have a higher purpose and different priorities. We come under new ownership, and it affects our entire approach to life. As Paul later writes,

> For his sake *I have suffered the loss of all things* and count them as rubbish, in order that I may gain Christ ... that I may know him and the power of his resurrection, and may share his sufferings, becoming like him in his death. (Phil. 3:8-10)

Thirdly, **it affects the way that Satan looks at us**. We no longer have to be pawns in his chess game, for our lives have been 'hidden with Christ in God' (Col. 3:3). Outside of Christ, we are effectively defenceless against his attacks:

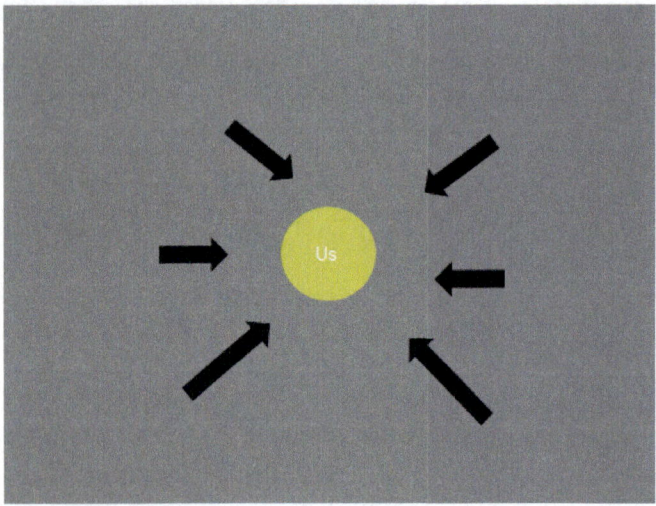

'Hidden' in Christ, however, the picture is radically different:

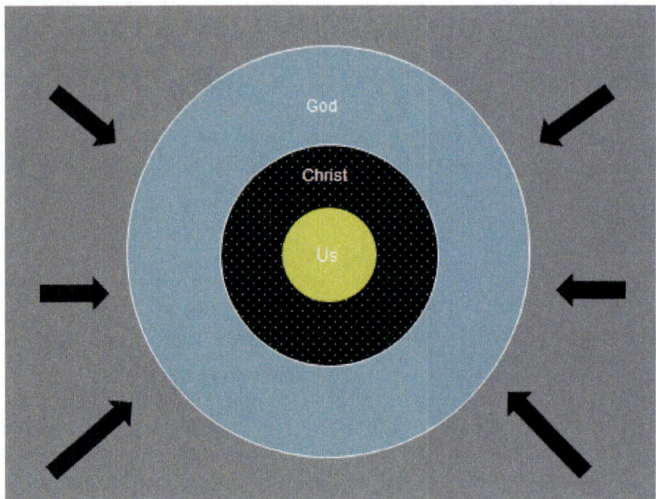

This explains the importance of believers' baptism. In stepping into the water we 'put on Christ as a garment' (Gal. 3:27 NEB), becoming completely immersed and identified with him. The original Greek verb was often used for dyeing an object a completely different colour.

The diagram we have just seen also highlights something else truly astonishing. Being adopted in Christ means that we now 'participate in the divine nature' (2 Peter 1:4 NIV). Our identity, in some remarkable way, is placed *inside* of God's. We acquire a new purpose and power for living.

Although we see this can be partially fulfilled in our earthly lives, its total consummation will only be in the future. Now our minds are being transformed steadily (Rom. 12:2), but we will one day become fully *like* Jesus:

> For he knew all about us before we were born and he destined us from the beginning to share *the likeness of his Son*. This means the Son is the oldest among a vast family of brothers and sisters who will become *just like him*. (Rom. 8:29, *Passion Translation*)

> Dear friends, now we are children of God, and what we will be has not yet been made known. But we know that when Christ appears, *we shall be like him*, for we shall see him as he is. (1 John 3:2 NIV)

If we have received Christ, we are no longer the people we once were. We have been born again with a new identity. 'As a man thinks, so he is' (Prov. 23:7). For this reason we are to be 'transformed by the renewal of your mind, that by testing you may discern what is the will of God, what is good and acceptable and perfect' (Rom. 12:2).

5. We are **one** with each other in Christ

This change of identity has other consequences, as well. Just as we are now **one** with Christ, we are also ***united together as a single body.***

> I pray not only for these,
> but for those also
> who through their words will believe in me.
> May they all be **one**.
> Father, may they be **one** in us,
> as you are in me and I am in you,
> so that the world may believe it was you who sent me.
> I have given them the glory you gave to me,
> that they may be **one** as we are **one**. ...
> may they be so completely **one**
> that the world will realise that it was you who sent me
> and that I have loved them as much as you loved me.
> (John 17:20-23, *Jerusalem Bible*).

Through Jesus's **one** sacrifice, therefore, we have been made **one** people. Because his blood is the only grounds through which we are put right with the Father, we are all **equal** in his sight. Jesus illustrated this fundamental equality in the parable of the labourers in the vineyard who all receive **one** denarius no matter how much of the day they had been working (Matt. 20:1-16). This means that if we have received him as Saviour, we have equal standing before God, regardless of whether we are the President of the United States, or the poor woman who cleans latrines with her bare hands in Pakistan.

Paul explains this as follows:

> For as many of you as were baptized into Christ have put on Christ. There is neither Jew nor Greek, there is neither slave nor free, there is no male and female, for you are all **one** in Christ Jesus. (Gal. 3:27-28)

This equality has a practical impact on the way we should live our lives. Paul tells the Ephesians to 'walk in a manner worthy of the calling to which you have been called, with all humility and gentleness, with patience, bearing with one another in love, eager to maintain the **unity** of the Spirit in the bond of peace.'

He then underlines this as follows:

> There is **one** body and one Spirit—just as you were called to the **one** hope that belongs to your call—**one** Lord, one faith, **one** baptism, **one** God and Father of all, who is over all and through all and in all. (Eph. 4:4-6)

This gives a completely different concept of identity to our modern Western individualism. Rather, members of the body of Christ *belong to one another*:

> For as in **one** body we have many members, and the members do not all have the same function, so we, though many, are **one** body in Christ, and individually members **one** of another. (Rom. 12:4-5)
>
> For in **one** Spirit we were all baptized into **one** body—Jews or Greeks, slaves or free—and all were made to drink of **one** Spirit. (1 Cor. 12:13)

Indeed, the church in its infancy interpreted this oneness in a radical way:

> Now the full number of those who believed were of **one** heart and soul, and no one said that any of the things that belonged to him was his own, but they had everything in common. ... There was not a needy person among them, for as many as were owners of lands or houses sold them and brought the proceeds of what was sold and laid it at the apostles' feet, and it was distributed to each as any had need. (Acts 4:32-35)

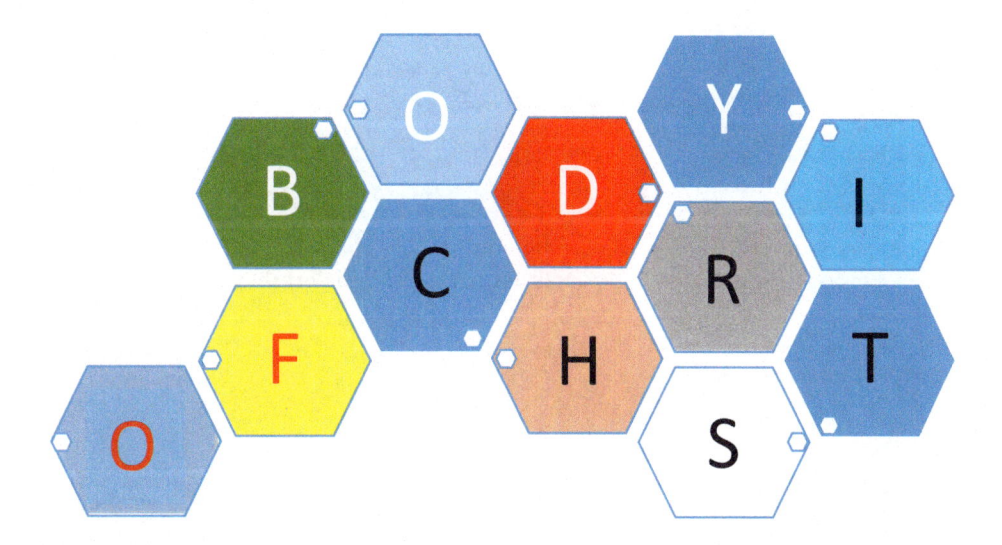

There are clear implications for the way believers should live their lives today. We all share the same spiritual DNA. We are no longer isolated individuals, but we have been drawn together in Christ, who is our life.

Ultimately, all forms of arrogance are an affront to God. We are to minister to all our brothers and sisters within the body of Christ with the heart of a servant, as a template for the way we are called to treat the whole of humanity. This is especially true of our dealings with those of other denominations and those of other doctrinal viewpoints, who deserve particular honour and respect (Luke 9:49-50; Rom. 14:1-21). True humility is to see the face of God in our estranged brother (Gen. 33:10).

The true church, then, is called to radical humility and servanthood. We are to model an upside-down kingdom where strong is weak and weak is strong. We are to prefer others before ourselves, and to place the lowliest among us on the highest pedestal. As Jesus reminds us, 'as you did it to one of the least of these my brothers, you did it to me' (Matt. 25:40).

6. We need to make God number **one** in our lives

Because God is an all-encompassing God, our approach to him needs to be all-encompassing. We cannot come to him with half measures or present to him anything less than our whole lives. God hates mixture, and demands an all-or-nothing response from us. The passage which we have just read in the previous section from Acts chapter 4 would scarcely be thinkable in most of today's church. It is not appropriate that we should only give him *part* of ourselves back to a God who has given *all* of himself for us.

There are some strong positive models for us to follow in the Old Testament:

> Then the people rejoiced because they had given willingly, for with *a whole heart* they had offered freely to the LORD. David the king also rejoiced greatly.
> (1 Chron. 29:9)

Similarly in the New Testament we see some remarkable examples:

> Jesus looked up and saw the rich putting their gifts into the offering box, and he saw a poor widow put in two small copper coins. And he said, "Truly, I tell you, this poor widow has put in more than all of them. For they all contributed out of their abundance, but she out of her poverty put in *all she had to live on.*" (Luke 21:1-4)

This, then, should be the heart cry of our prayers:

Double-Mindedness

The Bible warns about seesawing between two different attitudes towards God. Elijah bewails the people of Israel when he says, "How long will you go limping between two different opinions?" (1 Kings 18:21). Jesus warns us that "No one who puts his hand to the plough and looks back is fit for the kingdom of God" (Luke 9:62). The writer to the Hebrews tells us that those who 'shrink back' are destroyed (Heb. 10:39). In the same way Paul describes the dangers of being 'tossed back and forth by the waves, and blown here and there by every wind of teaching and by the cunning and craftiness of people in their deceitful scheming' (Eph. 4:14 NIV).

If any of you lacks wisdom, let him ask God, who gives generously to all without reproach, and it will be given him. But let him ask in faith, with no doubting, for the one who doubts is like a wave of the sea that is driven and tossed by the wind. For that person must not suppose that he will receive anything from the Lord; he is a double-minded man, unstable in all his ways. (James 1:5-8).

> ಸಚ
> Teach me your way, LORD, that I may rely on your faithfulness; give me an *undivided* heart, that I may fear your name.
> (Ps. 86:11 NIV)
> ಸಚ

God, in turn, has given us clear promises of blessing in response:

> ಸಚ
> You will seek me and find me, when you seek me with *all* your heart.
> (Jer. 29:13)
> ಸಚ

We need, therefore, to keep **one** focus in our lives, and that is 'the upward call of God in Christ Jesus' (Phil. 3:14). This is the challenge posed to us by the writer to the Hebrews:

> ಸಚ
> Therefore, since we are surrounded by so great a cloud of witnesses, let us also lay aside every weight, and sin which clings so closely, and let us run with endurance the race that is set before us, looking to Jesus, the founder and perfecter of our faith, who for the joy that was set before him endured the cross, despising the shame, and is seated at the right hand of the throne of God.
> (Heb. 12:1-2)
> ಸಚ

Following Christ is not a lifestyle choice, therefore. On the contrary, it will cost us *everything*:

> ಸಚ
> 'For which of you, desiring to build a tower, does not first sit down and count the cost, whether he has enough to complete it? Otherwise, when he has laid a foundation and is not able to finish, all who see it begin to mock him, saying, 'This man began to build and was not able to finish.'
>
> Or what king, going out to encounter another king in war, will not sit down first and deliberate whether he is able with ten thousand to meet him who comes against him with twenty thousand? And if not, while the other is yet a great way off, he sends a delegation and asks for terms of peace. So therefore, *any one of you who does not renounce all that he has cannot be my disciple.*'
> (Luke 14:28-33)
> ಸಚ

It is this dogged determination to push through despite everything thrown against us that marks the essence of a victorious, faith-filled life. Faced with every misfortune possible, Job is still adamant that '*even if* he slays me, I will hope in him' (Job 13:15 NET). Similarly, Shadrach, Meshach and Abednego, threatened by Nebuchadnezzar with being thrown into the blazing furnace for not worshipping the idolatrous statue, give a very uncompromising reply:

> ಸಚ
> 'the God we serve is able to deliver us from it, and he will deliver us from Your Majesty's hand. But *even if he does not*, we want you to know, Your Majesty, that we will not serve your gods or worship the image of gold you have set up.' (Dan. 3.17-18 NIV)
> ಸಚ

We need to be ruthless, then, in pulling down the idols of power, money, greed, sex and success which are attempting to suffocate us (Rom. 8:13). Our hearts are God's sanctuary, and there should be room for nothing else. Winning over the Promised Land of our souls requires total co-operation with God's Spirit, and there should be no place for compromise with the forces that seek to destroy us from within. Failure to do so comprehensively may leave us with a 'thorn in the side' which risks becoming a constant stumbling block in our Christian walk (Num. 33:55).

A popular acronym for 'faith' is '**F**orsaking **A**ll **I** **T**rust **H**im'. It presents a powerful challenge. Are we willing to forsake all for Jesus, despite the cost? Are we willing to trust him with everything? Are we willing to lay down our lives for him? This is a choice each one of us has to make in our lives. As John the Baptist once said, 'he must increase, but I must decrease' (John 3:30).

Resetting our priorities:

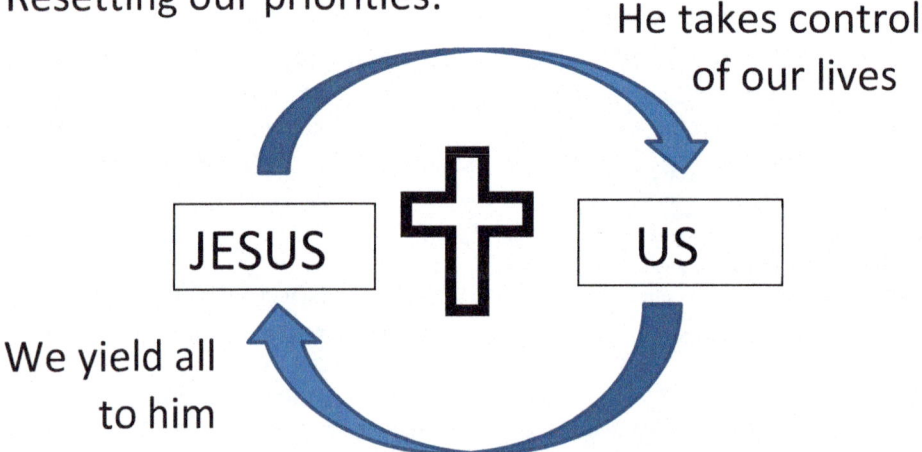

He takes control of our lives

JESUS ✝ US

We yield all to him

Let us summarise all that we have covered so far. There is **one** God, the creator of the entire universe. He has expressed himself through **one** set of laws governing the whole of creation, nature and society. We have rebelled against these laws but God has provided **one** means of putting us back into alignment with him through the death of Jesus on the cross.

Accepting Jesus as our Saviour makes us **one** with many others across history who have made the same choice. Together we need to serve God with **one** heart and share the good news of his salvation with **one** voice.

Nothing short of **total** commitment to him will bring about the purpose and destiny that God wants to achieve in our lives. This should be the **one** outstanding goal of our lives.

This lifelong challenge provides the basis for a powerful hymn by Theodore Monod (1836-1921):

ONE: THE NUMBER OF IDENTITY

Oh, the bitter shame and sorrow,
That a time could ever be,
When I let the Saviour's pity
Plead in vain, and proudly answered,
All of self, and none of Thee,
All of self and none of Thee.

Yet He found me; I beheld Him
Bleeding on the cursed tree;
Heard Him pray, Forgive them, Father,
And my wistful heart said faintly,
Some of self, and some of Thee,
Some of self, and some of Thee.

Day by day His tender mercy,
Healing, helping, full and free,
Sweet and strong, and ah! so patient,
Brought me lower while I whispered,
Less of self, and more of Thee,
Less of self, and more of Thee.

Higher than the highest heavens,
Deeper than the deepest sea,
Lord, Thy love at last hath conquered;
Grant me now my heart's petition,
None of self, and all of Thee,
None of self, and all of Thee.

Chapter Two

Two

The Number of Relationship

1. Two as Everlasting Love

As we have already seen, the most profound truth in our universe is the deep relationship between Father and Son, which lies at the very heart of God's nature. This inner self-giving love takes us back beyond time and space to the very foundations of eternity. We see hints of this in Proverbs chapter 8:

> When he established the heavens, I was there;
> when he drew a circle on the face of the deep,
> when he made firm the skies above,
> when he established the fountains of the deep,
> when he assigned to the sea its limit,
> so that the waters might not transgress his command,
> when he marked out the foundations of the earth,
> then *I was beside him, like a master workman*,
> and *I was daily his delight*,
> rejoicing before him always,
> rejoicing in his inhabited world
> and delighting in the children of man. (Prov. 8:27-31)

Jesus reveals the depths of this love relationship more fully in John chapter 17:

The Mystery of God

The Bible tells us that *God is light*. Light, both visible and invisible, can be described in **two** possible ways: either as waves or as particles. Both explanations are true, and yet appear to contradict each other. In the same way, God is one and yet more than one.

Many descriptions of the 'angel of the LORD' in the Old Testament and of Christ in the New Testament raise the idea of a being alongside the Father who is also 'God'. This enigma finds its fullest expression in John 1.1: 'In the beginning was the Word, and the Word was *with* God, and the Word *was* God.'

How can the Word both *be* 'God' and yet also *with* God? In fact there are many similar verses in the Bible, going right back to Genesis 1:26-27: 'Then God said, "Let us make man in *our* image ... So God created man in *his* own image.' This apparent contradiction points to a profound mystery at the heart of God's being, and yet is vital for our salvation.

No one has ever seen God; **the only God, who is at the Father's side**, *he has made him known.* (John 1.18)

"Father, glorify me in your own presence with the glory that I had with you before the world existed ... my glory that you have given me because *you loved me before the foundation of the world*." (John 17:5, 24)

With a few exceptions, almost *every* New Testament book from John's Gospel onwards begins by presenting this deep relationship between Father and Son. In Paul's letters, for example, they appear as *joint* sources of blessing to believers, beginning from Romans 1:7, which reads, 'Grace to you and peace from God our Father *and* the Lord Jesus Christ'.

This intimate bond shines out most strongly in verse 18 of the first chapter of John's Gospel. In older translations it presents the Son as being in the Father's bosom, a position of great intimacy. In the more recent *Passion Translation*, the verse reads as follows:

No one has ever gazed upon the fullness of God's splendour except the *uniquely beloved Son*, who is cherished by the Father and held close to his heart. Now he has unfolded to us the full explanation of who God truly is!

God's greatest desire for us is to be drawn into this love relationship, which involves trusting both in Father and Son equally (John 14:1), through which we may gain eternal life (John 17:3). This invitation to invite Father and Son into the innermost recesses of our hearts is addressed to each one of us personally:

"If anyone loves me, he will keep my word, and my Father will love him, and **we** will come to him and make our home with him." (John 14:23)

2. **Two** as Covenant Relationship

The relationship that God wants with us is not the remote subordination of master and slave. Nor is it a deep but occasional long-distance connection, like a cherished uncle who is visited once a year. Rather, he wants us to walk with him on a daily basis, and to live out our lives completely in him. Just as Jesus shares a deep intimacy with the Father, it is God's desire that we should also share that intimacy. There are a number of passages in the Old Testament that touch on this profound relationship, as we see below:

> O Lord, you have searched me and known me!
> You know when I sit down and when I rise up;
> you discern my thoughts from afar.
> You search out my path and my lying down
> and are acquainted with all my ways.
> Even before a word is on my tongue,
> behold, O Lord, you know it altogether.
> You hem me in, behind and before,
> and lay your hand upon me.
> (Ps. 139:1-5)

> Set me as a seal upon your heart,
> as a seal upon your arm,
> for love is strong as death,
> jealousy is fierce as the grave.
> Its flashes are flashes of fire,
> the very flame of the Lord.
> Many waters cannot quench love,
> neither can floods drown it.
> If a man offered for love
> all the wealth of his house,
> he would be utterly despised.
> (Song of Solomon 8:6-7)

> Deep calls to deep
> at the roar of your waterfalls;
> all your breakers and your waves
> have gone over me.
> By day the Lord commands his steadfast love,
> and at night his song is with me,
> a prayer to the God of my life.
> (Ps. 42:7-8)

> "Fear not, for I have redeemed you;
> I have called you by name, you are mine.
> When you pass through the waters, I will be with you;
> and through the rivers, they shall not overwhelm you;
> when you walk through fire you shall not be burned,
> and the flame shall not consume you.
> (Is. 43:1-2)

TWO: THE NUMBER OF RELATIONSHIP

Above: Michelangelo's celebrated portrayal of the Creation of Adam by God on the ceiling of the Sistine Chapel in Rome.

Below: A stained glass window depicting Adam and Eve from the Cathedral of St. Michael and St. Gudula in Brussels.

This bond of love between God and his church is expressed in two significant ways. Firstly, the Bible describes us as **God's children**. We have been adopted together into a family with Jesus through his death, by which we can all now address God as 'Father'.

There are several verses in the New Testament that draw attention to this wonderful security we can enjoy, knowing God's fatherly protection in every situation:

> ৪০৩
>
> For all who are led by the Spirit of God are sons of God. For you did not receive the spirit of slavery to fall back into fear, but you have received the Spirit of adoption as sons, by whom we cry, "Abba! Father!" The Spirit himself bears witness with our spirit that we are *children of God*, and if children, then heirs—heirs of God and fellow heirs with Christ ... (Rom. 8:14-17)
>
> See what kind of love the Father has given to us, that we should be called *children of God*; and so we are. ... Beloved, we are God's children now, and what we will be has not yet appeared; but we know that when he appears we shall be like him, because we shall see him as he is.
> (1 John 3:1-2)
>
> ৪০৩

The second way of looking at this new relationship is as a **marriage**. Although this image may highlight different aspects of our relationship with God (in comparison with sonship) it may simply be a different side of the same coin, as God implies to Jeremiah:

> ৪০৩
>
> "'I said,
> How I would set you among my *sons* ...
> And I thought you would call me, *My Father*,
> and would not turn from following me.
> Surely, as a treacherous *wife* leaves her *husband*,
> so have you been treacherous to me, O house of Israel,
> declares the LORD.'" (Jer. 3:19-20)
>
> ৪০৩

Many of the Old Testament passages concerning the 'bride' emphasise the covenant relationship through which God undertakes to protect Israel, cover her and provide for her in every sphere, as we see on the next page.

In the New Testament it is Jesus who is repeatedly described as the 'bridegroom' (see, for example, Matthew 9.15 and 25:10) who goes to prepare a place for us:

> ৪০৩
>
> "In my Father's house are many rooms. If it were not so, would I have told you that I go to prepare a place for you? And if I go and prepare a place for you, I will come again and will take you to myself, that where I am you may be also." (John 14:2-3)
>
> ৪০৩

This 'wedding' reaches its consummation in the final pages of Revelation, where bride and bridegroom are united for ever in a dramatic climax to the whole Bible adventure. God's plan for the ages is complete, and the bride shines with the glory of God (Rev. 21:9-11).

Bride and Bridegroom

ஐௐ

"For your Maker is your husband,
the Lord of hosts is his name;
and the Holy One of Israel is your Redeemer,
the God of the whole earth he is called.
For the Lord has called you
like a wife deserted and grieved in spirit,
like a wife of youth when she is cast off,
says your God."
(Is. 54:5-6)

ஐௐ

ஐௐ

"You shall be called My Delight Is in Her,
and your land Married;
for the Lord delights in you,
and your land shall be married.
For as a young man marries a young woman,
so shall your sons marry you,
and as the bridegroom rejoices over the bride,
so shall your God rejoice over you."
(Is. 62:4-5)

ஐௐ

"When I passed by you again and saw you, behold, you were at the age for love, and I spread the corner of my garment over you and covered your nakedness; I made my vow to you and entered into a covenant with you, declares the Lord God, and you became mine."
(Ezek. 16:8)

ஐௐ

ஐௐ

"And in that day, declares the Lord, you will call me 'My Husband,' … And I will betroth you to me forever. I will betroth you to me in righteousness and in justice, in steadfast love and in mercy. I will betroth you to me in faithfulness. And you shall know the Lord."
(Hos. 2:16, 19-20)

ஐௐ

And I saw the holy city, new Jerusalem, coming down out of heaven from God, prepared as a bride adorned for her husband. (Rev. 21:2)

3. **Two** as a Universal Template

If the universe is founded on the principle of love and relationship, rather than on the whims of a solitary and isolated lawmaker, we should not be surprised to see this reflected in the natural world around us. Physicists tells us that, at the very outset of the universe, only **two** elements existed, hydrogen and helium, out of which all the other elements were formed. The most basic of these, hydrogen, which makes up over 90 per cent of all the atoms in the universe, consists in its simplest form of just **two** particles: an electron orbiting around one proton. Pure hydrogen normally consists of **two** of these hydrogen atoms linked together (H_2).

Moreover, the vast majority of the air we breathe, which is mainly oxygen and nitrogen, also consists of similarly paired molecules. Indeed, despite 'non-binary' being the current buzzword, everything that God creates in the universe itself is founded on pairings and polarities between opposites: positive versus negative, acid versus alkali, matter versus anti-matter, 'up' quarks versus 'down' quarks, one versus zero, and so on. These are the principles that make electricity work and cause computer programmes to run.

Likewise, the Bible is a book of binary opposites: light is set up against darkness, truth against falsehood, and life against death. And this clear process of separation, division, contrast and antithesis is evident from the very first page of the Bible. God *speaks* and separates the light from the darkness. He separates the earth from the sky and the land from the sea. Genesis is a series of separations into complementary pairs.

The culminating act of this process of separation in Genesis 1 is when God creates a fundamental distinction within humanity that reflects his own innermost being:

> Then God said, "Let *us* make man in *our* image, after *our* likeness. And let them have dominion over the fish of the sea and over the birds of the heavens and over the livestock and over all the earth and over every creeping thing that creeps on the earth."
> So God created man in his own image,
> in the image of God he created him;
> *male* and *female* he created them.
> (Gen. 1:26-27)

Two is Better than One

An atom of hydrogen, the most basic and plentiful substance in the universe, is fundamentally unstable on its own and 'seeks' out a partner:

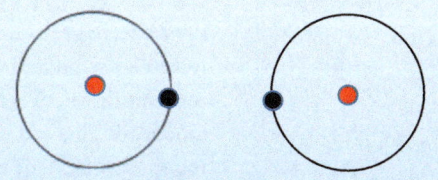

When two hydrogen atoms get close enough together to share their electrons, the result is more stable:

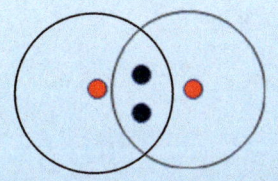

The result gives us what is called a 'covalent bond' and can be represented in a 'Lewis diagram' as **H:H**. Oxygen atoms behave in the same manner. All the oxygen we breathe consists of these paired atoms.

The diagrams below show how pairings operate in a different manner in a magnetic (left) or electric (right) field. With a magnetic field, similar poles repel each other, but opposites attract, linking the field lines together. A similar phenomenon occurs between positive and negative electric charges, causing current to flow from positive to negative. This provides a clear blueprint for how God has structured the relationships between male and female, creating a secure environment for families to be created and nurtured. This in turn offers us a picture of Christ's love for his bride, the church (Eph. 5:31-32).

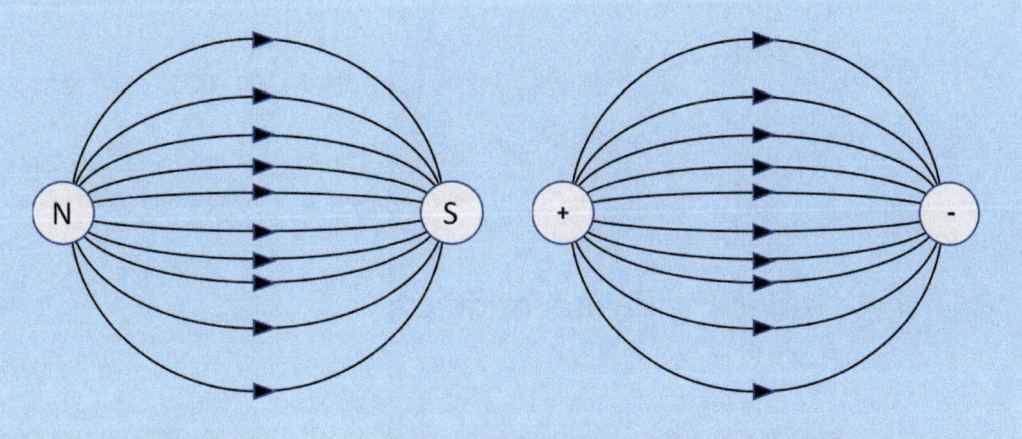

Then the man said,
"This at last is bone of my bones
   and flesh of my flesh;
she shall be called Woman,
   because she was taken out of Man." Therefore a man shall leave his father and his mother and hold fast to his wife, and they shall become one flesh. (Gen. 2:23-24)

As we have already seen in the relationship between Father and Son, there is a deep interconnectedness in the heart of God. Gender is a primary reflection of God's image: it provides ultimate proof that God cannot be a solitary, monolithic entity: otherwise he would have produced isolated asexual beings which do not depend on each other.

The distinction between sexes is thus something very precious to God. Jesus warned us about not violating this order that God has set in place:

> "Have you not read that he who created them from the beginning made them male and female, and said, 'Therefore a man shall leave his father and his mother and hold fast to his wife, and the two shall become one flesh'? So they are no longer two but one flesh. What therefore God has joined together, let not man separate."
> (Matt. 19:4-6)

The second chapter of Genesis throws more light on this. Because God removes something from Adam in order to create Eve, he is incomplete without her. Something is absent which can only be restored in togetherness.

As we have seen already, the relationship between husband and wife is a reflection of the relationship between Father and Son in the Godhead. This can easily be seen by comparing the structure of the following verses:

> No one knows the Son except the Father, and no one knows the Father except the Son and anyone to whom the Son chooses to reveal him. (Matt. 11:27)
>
> For the wife does not have authority over her own body, but the husband does. Likewise the husband does not have authority over his own body, but the wife does. (1 Cor. 7:4)
>
> Nevertheless, in the Lord woman is not independent of man, nor is man independent of woman. For as woman came from man, so also man is born of woman. But everything comes from God. (1 Cor. 11:11-12 NIV)

We can see from this that the interdependency of marriage is an inner reflection of the life of God himself:

Marriage reflecting divine intimacy:

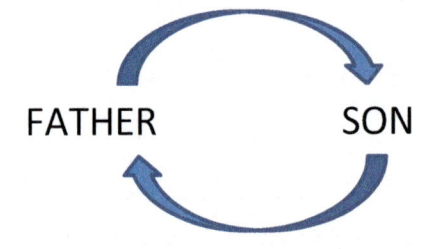

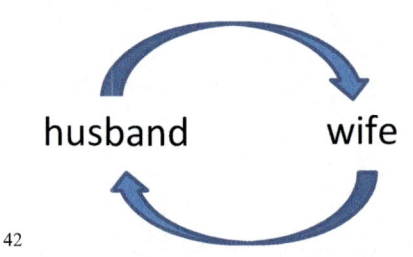

FATHER ⇌ SON   husband ⇌ wife

Several passages in the Old Testament books reflect upon this principle of mutual support:

> **Two** are better than one, because they have a good reward for their toil. For if they fall, one will lift up his fellow. But woe to him who is alone when he falls and has not another to lift him up! Again, if **two** lie together, they keep warm, but how can one keep warm alone? And though a man might prevail against one who is alone, **two** will withstand him ...
> (Ecc. 4:9-12)

In the Apocrypha, too, we find the same principles spelt out, with a wider application:

> Good is the opposite of evil;
> and life the opposite of death;
> so the sinner is the opposite of the godly.
> Look at all the works of the Most High; they come in pairs, one the opposite of the other.
> (Sirach 33:14-15 NRSV)

> All things are in pairs, each the opposite of the other,
> but nothing the Lord made is incomplete.
> Everything completes the goodness of something else.
> Could anyone ever see enough of this splendour? (Sirach 42:24-25 GNB)

For this reason, it is worth noticing that, just as God created everything in mating pairs, Jesus uses this as a model as a template for the preaching of the gospel. As two was the blueprint of fruitfulness for God's *original* creation, so two is also the blueprint for the *new* creation inaugurated by Jesus:

> After this the Lord appointed seventy-two others and sent them on ahead of him, **two by two**, into every town and place where he himself was about to go.
> (Luke 10:1)

Part of the strength of this approach is that setting into pairs can compensate for errors, weaknesses or defects in a single individual:

> As iron sharpens iron, so one person sharpens another. (Proverbs 27:17 NIV)

> Do two people walk hand in hand if they aren't going to the same place?
> (Amos 3:3, *The Message*)

We can see a correlation with this in the very text of scripture itself. Many Biblical statements are set into pairs which balance or contrast with one another. A classic instance of this is Job 1:21:

> ☙❧
>
> "Naked I came from my mother's womb, and naked shall I return. The LORD gave, and the LORD has taken away; blessed be the name of the LORD."
> (Job 1:21)
>
> ☙❧

Another famous example is the first eight verses of Ecclesiastes chapter 3:

> ☙❧
>
> For everything there is a season, and a time for every matter under heaven:
> a time to be born, and a time to die;
> a time to plant, and a time to pluck up what is planted;
> a time to kill, and a time to heal;
> a time to break down, and a time to build up;
> a time to weep, and a time to laugh;
> a time to mourn, and a time to dance;
> a time to cast away stones, and a time to gather stones together;
> a time to embrace, and a time to refrain from embracing;
> a time to seek, and a time to lose;
> a time to keep, and a time to cast away;
> a time to tear, and a time to sew;
> a time to keep silence, and a time to speak;
> a time to love, and a time to hate;
> a time for war, and a time for peace.
> (Ecc. 3:1-8)
>
> ☙❧

Sometimes such contrasts are set in very stark relief with each other, as we see in Luke Chapter 6, verses 20-26:

> "**Blessed are you** who are poor,
> for yours is the kingdom of God.
> "**Blessed are you** who are hungry now,
> for you shall be satisfied.
> "**Blessed are you** who weep now,
> for you shall laugh.
> "**Blessed are you** when people hate you
> and when they exclude you ... on account of
> the Son of Man!..."

> "But **woe to you** who are rich,
> for you have received your consolation.
> "**Woe to you** who are full now,
> for you shall be hungry.
> "**Woe to you** who laugh now,
> for you shall mourn and weep.
> "**Woe to you**, when all people speak well of you,
> for so their fathers did to the false prophets."

Applying these principles to our lives can sharpen our thinking and give us a deeper insight into situations. In Job we are reminded that 'true wisdom has **two** sides' (Job 11:6 NIV). Jesus taught us to be 'as wise as serpents and innocent as doves' (Matt. 10:16). Proverbs reminds us of the importance of exploring *both* sides of an argument:

> The one who states his case first seems right,
> until the other comes and examines him.
> (Proverbs 18:17)

This principle is important in the way that we read scripture and interpret it at both the largest and the smallest levels. Many of the great truths of the Bible are balanced by equal and opposite truths which need to be held in tension with each other: for instance, predestination versus free will, judgement against sin versus mercy for sinners, or God as one versus God as more than one. So often we need **two** angles to get a real sense of perspective.

In the end, every complementary pair of attributes finds its perfect match in Jesus, who is the ultimate expression of the balance and wholeness that God intended mankind to possess. He alone is our mentor and model for addressing every question we face in life. He is everything and yet made himself nothing, being at once both king and yet a servant, lion and yet a lamb, Son of God and yet Son of Man. In the light of this Paul was able to declare with confidence that Christ is the total answer in *every* situation, however easy or however difficult:

> I have learned in whatever situation I am to be content. I know how to be brought low, and I know how to abound. In any and every circumstance, I have learned the secret of facing plenty and hunger, abundance and need. I can do *all things* through him who strengthens me.
> (Phil. 4:11-13)

Two as Confirmation

Hebrew poetry very often consists of matching pairs, where one line is confirmed and amplified by the next. For instance, in Psalm 89, the second half of verse 1 expands on the first, while the second verse restates the first in slightly different terms:

I will sing of the steadfast love of the LORD, for ever;
   with my mouth I will make known your faithfulness to all generations.
For I said, "Steadfast love will be built up for ever;
   in the heavens you will establish your faithfulness."

In a sense the same is true on a much bigger scale between the Old and New Testaments, or, to follow the old adage, 'the New is in the Old concealed; the Old is in the New revealed.' The underlying principle builds on the Biblical doctrine that every matter should be established by two or three witnesses (Num. 35:30). This twofold pattern of witness is reflected elsewhere in the presence of **two** cherubim above the Ark, **two** divine witnesses at Jesus's baptism, **two** Old Testament prophets at his transfiguration, **two** angels at the resurrection and ascension of Jesus in Luke, John and Acts, **two** witnesses in Revelation, and ultimately **two** comings of the Messiah.

*"If I do judge, my judgement is true, for it is not I alone who judge, but I and the Father who sent me. In your Law it is written that the testimony of **two** people is true. I am the one who bears witness about myself, and the Father who sent me bears witness about me." (John 8:16-18)*

Two as Emphasis

God sometimes repeats names to attract attention. For instance, we find 'Abraham, Abraham' (Gen. 22:11), 'Jacob, Jacob' (Gen. 46:2), 'Moses, Moses' (Exodus 3:4), 'Samuel, Samuel' (1 Sam. 3:10), 'Martha, Martha' (Luke 10:41), 'Simon, Simon' (Luke 22:31), and 'Saul, Saul' (Acts 9:4). Also, Jesus prefaces many of his statements in John's Gospel with 'Amen, Amen', as if to underline them (see also Numbers 5:22).

Hebrew uses repetition to show progressive increase: thus we find 'from glory to glory' (2 Cor. 3:18); 'from strength to strength' (Psalm 84:7); 'from faith to faith' (Romans 1:17); and 'grace upon grace' (John 1:16). Repetition can also express superlatives: as in 'God of gods' (Deut. 10:17), 'King of Kings' and 'Lord of Lords' (1 Tim. 6:15; Rev. 19:16) as well as 'Song of Songs'.

However, I suggested in my book *But is he God?* that repetitions of the divine name within the same sentence may point to the Father/Son relationship *within* the Godhead. Examples include:

- Then *the* LORD rained on Sodom and Gomorrah sulphur and fire from *the* LORD out of heaven (Gen. 19:24)
- *The* LORD answered Moses, 'Is *the* LORD's arm too short?' (Num. 11:23 NIV)
- *The* LORD declares to you that *the* LORD will make you a house (2 Sam. 7:11)

The LORD *... proclaimed the name of the* LORD. *... "The* LORD, *the* LORD, *a God merciful and gracious, slow to anger, and abounding in steadfast love and faithfulness ...* (Ex. 34:5-6)

Two as Contrast

Over and over again in the Bible we see the struggle between opposites played out against each other, where God's way of doing things is contrasted with man's way of doing things. We see this represented in personal terms through competition between brothers in Genesis (Cain and Abel, Ishmael and Isaac, Esau and Jacob). We also see it visually as two trees in the Garden of Eden (the tree of life and the tree of knowledge), two women in Proverbs (Wisdom and Folly) and two cities in Isaiah and Revelation (Babylon and Jerusalem). The tension between these themes is worked out relentlessly throughout scripture, almost like a great symphony.

The same is true in the New Testament. In Paul's writings we see the flesh versus the Spirit, the law versus grace, and the first Adam versus the second Adam, and in John's writings, light versus darkness and the heavenly versus the earthly. In the parables of Jesus we have the narrow and wide gates, the house on the rock and the house on the sand, the two sons, the Pharisee and the tax collector, and so on. Ultimately these point to two kingdoms, the kingdom of God and the kingdom of this world. The conflict between these two kingdoms is something we experience on a daily basis in our lives, and is never fully resolved until the triumphant final closing chapters of the Bible.

Elijah came near to all the people and said, "How long will you go limping between two different opinions? If the LORD is God, follow him; but if Baal, then follow him." (1 Kings 18:21)

Two as Separation

Separation is an important theme throughout scripture. Firstly, it is important in the act of creation. God *separates* the light from the darkness, the sea from the dry land, and so on.

Secondly, it is important in redemption. God divided the Red Sea and led the Israelites through with a wall of water on either side. The same happened in crossing the Jordan into the Promised Land. And when Jesus died on the cross, the veil of the temple which blocked off access to the Holy of Holies was torn apart, pointing to the fact that access to God's presence is now open to all.

The other side to this equation can be seen in Genesis 15:9-21, where God underlines his promise to Abraham by walking between the divided carcasses of slaughtered animals, showing that he alone would face the consequences if the terms of the covenant were broken by Abraham's descendants.

Finally, separation takes place at the final judgement, as shown in the parables of the wheat and the tares and the sheep and the goats, reminding us that there are ultimately **two** eternal destinies. In addition, separation plays a vital role in purifying the believer from the contamination of the world and setting us apart for God's exclusive purposes. God's Word acts like a surgeon's knife, cutting out the cancer of sin and making us ready to serve him wholeheartedly.

For the word of God is living and active, sharper than any two-edged sword, piercing to the division of soul and of spirit, of joints and of marrow, and discerning the thoughts and intentions of the heart. (Heb. 4:12)

4. **Two** as divine symmetry

We noticed in the previous section how many statements in the Bible are arranged in pairs. This reflects something deep within God's nature and the nature of creation. The number two, as well as expressing *outward* relationship, reminds us of the crucial need for the *inward* relationship of balance in our lives. The Song of Solomon, describing the beautiful proportions of the bride and the symmetry between her different features, comments that 'You are altogether beautiful, my love; there is no flaw in you' (Song 4:7).

Symmetry describes an inner relationship between two halves that are perfectly proportioned against each other. We see many examples across the natural world, whether we are looking at flowers, butterflies, or the design of the human body.

Human beings have been fascinated with palindromes, where words are spelt the same way in both directions. It is striking, therefore, that the deepest and most intimate relationship word in the Bible, ABBA ('Daddy': an extraordinary and revolutionary way to address God), is an exact palindrome: it reads the same backwards as forwards. While this may just be a happy coincidence, it does remind us that God stands outside time. He is the same forwards and backwards, eternally faithful and eternally consistent, even outside the realm of time and space. We will see in later chapters how he demonstrates his nature through symmetrical shapes such as squares, cubes and crystals. He is the Alpha and Omega, the Beginning and the End.

Scripture is full of symmetrical structures and patterns. These help to express and amplify various aspects of Biblical truth. For instance, symmetry may express harmonious mutual relationships. We can see this in two of the statements we considered earlier:

no one knows the Son except the Father,

and no one knows the Father except the Son (Matt. 11:27)

The Ordered Cosmos

Many laws of physics and chemistry are descriptions of symmetry. Matter is reflected by antimatter, positive by negative, and so on. The same appears to be true of the universe itself. Current scientific models predict that cosmic background radiation should be evenly spread. Surprisingly it is not so. In fact it seems to line up with the plane in which the earth travels round the sun, with a probability of less than 0.1 percent of this happening by chance. Some physicists were so disturbed by this that they dubbed it the 'axis of evil'! One leading atheist physicist, Laurence Krauss, put his concern like this: 'We're looking out at the whole universe. There's no way there should be a correlation of structure with our motion of the earth around the sun — the plane of the earth around the sun — the ecliptic. That would say we are **truly the centre of the universe.**'[2]

*And when you look up into the sky and see the sun, moon, and stars—all the forces of heaven— don't be seduced into worshiping them. The LORD your God **gave them to all the peoples of the earth**.* (Deut. 4:19 NLT)

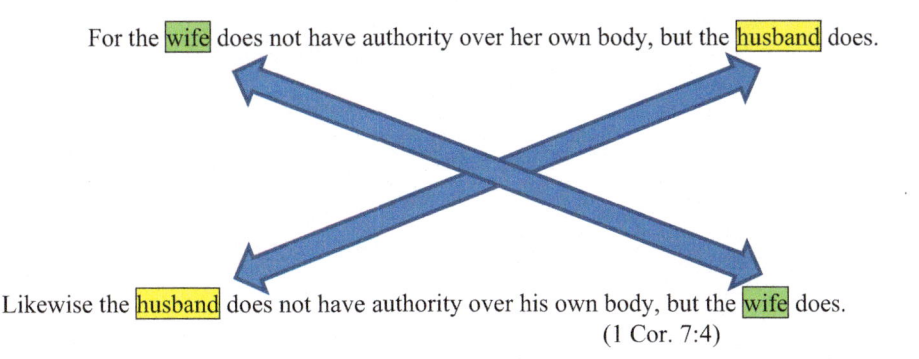

For the wife does not have authority over her own body, but the husband does.

Likewise the husband does not have authority over his own body, but the wife does.
(1 Cor. 7:4)

The technical name for this device is a 'chiasm' because of its resemblance to a Greek letter x, or 'chi'. The symmetrical structure of such patterns makes them well-suited to express the themes of judgement and reward. We can see this clearly in the following verses:

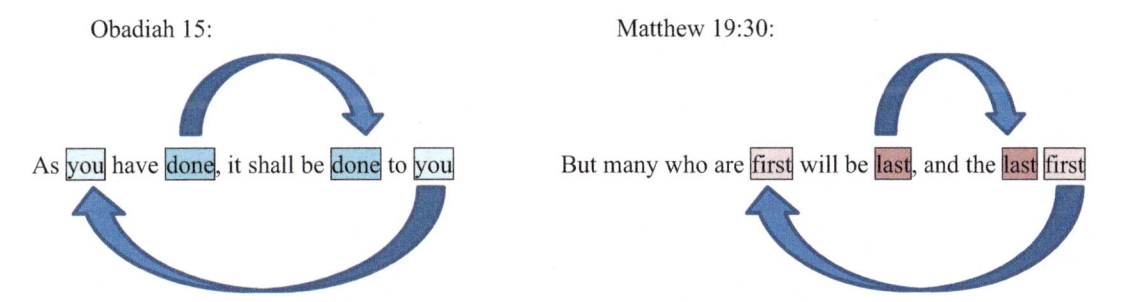

Obadiah 15:

As you have done, it shall be done to you

Matthew 19:30:

But many who are first will be last, and the last first

The palindromic name of God, ABBA, is often a helpful way of laying out such constructions:

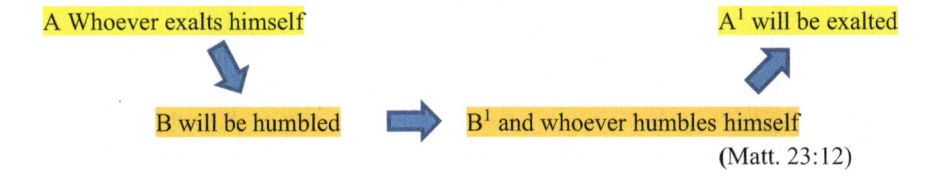

A Whoever exalts himself

B will be humbled

B¹ and whoever humbles himself

A¹ will be exalted

(Matt. 23:12)

It is natural that verses expressing the 'Divine Exchange' that we considered in Chapter One should take this format:

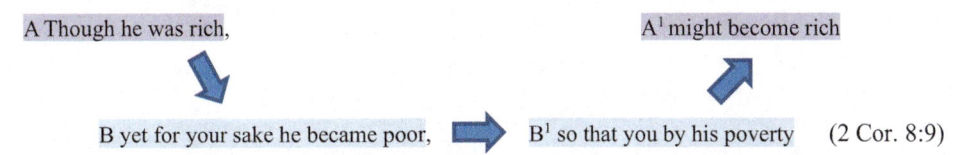

A Though he was rich,

B yet for your sake he became poor,

B¹ so that you by his poverty

A¹ might become rich

(2 Cor. 8:9)

The writer C.S. Lewis uses a similar construction in his book *Mere Christianity*:

A The Son of God   A¹ to become sons of God

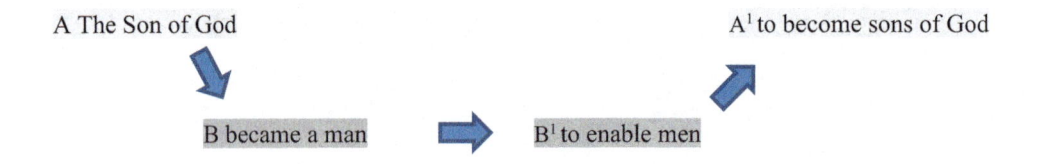

      B became a man ⟹ B¹ to enable men

It follows that this format lends itself beautifully to verses which express the parabola of redemption:

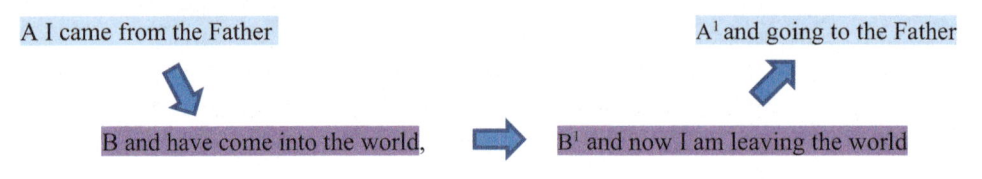

A I came from the Father   A¹ and going to the Father

    B and have come into the world, ⟹ B¹ and now I am leaving the world

(John 16.28)

In a sense, we join this parabola through baptism: we join Christ in his death as we go down into the water, and we are raised back up with him as we come out of the water.

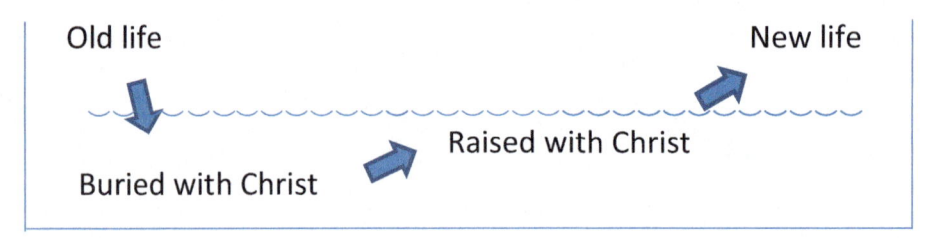

Old life → **Buried with Christ** → **Raised with Christ** → **New life**

The power of symmetry in displaying the cross as a dramatic turning-point in the history of mankind is demonstrated forcefully by Bach in his B minor Mass. By positioning the *Crucifixus* as the very centre of his setting of the Creed, and placing the Creed at the heart of his entire work, he creates a formidable musical arch shape. Immediately following the *Crucifixus*, the next movement, *Et resurrexit*, begins in the soprano part with a sequence of pitches arranged in an exact palindrome, showing that death itself has been sent into reverse:

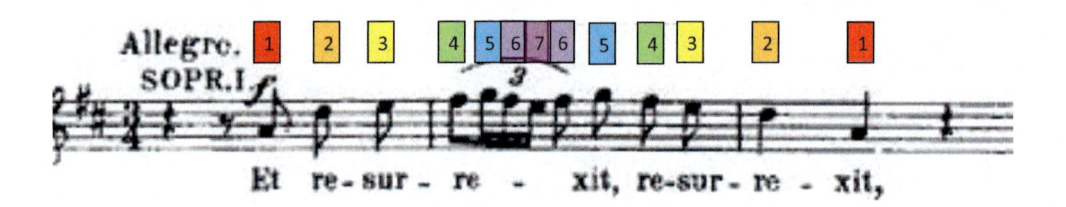

[Musical notation: Allegro, SOPR.I — Et re-sur-re-xit, re-sur-re-xit, with pitches numbered 1 2 3 4 5 6 7 6 5 4 3 2 1]

TWO: THE NUMBER OF RELATIONSHIP

The palindrome ΝΙΨΟΝ ΑΝΟΜΗΜΑΤΑ ΜΗ ΜΟΝΑΝ ΟΨΙΝ ("Wash [your] sins, not only [your] face"), supposedly by the church father Gregory of Nazianzus, appears on a holy water font (see above) near the great cathedral of Hagia Sophia in Constantinople (now Istanbul) and many other orthodox churches from the Byzantine period (photo by Christine Kekka). A variant form also appears in a number of churches across Western Europe, such as the font at St Martin at Ludgate in London (pictured below, photographed by Andrew Abbott). Water in scripture often pictures the reversal and cleansing of sin.

Another symmetrical arrangement appears in the second half of the book of Isaiah (chapters 40 to the end of the book, sometimes called 'Deutero-Isaiah'). The whole of Isaiah is intriguing in itself in that the number of chapters in the two clearly divided sections correspond exactly to the number of books in the whole Bible (39 plus 27, making a total of 66 in all). Still more intriguing, as David Pawson points out, is that the exact **middle** verse of the **middle** chapter of the second section of Isaiah contains one of the most profound passages in the whole Bible and is a direct pointer to the cross:

> All we like sheep have gone astray;
> we have turned—every one—to his own way;
> and the LORD has laid on him
> the iniquity of us all. (Is. 53:6)[3]

Sceptics may point out here that chapters and verses were not added until centuries after the completion of the Bible. But we should remember that there are no coincidences with God, whose providential hand is not necessarily just restricted to the original texts themselves, even if these added 'extras' are of secondary importance.

Indeed, if we compare the beginning and ending of the Bible as a whole we can see the same symmetrical crossover shape appearing. In many ways Revelation might be seen as Genesis through a mirror. Both make prominent use of the sun, moon and twelve stars as symbols for the tribes of Israel (Gen. 37:9-10; Rev. 12:1), and both have interesting points of contact between the beginning and end of the respective books:

Genesis (end)

- Naming and numbering of the tribes of Israel (46:8-27)
  ↓
- Jacob standing before Pharoah's throne; seven years of famine and economic turmoil (47:7-26)
  ↓
- Jacob's prophecy over the sons of Israel: blessing and rebuke (49:1-27)
  ↓
- "God meant it for good ... that many people should be kept alive" (50:20)

Revelation (beginning)

- Naming and numbering of the tribes of Israel (7:4-8)
  ↑
- Christ standing before God's throne; seven seals; famine and economic turmoil (chapters 5 and 6)
  ↑
- Christ's letters to the seven churches: blessing and rebuke (2:1-3:22)
  ↑
- "I am alive for evermore, and I have the keys of Death and Hades" (1:18)

These similarities are even more marked if we compare the books at their opposite end:

TWO: THE NUMBER OF RELATIONSHIP

Genesis (beginning)

CREATION (1:1-2:25)
Creation of the heavens and the earth (2:1)
Tree of life (2:9); River (2:10); Gold (2:11)
Precious Stones (2:12)
Adam and Eve (2:22-23)

↓

THE ORIGINAL FALL OF MAN (3:1-3:24)
First deception of mankind (3:1-3:7)
Judgement on Satan and rebellious humanity (3:14-19)

↓

GENERATIONS OF ADAM (4:1-5:32)
Lifespans of up to 1,000 years (5:5, 20, 27)
Enoch translated to heaven (5:24)

↓

UNIVERSAL JUDGEMENT (6:1-7:24)
Humanity set against God (6:5)
Nephilim drowned in flood (6:4; 7:21-23)

↓

THE SAVED REMNANT ON EARTH (8:1-10:32)
Worship offered to God (8:20)
Remnant becomes a multitude (10:1-10:32)

↓

JUDGEMENT ON BABEL (11:1-9)
A tower with its top in the heavens (11:4)
"Let us make a name for ourselves" (11:4)
God acts against the city (11:6-9)

↓

THE RIGHTEOUS AND THE WICKED (11:10-19.29)
Abraham set apart as firstfruits of mankind (12:1-3)
In you all the families of the earth will be blessed (12:3)
Angelic Intermediaries (19.1)
Sexual immorality of Sodom (19:4-9)
Fire from heaven (19:24)
Sodom and Gomorrah destroyed (19:25)

Revelation (end)

NEW CREATION (21:1-22:21)
Creation of a new heaven and a new earth (21:1)
Tree of life (22:2); River (22:1); Gold (21:18, 21)
Precious Stones (21:11, 18-21)
Christ and his Bride (21:9)

↑

THE FINAL FALL OF MAN (20:7-15)
Final deception of mankind (20:7-8)
Judgement on Satan and rebellious humanity (20:9-15)

↑

MILLENIUM OF CHRIST (20:1-6)
Saints reign with Christ for 1,000 years (20:4-6)
Martyrs translated to earth (20:4)

↑

JUDGEMENT ON THE NATIONS (19:11-21)
Humanity set against God (19:19)
Beast and false prophet destroyed in battle (19:20)

↑

THE SAVED REMNANT IN HEAVEN (19:1-10)
Worship offered to God (19:1-8)
Remnant has become a multitude (19:1,6)

↑

JUDGEMENT ON BABYLON (17:1-18:24)
Her sins are heaped high as heaven (18:5)
She glorified herself (18:7)
God acts against the city (18:8)

↑

THE RIGHTEOUS AND THE WICKED (14:1-16.21)
144,000 'redeemed from mankind as firstfruits' (14.1-4)
An eternal gospel to… those who dwell in the earth (14.6)
Angelic Intermediaries (15.1)
Sexual immorality of Babylon (14:8)
Fire from heaven (16:8)
Cities of the nations destroyed (16:19)

Furthermore, both Genesis and Revelation are rich in their own internal symmetries, both on a small and a large scale. For example, the climactic statement of Genesis Chapter One in verse 27 follows the pattern of some of the verses we have been considering, the mirror formation presenting the idea that mankind was intended as God's 'image' or 'reflection' on the earth:

>   A   God created man
>   B   in his own image,
>   B¹ in the image of God
>   A¹ He created him

This arch however appears within a much larger symmetrical formation:

A God created the heavens and the earth (1:1)
    B There was evening and there was morning (1:5 etc.)
        C God saw that it was good (1:10 etc.)
            D Plants yielding seed (1:11-12)
                E Birds fill the heavens (1:20)
                    F Beasts of the earth (1:24-25)
                        G Dominion over every living thing (1:26)
                            H God created man (1:27)
                                I in his own image,
                                I¹ in the image of God
                            H¹ He created him
                        G¹ Dominion over every living thing (1:28)
                    F¹ Every beast of the earth (1:30)
                E¹ Every bird of the heavens (1:30)
            D¹ Every green plant for food (1:30)
        C¹ God saw that it was very good (1:31)
    B¹ There was evening and there was morning (1:31)
A¹ God finished creating the heavens and the earth (2:1-2)

Chapters 2 and 3, meanwhile, trace out another large-scale arch formation:

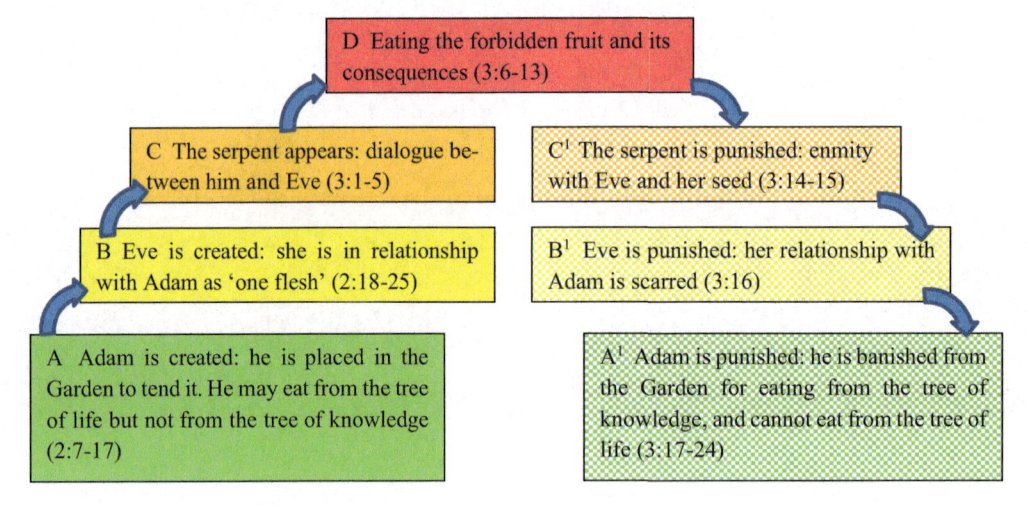

D Eating the forbidden fruit and its consequences (3:6-13)

C The serpent appears: dialogue between him and Eve (3:1-5)

C¹ The serpent is punished: enmity with Eve and her seed (3:14-15)

B Eve is created: she is in relationship with Adam as 'one flesh' (2:18-25)

B¹ Eve is punished: her relationship with Adam is scarred (3:16)

A Adam is created: he is placed in the Garden to tend it. He may eat from the tree of life but not from the tree of knowledge (2:7-17)

A¹ Adam is punished: he is banished from the Garden for eating from the tree of knowledge, and cannot eat from the tree of life (3:17-24)

But just as we considered 'wheels within wheels' earlier in the book, so here we see 'arches within arches' that nestle inside each other like Russian dolls. Chapters 2 and 3 both have their own individual arch shapes:

Genesis Chapter Two:

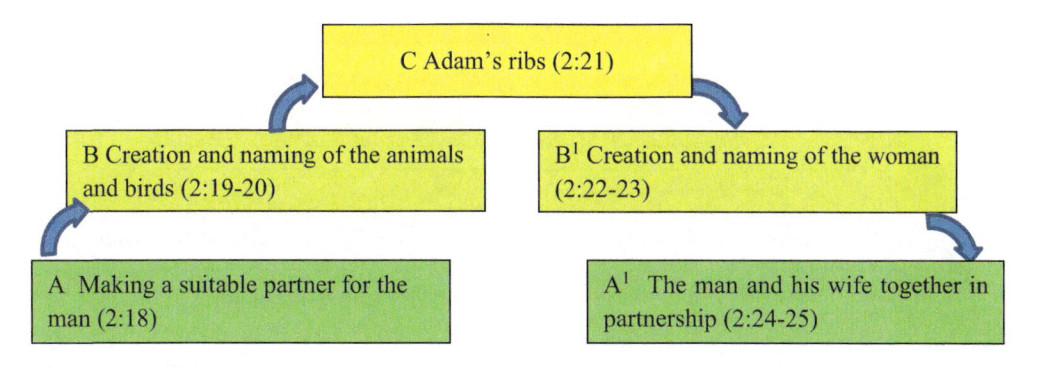

- C Adam's ribs (2:21)
- B Creation and naming of the animals and birds (2:19-20)
- B¹ Creation and naming of the woman (2:22-23)
- A Making a suitable partner for the man (2:18)
- A¹ The man and his wife together in partnership (2:24-25)

Genesis Chapter Three:

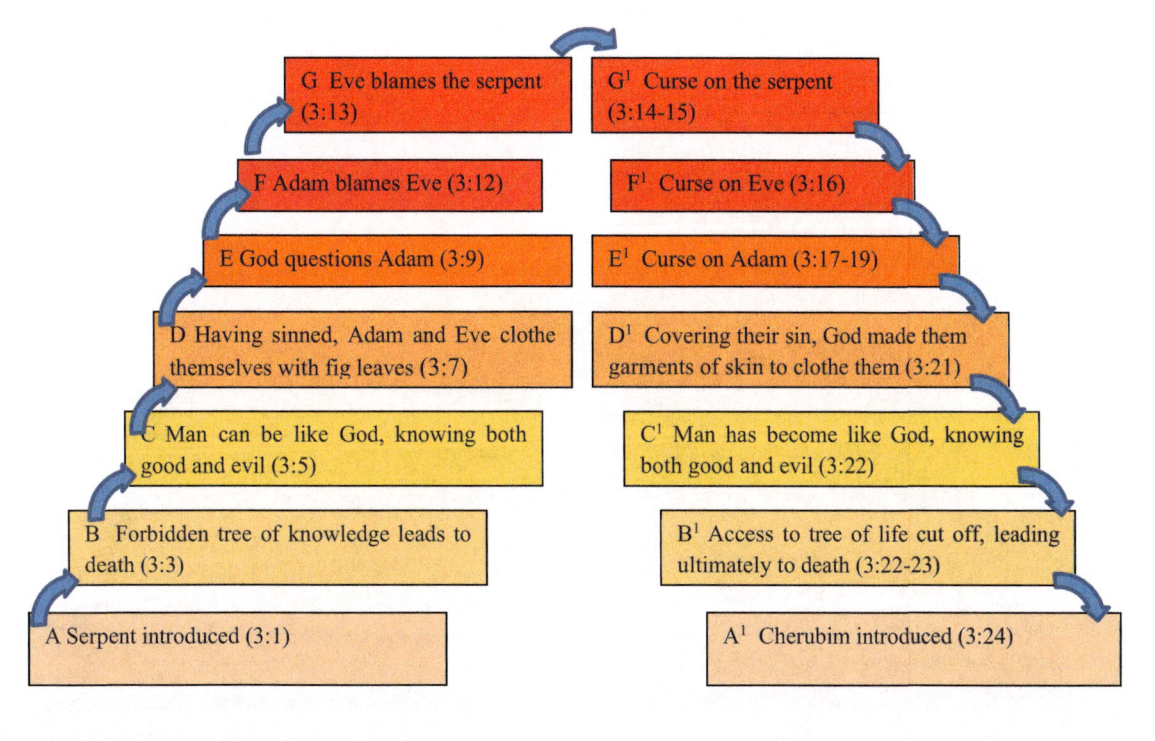

- G Eve blames the serpent (3:13)
- G¹ Curse on the serpent (3:14-15)
- F Adam blames Eve (3:12)
- F¹ Curse on Eve (3:16)
- E God questions Adam (3:9)
- E¹ Curse on Adam (3:17-19)
- D Having sinned, Adam and Eve clothe themselves with fig leaves (3:7)
- D¹ Covering their sin, God made them garments of skin to clothe them (3:21)
- C Man can be like God, knowing both good and evil (3:5)
- C¹ Man has become like God, knowing both good and evil (3:22)
- B Forbidden tree of knowledge leads to death (3:3)
- B¹ Access to tree of life cut off, leading ultimately to death (3:22-23)
- A Serpent introduced (3:1)
- A¹ Cherubim introduced (3:24)

Moreover, the *second* of these arches can itself be broken into **two** adjacent arches, as we see laid out on the next page:

The Fall of Man:

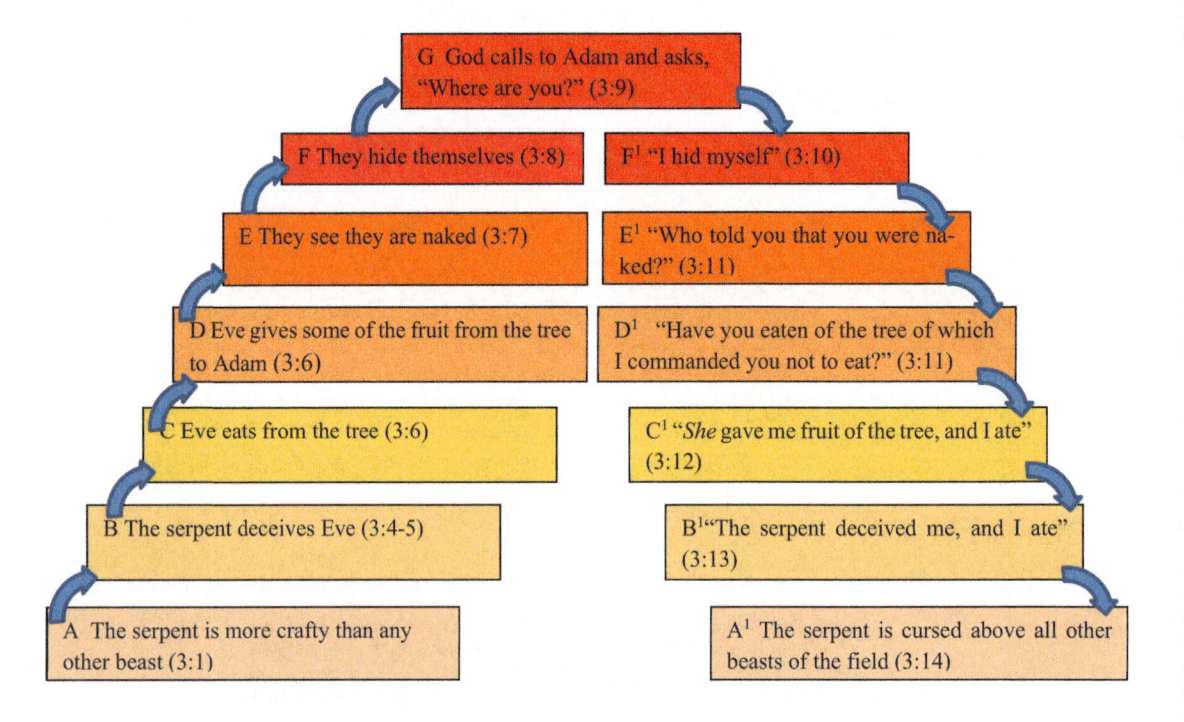

- G God calls to Adam and asks, "Where are you?" (3:9)
- F They hide themselves (3:8)
- F¹ "I hid myself" (3:10)
- E They see they are naked (3:7)
- E¹ "Who told you that you were naked?" (3:11)
- D Eve gives some of the fruit from the tree to Adam (3:6)
- D¹ "Have you eaten of the tree of which I commanded you not to eat?" (3:11)
- C Eve eats from the tree (3:6)
- C¹ "*She* gave me fruit of the tree, and I ate" (3:12)
- B The serpent deceives Eve (3:4-5)
- B¹ "The serpent deceived me, and I ate" (3:13)
- A The serpent is more crafty than any other beast (3:1)
- A¹ The serpent is cursed above all other beasts of the field (3:14)

The Judgement on Man:

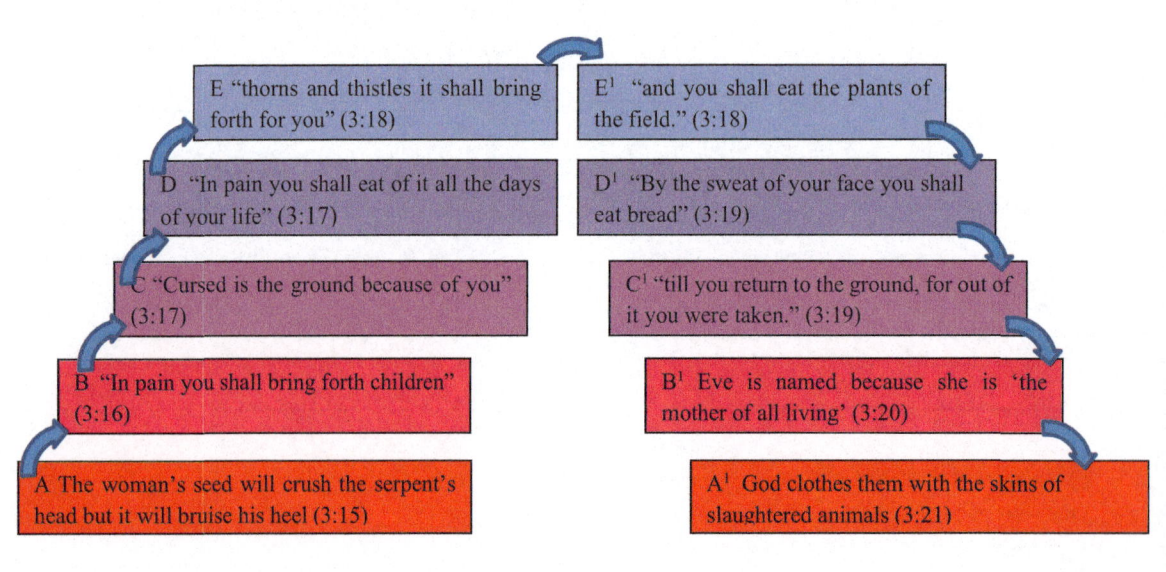

- E "thorns and thistles it shall bring forth for you" (3:18)
- E¹ "and you shall eat the plants of the field." (3:18)
- D "In pain you shall eat of it all the days of your life" (3:17)
- D¹ "By the sweat of your face you shall eat bread" (3:19)
- C "Cursed is the ground because of you" (3:17)
- C¹ "till you return to the ground, for out of it you were taken." (3:19)
- B "In pain you shall bring forth children" (3:16)
- B¹ Eve is named because she is 'the mother of all living' (3:20)
- A The woman's seed will crush the serpent's head but it will bruise his heel (3:15)
- A¹ God clothes them with the skins of slaughtered animals (3:21)

There is an interesting contrast between these two segments. Whereas the first arch begins and ends with the serpent, the second arch appears to begin and end with Christ, by offering pointers towards his sacrifice on our behalf on the cross, defeating Satan through his death and 'covering' our sins through his blood. Within this great tragedy, therefore, there are already seeds of hope.

The Babel account, describing man's renewed rebellion against God in Chapter 11, also shows an outward symmetry, almost creating a miniature 'tower' in its own right. Here we should notice that, just as in the first part of Genesis Chapter 3, it is God's intervention that marks the apex of the tower:

```
                    the LORD came down (v.5)
            a city and a tower (v.4)      the city and the tower (v.5)
        let us build ourselves (v.4)      the children of man had built (v. 5)
    Come, let us make bricks (v.3)        Come, let us go down (v.7)
    one another (v.3)                     one another (v.7)
    settled there (v.2)                   dispersed them from there (v. 8)
    one language (v.1)                    the language (v.9)
the whole earth (v.1)                     all the earth (v.9)
```

The same is true of the flood story. This becomes particularly apparent if we map out the timings of the different segments of the story, which give a clear indication of an underlying pattern, in that they are again reflected around a central point:

```
            A: Seven days waiting to enter Ark (7:4)
              B: Second reference to seven days waiting (7:10)
                C: 40 days (7:17)
                  D: 150 days (7:24)
                    E: God remembers Noah (8:1)
                  D¹: 150 days (8:3)
                C¹: 40 days (8:6)
              B¹ Seven days waiting for dove (8:10)
            A¹: Second seven days waiting for dove (8:12)
```

But this is concealed within a much larger arch which very appropriately traces a rainbow shape:

The Rainbow Shape in the Story of the Flood

A   Noah is born (5:28-29)
  B   The curse on the ground (5:29)
    C   Sin takes hold of the earth (6:1-5)
      D   Noah described (6:9)
        E   Noah's three sons (6:10)
          F   First mention of the ark (6:14-16)
            G   The future flood (6:17)
              H   God's covenant with Noah and all creatures (6:18-20)
                I   Food on the ark (6:21)
                  J   Noah's obedience (6:22)
                    K   Command to enter the ark (7:1)
                      L   7 days wait for flood promised (7:4-5)
                        M   7 days wait for flood fulfilled (7:7-10)
                        N   Noah and the animals enter the ark (7:11-15)
                          O   God shuts Noah in (7:16)
                            P   Interval of 40 days (7:17)
                            Q   The waters prevail (7:17-18)
                              R   Mountain peaks covered (7:19-20)
                                S   Waters increase for 150 days (7:21-24)
                                T   **God remembers Noah** (8:1)
                              S^1 Waters subside for 150 days (8:1-3)
                            R^1 Mountain peaks reappear (8:4-5)
                        Q^1 The waters abate (8:5)
                      O^1 Noah opens the window of the ark (8:6)
                    N^1 Noah releases a raven and dove from the ark (8:7-9)
                  M^1 7 days waiting for waters to subside (8:10-11)
                L^1 7 more days waiting for waters to subside (8:12-13)
              K^1 Command to leave the ark (8:15-17)
            J^1 Noah's obedience (8:18-19)
          I^1 Food after the ark (9:3-4)
        H^1 God's covenant with Noah and all creatures (9:8-11)
      G^1 No future flood (9:11-15)
      F^1 Final mention of the ark (9:18)
    E^1 Noah's three sons (9:19)
    D^1 Noah is described again (9:20)
    C^1 Sin takes hold once more (9:21-24)
  B^1 The curse on Canaan (9:25)
A^1 Noah dies (9:29)

Within this rainbow, a striking miniature rainbow appears after Noah and his family emerge from the Ark:

```
A    "Whoever sheds
 B    the blood
  C    of man
  C¹   by man
 B¹   his blood
A¹   shall be shed ..."
```

Just as we saw in the story of the Fall, this may contain another extraordinary pointer to Christ's work on the cross. On the surface the verse simply appears to mandate capital punishment for murder. But it is conceivable that it goes far beyond this. It is God who, above all, takes life and gives it; God who put into place the law of sin and death; God who allowed the flood and many subsequent acts of judgement as punishments for sin, causing loss of life on a massive scale. This passage may also be hinting that, in response to all this, God would later be willing to taste death for himself in Christ, to face his own judgement and penalty for the sin of the whole world.

The first few chapters of Genesis, then, contain many patterns and structures below the surface that may aid our understanding of God's ultimate purposes in the stories and how they stand in the great drama of redemption. And it is not the only book of the Bible to display such features. Many other books display such features, Esther being a prime example, even if these are not immediately apparent at surface level to the reader.

But what of Revelation? Many Christians shy away from this book because of its strange images, bizarre symbolism, and a dream-like quality in which sequences of events seem to recycle themselves in ever more dramatic ways.

Yet for all its difficulties, it is full of the most remarkable symmetries and number patterns that would repay a lifetime of study. As we show on the next two pages, there are remarkable correspondences between the first and second halves which are all the more striking given that the book was revealed to John as a series of supernatural visions. These correlations help to throw light on some of the great mysteries of the book: why the trumpet and bowl judgements are so similar, why there should be **two** beasts and not just one, why the 144,000 saints appear twice, in two different contexts, and so on.

In particular, this twofold patterning helps to draw attention to the main theme of the book, Christ's ultimate triumph over Satan, which is laid out clearly in 12:10, the verse which stands at the apex of the entire pyramid. As such, it provides extra comfort and reassurance to those suffering from the fires of persecution. Help is on its way!

12.10 And I heard a loud voice in heaven, saying, "Now the salvation and the power and the kingdom

THE COSMIC BATTLE (12:1-10)

Satan cast down from heaven to earth (12:9)
Woman given sanctuary for 42 months (12:6)
Woman's offspring (Jesus), threatened by dragon (12:4-5)
Seven heads and ten horns (12:3)

THE TWO WITNESSES (11:1-12)

Worshippers of God (11:1)
Two witnesses, 42 months (11:2-3)
Fire from their mouths (11:5)
Breath and the punishment of death (11:5)
Miracles (11:6)
Beast from the abyss wages war against them (11:7)
Every people, tribe, language and nation (11:9)
Witnesses resurrected (11:11)

144,000 SAINTS AND SEVEN TRUMPETS (7:1-10:11 & 11:13-19)

Foreheads marked (7:3)
144,000 saints (7:4)
Every nation, tribe, people and language (7:9)
Elders and living creatures (7:11)
Worshipped God (7:11)
Comfort for those who have worshipped the Lamb (7:13-17)
Rest for the righteous (7:17)
Seven angels given seven trumpets (8:2)
The smoke of the incense ... rose before God (8:4)
First trumpet affects the earth (8:7)
Second trumpet affects the sea: a third becomes blood, and a third of creatures in the sea die (8:8-9)
Third trumpet affects the rivers and springs: they become bitter (8:10-11)
Fourth trumpet affects sun, moon and stars (8:12)
Fifth trumpet causes the sun and air to be darkened (9:2)
Sixth trumpet releases angels bound at the river Euphrates (9:14)
Three plagues out of the mouths of the horses (9:17,18)
They did not repent of their murders (9:21)
A great earthquake, and a tenth of the city fell (11:13)
Seventh trumpet: loud voices proclaim the coming of Christ's kingdom (11:15)
Flashes of lightning, rumblings, peals of thunder, an earthquake, and heavy hail (11:19)

Revelation Symmetry

JUDGEMENT FROM THE THRONE (4:1-6:17)

A door standing open in heaven (4:1)
A throne stood in heaven, with one seated on the throne (4:2)
Round the throne were twenty-four thrones (4:4)
Twenty-four elders (4:4)
Peals of thunder (4:5)
Four living creatures (4:6-8)
"Worthy are you, our Lord and God, to receive glory and honour and power" (4:11)
Appearance of the Lamb (5.6)
A kingdom and priests to our God, and they shall reign (5:10)
Myriads of myriads and thousands of thousands (5:11)
Fell down and worshipped (5:14)
The scroll is opened (6:1)
Behold, a white horse! And its rider had a bow, and a crown was given to him, and he came out conquering, and to conquer (6:2)
Its rider was permitted to take peace from the earth, so that people should slay one another (6:4)
Death and Hades (6:8)
The souls of those who had been slain for the word of God (6:9)
How long before you will judge and avenge our blood? (6:10)
Kings of the earth ... great ones ... generals and the rich and the powerful, and everyone, slave and free (6:15)
The wrath of the Lamb (6:16)

THE CHURCH OF GOD (1:9-3:22)

I saw seven golden lampstands (1:12)
His face was like the sun shining in full strength (1:16)
I have the keys of Death (1:18)
To the one who conquers I will grant to eat of the tree of life (2:7)
The book of life (3:5)
I will write on him the name of my God (3:12)
The city of my God, the new Jerusalem (3:12)

THE COMING KING (1:1-1:8)

God gave...to show to his servants the things that must soon take place (1:1)
He made it known by sending his angel (1:1)
Blessed is the one who reads aloud the words of this prophecy ... and who keep what is written in it (1:3)
The time is near (1:3)
He is coming with the clouds (1:7)
"I am the Alpha and the Omega," says the Lord God, "who is and who was and who is to come, the Almighty." (1:8)
Write what you see in a book and send it to the seven churches (1:11)

and the authority of his Christ have come, for the accuser of our brothers has been thrown down"

THE COSMIC BATTLE (12:10-13.1)

Satan cast down from heaven to earth (12:12-13)
 Woman given sanctuary for 42 months (12:14)
  Woman's offspring (followers of Jesus), threatened by dragon (12:17)
   Ten horns and seven heads (13:1)

THE TWO BEASTS (13:1-18)

Worshippers of the dragon and the beast (13:4)
Two beasts, 42 months (13:5)
Fire from heaven (13:13)
Breath and the punishment of death (13:15)
Miracles (13:14)
Beast wages war against the saints (13:7)
Every tribe, people, language and nation (13:7)
Beast resurrected (13:3,12,14)

144,000 SAINTS AND SEVEN BOWLS (14:1-16:21)

Foreheads marked (13:16)
144,000 saints (14:1)
Every nation, tribe, language and people (14:6)
Elders and living creatures (14:3)
Worship God (14:7)
Torment for those who have worshipped the beast (14:9-11)
Rest for the righteous (14:13)
Seven angels given seven bowls (15:6-7)
The sanctuary was filled with smoke from the glory of God (15:8)
First bowl affects the earth (16:2)
Second bowl affects the sea: it becomes blood, and every living creature in the sea dies (16:3)
Third bowl affects the rivers and springs: they become blood (16:4)
Fourth bowl affects the sun (16:8)
Fifth bowl causes the kingdom of the beast to be darkened (16:10)
Sixth bowl dries up the the river Euphrates, enabling kings from the east to cross (16:12)
Three unclean spirits out of the mouths of the dragon, beast and false prophet (16:13)
They did not repent of their deeds (16:11)
A great earthquake ... and the cities of the nations fell (16:18-19)
Seventh bowl: a loud voice in heaven proclaims, "It is done!" (16:17)
Flashes of lightning, rumblings, peals of thunder, a great earthquake, and great hail (16:18,21)

JUDGEMENT FROM THE THRONE (19:1-20:15)

I saw heaven opened (19:11)
God who was seated on the throne (19:4)
I saw thrones, and seated on them were those to whom the authority to judge was committed (20:4)
Twenty-four elders (19:4)
Peals of thunder (19:6)
Four living creatures (19:4)
"Salvation and glory and power belong to our God" (19:1)
Appearance of the Bride of the Lamb (19.7-8)
Priests of God and of Christ, and they will reign (20:6)
A great multitude (19:1,6)
Fell down and worshipped (19:4)
Books were opened (20:12)
Behold, a white horse! The one sitting on it is called Faithful and True, and in righteousness he judges and makes war (19:11)
Satan will be released ... and will come out to deceive the nations ... to gather them for battle (20:7-8)
Death and Hades (20:13-14)
The souls of those who had been beheaded ... for the word of God (20:4)
He has judged the great prostitute ... and has avenged on her the blood of his servants (19:2)
Kings ... captains ... mighty men ... all men, both free and slave, both small and great (19:18)
The wrath of God the Almighty (19:15)

THE CHURCH OF GOD (21:1-22:5)

The city was pure gold (21:18)
The city has no need of sun or moon to shine on it ... its lamp is the Lamb (21:23)
Death shall be no more (21:4)
I will give from the spring of the water of life ... The one who conquers will have this heritage (21:6-7)
The Lamb's book of life (21:27)
His name will be on their foreheads (22:4)
The holy city, new Jerusalem, coming down out of heaven from God (21:2)

THE COMING KING (22:6-22:21)

God sent...to show his servants what must soon take place (22:6)
I, Jesus, have sent my angel (22:16)
Blessed is the one who keeps the words of the prophecy of this book (22:7)
The time is near (22:10)
He is coming soon (22:20)
"I am the Alpha and the Omega, the first and the last, the beginning and the end." (22:13)
I, Jesus, have sent my angel to testify ... for the churches (22:16)

Finally, we should note that the fact that Revelation seems to shadow the events of Genesis in reverse hints at the possibility that the entire course of history, viewed from a Biblical perspective, follows a symmetrical shape, in which we ourselves are still active participants:

CREATION OF HEAVEN AND EARTH			
Adam and Eve in the Garden of Eden			
2,000 YEARS +	Adam to Abraham	One language → many languages	
BIRTH OF ISRAEL: Abraham, Isaac, Jacob, Joseph			
2,000 YEARS +	Abraham to Christ	-- 400 year silence in the Biblical record --	
^	^	EXODUS AND RETURN TO PROMISED LAND	
^	^	Cycles of disobedience: Joshua to Samuel	God's Kingdom
^	^	SAUL (40 years) DAVID (40 years) SOLOMON (40 years)	United Kingdom
^	^	Cycles of disobedience: Rehoboam to Zedekiah	Divided Kingdom
^	^	EXILE AND RETURN TO PROMISED LAND	
^	^	-- 400 year silence in the Biblical record --	
BIRTH OF CHURCH: The Coming of Jesus			
2,000 YEARS +	First Coming to Second Coming	One church → many denominations	
Christ (the second Adam) in the Millenium			
CREATION OF NEW HEAVEN AND NEW EARTH			

Two points can be made here. Firstly, it is worth noticing that the exact midpoint of the chart marks the summit of Israel's history, where King David became ruler in Jerusalem, halfway between Abraham and Christ. In the light of this the re-establishment of Israel in 1948 as an independent nation, and the subsequent restoration of Jerusalem as its capital, is a highly significant event (Luke 21:24). We should never forget that the climax of the Bible is the *New* Jerusalem coming down from heaven to earth, with Jesus, Son of David, ruling as its new king.

Secondly, although the timings given here are very approximate, it is very clear that from our vantage-point in history we have almost reached the bottom of the chart. We need to be preparing for the return of Christ and to understand the urgency of sharing that message with others.

The Head of the Corner

At the very heart of the Bible we find Psalm 118. It occurs at almost exactly the halfway point in the Bible in terms of chapter numbers, and is sandwiched in between the **shortest** chapter in the Bible, Psalm 117 (which occurs at the exact midpoint) and the **longest** chapter in the Bible, Psalm 119.

It begins and ends with same phrase ('Oh give thanks to the Lord, for he is good; for his steadfast love endures for ever!'), and the central axis of the Psalm introduces a threefold description of God which might be considered a symmetrical pointer to the Trinity:

"The right hand of the LORD does valiantly,
    the right hand of the LORD exalts,
  the right hand of the LORD does valiantly!"

Adding the 594 chapters up to the midpoint at Psalm 117 and the 594 chapters from Psalm 118 to the end of the Bible together makes a total of 1188. It is intriguing, then, that Psalm 118 verse 8 says 'it is better to take refuge in the Lord than to trust in man' which might be summed up as a central theme of scripture. This in turn occurs just after the halfway point of a symmetrical structure covering the first part of the Psalm, arranged in a 3+2+2+3 pattern:

Let Israel say,
  "His steadfast love endures for ever."
Let the house of Aaron say,
  "His steadfast love endures for ever."
 Let those who fear the LORD say,
  "His steadfast love endures for ever."
Out of my distress I called on the LORD;
  the LORD answered me and set me free.
The LORD is on my side; I will not fear.
  What can man do to me?
The LORD is on my side as my helper;
  I shall look in triumph on those who hate me.

It is better to take refuge in the LORD
  than to trust in man.
It is better to take refuge in the LORD
  than to trust in princes.
All nations surrounded me;
  in the name of the LORD I cut them off!
They surrounded me, surrounded me on every side!
  in the name of the LORD I cut them off!
They surrounded me like bees;
  ....they went out like a fire among thorns;
  in the name of the LORD I cut them off!

Eight verses from the *end* of the Psalm we also find the words 'the stone that the builders rejected has become the *cornerstone*.' This describes the first stone set in a building, against which the place of all the other stones is determined. Like the keystone of an arch, it is appropriate both for the mirror-like constructions present and for a Psalm almost exactly halfway through scripture, and it reappears no less than five times in the New Testament in reference to Christ. This verse, therefore, places Jesus at the apex of the Bible that we have today.

If we now turn back to the exact middle chapter of the Bible, Psalm 117, we find it to be the **shortest** chapter in the Bible, and yet occurring in the **largest** book (Psalms). There are exactly 595 chapters up to and including this middle chapter. The number 595 is a palindromic number (it reads the same backwards as forwards). The Psalms immediately before and after both speak powerfully of how God delivers from death.

Calculating the exact middle *verse* in Scripture takes us to a slightly different place, at Psalm 103.1-2. There are exactly 15,551 verses up to and including the first of these verses. 15551 is again a palindromic number. The Psalm beforehand is a powerful cry for deliverance and the Psalm continuing on from these verses a thanksgiving for that deliverance.

Are these patterns real, or mere coincidences? Chapters and verses were not added until centuries after the Bible was finished, and so might be considered a fanciful irrelevance. But it is intriguing that the total number of chapters in the Old Testament (929) and the total number of books in the Bible (66) are also palindromic numbers, appropriate to a God who declares 'the end from the beginning' (Is. 46:10).

All this, of course, may be fascinating to look at on paper, but beyond what we have just said, what are the practical applications of Biblical symmetry in our everyday walk with God?

1. It should have an impact on **the choices that we make in our lives**. There is a symmetry between cause and effect: what goes out comes back in, and what goes up must come down (Ecc. 1:5-7). We reap what we sow. As Paul writes to the Galatians:

> ಸಾರ
> The one who sows to his own flesh will from the flesh reap corruption, but the one who sows to the Spirit will from the Spirit reap eternal life. (Gal. 6:8)
> ಸಾರ

To the Romans he writes:

> ಸಾರ
> Just as you once presented your members as slaves to impurity and to lawlessness leading to more lawlessness, so now present your members as slaves to righteousness leading to sanctification. (Rom. 6:19)
> ಸಾರ

Since actions have a habit of coming back upon us, we need to live our lives in such a way that we are planting the right seeds for the right harvest.

2. Symmetry should have **an impact in the way that we treat others**. Jesus said that 'whatever you wish that others would do to you, do also to them, for this is the Law and the Prophets' (Matt. 7:12). As we give, so also we receive. By the same token, our love for God needs to be outworked in our love for those around us. We should remember that Jesus summarised the Old Testament law in the form of **two** overriding commandments:

> ಸಾರ
> "You shall love the Lord your God with all your heart and with all your soul and with all your mind. This is the great and **first** commandment. And a **second** is like it: You shall love your neighbour as yourself. On these two commandments depend all the Law and the Prophets." (Matt. 22:37-40)
> ಸಾರ

In other words, our focus needs to be in **two** directions, both upward and outward, if we are to fully work out God's purpose in our lives. Cultivating quality relationships with others obviously plays a significant part in this. But our outward focus needs to spring first and foremost from a life of fellowship with God. To do this, we need to spend time in his presence each day, in worship, prayer, and the reading of his Word. The more we do this, the more we begin to catch his heart for the lives of others around us.

3. Symmetry reminds us of **the importance of forgiveness**. In the Lord's Prayer Jesus taught us the petition 'forgive us for our sins, *just as* we have forgiven those who sinned against us' (Matt. 6:12 NCV). If we want to experience a free flow God's grace in our lives, we need to be willing to allow that grace to flow out to others. Jesus reminds us that 'with the judgement you pronounce you will be judged, and with the measure you use it will be measured to you' (Matt. 7:2). In other words, we receive mercy to the extent that we have shown mercy. It is a case, once more, of reaping what we sow.

TWO: THE NUMBER OF RELATIONSHIP

Above: The Viceroy Butterfly, indigenous to much of North America, is marked by distinctive colours (photo by Doug Wechsler).

Below: NGC 6302, the so-called Butterfly Nebula, taken by the Hubble Space telescope, in the constellation Scorpio. The star at its centre is one of the hottest known in the universe, reaching temperatures of 250,000°C at its surface.

Palindromic Number Patterns

Many remarkable patterns exist in sums where numbers appear as mirror images of themselves. Some examples of the beautiful sequences that result are shown below:

$$1+1 = 1$$
$$1+2+1 = 2+2$$
$$1+2+3+2+1 = 3+3+3$$
$$1+2+3+4+3+2+1 = 4+4+4+4$$

$$121 = \frac{22 \times 22}{1+2+1}$$

$$12321 = \frac{333 \times 333}{1+2+3+2+1}$$

$$1234321 = \frac{4444 \times 4444}{1+2+3+4+3+2+1}$$

$$123454321 = \frac{55555 \times 55555}{1+2+3+4+5+4+3+2+1}$$

$$1,089 \times 9 = 9,801$$
$$10,989 \times 9 = 98,901$$
$$109,989 \times 9 = 989,901$$
$$1,099,989 \times 9 = 9,899,901$$

$$11^2 = 121$$
$$101^2 = 10201$$
$$1001^2 = 1002001$$
$$10001^2 = 100020001$$
$$100001^2 = 10000200001$$
$$1000001^2 = 1000002000001$$
$$10000001^2 = 100000020000001$$

Mirror number	Divided by	Equals	Divided again by	Equals
121	11	11	11	1
1234321	11	112211	11	10201
12345654321	11	1122332211	11	102030201
123456787654321	11	11223344332211	11	1020304030201

All these are examples of equations, where the value on one side of the equals sign adds up to the value on the other.

Although most of the examples listed above have no far-reaching significance beyond their simple beauty, some equations (such as $e = mc^2$) have literally changed the course of history.

The most significant equation that has ever been discovered arises from the following passage in the Old Testament:

> All we like sheep have gone astray;
>   we have turned—every one—to his own way;
> and the Lord has laid on him
>   the iniquity of us all. (Is. 53:6)

It led Paul to declare the following earth-shattering truth:

For our sake he made **him** to be **sin** who knew no sin, so that in him **we** might become the **righteousness of God** (2 Cor. 5:21).

It means that, on the cross, just as all our sin was put onto Jesus, so in turn, when we put our trust in Jesus, all his righteousness is transferred to us.

This, literally, is the equation which saved the world. The challenge to us is to choose to place ourselves on the other side of the equals sign. The decision is left entirely in our hands.

*For you know the grace of our Lord Jesus Christ, that though he was **rich**, yet for your sake he became **poor**, so that you by his **poverty** might become **rich**. (2 Cor. 8:9)*

4 Symmetry may be **an encouragement in our daily battle against the powers of darkness**. Isaiah chapter 14 offers a powerful reminder that every attempt to rise up against God always falls back on itself in the end. Just as Eve was deceived into thinking that she would become like God if she ate from the forbidden tree, so Satan himself was deceived into thinking that by killing Jesus on the cross his own kingdom would be established forever (1 Cor. 2:8). In the end, it will be *him* who is destroyed, and *God's* kingdom which will be established forever (Rev. 20:10; 21:1-4).

The two matching sides of the Revelation chart help us to make more sense of this. Its structure reflects the fact that Jesus needed to come on **two** separate occasions: firstly to achieve a *legal* victory over the powers of darkness, and secondly to enforce it as *absolute*. All Christians can live under this hope. We live both in the 'already' and the 'not yet'.

5 Symmetry places Christ **at a pinnacle in history**, towering over the span of time from Abraham to the present day, with BC and AD on either side of him, just as Moses and Elijah surrounded him on the Mount of Transfiguration, and two angels were with him at the resurrection and ascension. He stands as a colossus over time, and he needs to be a colossus in our lives if we are to get the right sense of perspective on our true purpose, and to understand our place in the wider scheme of things.

6 Symmetry teaches **us the vital importance of balance in our spiritual lives**. It was not just our outward relationships that were damaged by the fall but our inward relationships. God wants to restore that sense of proportion in our lives.

Physically, we have been created with two eyes, two ears, two arms, two lungs, two kidneys and two legs. But just as we need a balanced posture physically in order to stand upright, we also need a balanced posture spiritually. It has often been stated that 'all Word and you dry up; all Spirit and you blow up; but with the Word and the Spirit together you *grow up*.'

> A false balance is an abomination to the LORD, but a just weight is his delight (Proverbs 11.1)

Above all, we should notice that the Bible itself is divided into **two** complementary parts, based on **two** covenants: one with Israel, and one with the church, which completely interlock with each other. It is very tempting for Christians to focus all their study on the New Testament and only dip into the Old Testament occasionally. But this can result in an unbalanced conception of God where we minimise the seriousness of sin and judgement. Alternatively we can be so focused on keeping rules that we lose the revolutionary message of grace. Without both perspectives we can never fully understand power of the cross, where justice and mercy meet.

We should remember that Jesus came full of grace *and* truth (John 1:14, 17): they are both sides of the same coin, and we need both dimensions to be perfectly formed in our lives. Ultimately there is a real continuity of purpose through both sections: they are embedded within each other at the deepest level, just as Father and Son are two faces of a single and eternal Godhead.

Indeed, the often-repeated adage, 'the New is in the Old concealed; the Old is in the New revealed' can also be expressed in the relationship between Father and Son: ('the Son is in the Father concealed; the Father is in the Son revealed'). We need a deeper understanding of *both* parts of scripture to live fully rounded lives as believers.

The number two, therefore, is of crucial importance in our Christian walk. We should remember first and foremost that there are just **two** ultimate destinies for man: everlasting life in God's presence, or eternal separation from him. Because of the sin we inherited from Adam, we have no hope of the first and only a fearful expectation of the alternative.

But where man came in God's image and fell, so God came in man's image and triumphed (Phil. 2:5-11). Jesus's coming as a **second** Adam has given us a **second** chance to enter God's kingdom through a **second** birth (John 3:3). Out of this flows a restoration of the broken relationships in our lives: firstly our *upward* relationship with God, secondly our *outward* relationships with those around us, and finally the *inward* relationships within us, restoring the inner peace and balance that we so desperately need in our lives.

In becoming 'born again', instead of looking backwards to the mistakes of our past, we can look forward with hope and confidence to Christ's **second** coming in glory, when we will see the ultimate fulfilment of the promise in Genesis that 'the **two** will become **one** flesh' (Gen. 2:24), when Jesus is united forever with his bride, the church, and the broken pieces of creation are finally restored (Eph. 5:31-32; Rev. 21:9).

Chapter Three

Three

The Number of Fulfilment

1. There is one God in **three** persons

Up to now we have focused on the oneness of God, and the twofold relationship between Father and Son contained within that. However, the fullest revelation of God in the Bible is as *Trinity*: Father, Son and Holy Spirit, bound together in absolute union throughout the whole of eternity.

Although the word 'Trinity' never appears in the Bible, the threefold nature of God is apparent again and again throughout Scripture. He is *omnipotent* (all-powerful: Job 42:2); *omniscient* (all-knowing: 1 John 3:20); and *omnipresent* (filling the whole of space and time: Jer. 23:24). God is the one who *was*, who *is*, and who *is to come* (Rev. 4:8). Jesus Christ is the same *yesterday*, *today* and *forever* (Heb. 13:8).

To amplify this, the New Testament makes **three** essential statements about the nature of God. Firstly, that *God is spirit* (John 4:24): he may manifest himself in a particular way in one place at one time, but is not confined to that location. Far from being a static, solitary being, he fills the entire universe!

Secondly, it tells us that *God is light* (1 John 1:5). As we saw in the last chapter, light, both visible and invisible, can be described *either* as waves *or* as particles, just as God is one and yet more than one. Both explanations are true, and yet seem mutually contradictory. Although this goes beyond our ability to fully understand, we can experience its impact in extraordinary ways. We depend on the entire electromagnetic spectrum in our everyday lives, for example, but visible light is but a tiny fraction of it, as we see on the next page:

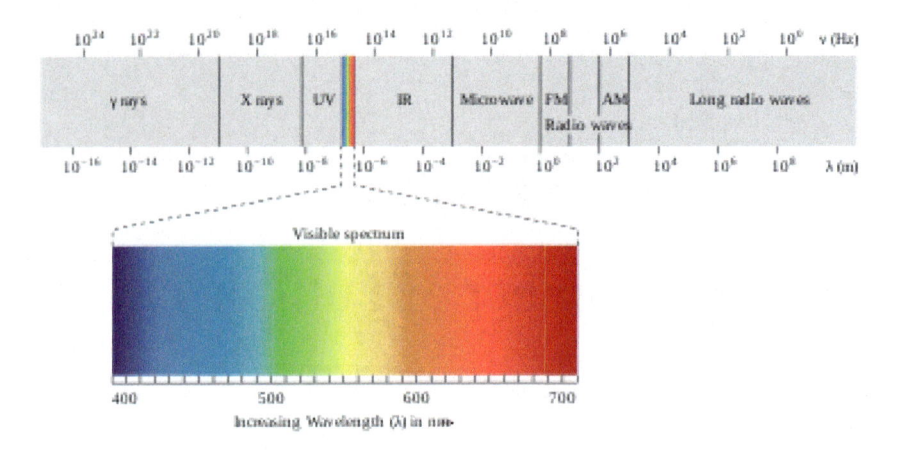

Thirdly, *God is love* (1 John 4:16): he is the embodiment of love, and therefore exists *within himself* as a relationship. As we have already noted, the Bible shows that he has revealed himself as **one** God in **three** persons. The clearest demonstration of this is at the end of Matthew's gospel, where a **single** name embraces all **three** persons of the Trinity:

> "Go therefore and make disciples of all nations, baptizing them in the name of the **Father** and of the **Son** and of the **Holy Spirit**" (Matt. 28:19)

This threefold activity in the life of the believer is spelt out more fully in John's Gospel:

> **Jesus** answered him, "If anyone loves me, he will keep my word, and **my Father** will love him, and *we will come to him* and make our home with him. ... But the Helper, **the Holy Spirit**, whom the Father will send *in my name*, he will teach you all things and bring to your remembrance all that I have said to you." (John 14:23-26)

Clearly we are dealing with a mystery here which is beyond human capacity to fathom. However, a possible insight into this interdependent relationship can be seen in the Menorah, the seven-branched candlestick described in Exodus 25:31-40. In its design it was unique: far from being assembled from different parts or put together from a variety of materials, it was fashioned from a single unbroken piece of pure gold, hammered into an intricate pattern of buds and branches. Its shape was also striking, appearing to trace out three concentric circles, with a single stem reaching down from the centre of the three circles to the base:

Not only does this outline trace out the 'wheels within wheels' that we noticed from the vision of the heavenly throne room in Chapter One, but it connects the centre of the wheels to the six-sided base, the number of man.

Could this be a pointer to the mystery of the Trinity and the incarnation? Beaten out of a single piece of incorruptible gold, the entire structure is described as being 'of one piece' with itself (Ex. 25:31), a striking anticipation of a phrase from the Nicene creed, where

Father and Son are said to be of 'one substance' (*homoousios*) with each other.

It would, admittedly, be an irony if the Temple, that most Jewish of places, contained a representation of God that most Jews would find blasphemous! Yet it is hard to escape the threefold patterning elsewhere in the Temple's design, with its **three** sections, arranged in exact arithmetical proportions to one another, each separated by a veil of **three** colours. This is even more the case in the Holy of Holies, whose length, breadth and height possessed identical measurements, and which portrayed the throne of God with two heavenly beings on either side, said, like the Menorah, to be 'of one piece' with each other (Ex. 25:19).

It is intriguing in this respect that when God reveals himself to Abraham in Genesis 18, Abraham sees **three** visitors, but addresses only one (verse 3). Here, as in the Holy of Holies, his two companions appear to be angels (19:1), but the strange interplay of pronouns in Hebrew still creates a sense of mystery ('they' alternates with 'he' in 18:9-10, seen clearly in the older King James Version, but often obscured in newer translations).

Similarly, when he reveals himself to Moses at the burning bush, he uses a unique name arranged in a symmetrical **threefold** pattern:

"**I am** who **I am**"
'ehyeh 'asher 'ehyeh
אֶהְיֶה אֲשֶׁר אֶהְיֶה
(Ex. 3:14)

Even the *Shema*, the bedrock of Jewish faith in the oneness of God that we considered in Chapter One, is arranged similarly with two flanks around a central hub, as follows:

The **LORD** our **God**, the **LORD** is one
(Deut. 6:4)

Indeed such threefold constructions can be found scattered across the Old Testament. Particularly well known is the Aaronic blessing in Numbers Chapter 6:

The **LORD** spoke to Moses, saying, "Speak to Aaron and his sons, saying, Thus you shall bless the people of Israel: you shall say to them,

The **LORD** bless you and keep you;
the **LORD** make his face to shine upon you and be gracious to you;
the **LORD** lift up his countenance upon you and give you peace.

"So shall they put my *name* upon the people of Israel, and I will bless them."
(Num 6:22-27)

Notice that the full expression of the *name* of the Lord here, as at the end of Matthew's gospel, contains **three** interlocking elements, a pointer to the full expression of God as Father, Son and Holy Spirit.

David Pawson, in *Unlocking the Bible*, has drawn attention to the hidden beauty of the three central verses.[4] There are 3 Hebrew words in the first sentence, 5 in the second and 7 in the third; there are 15 letters in the first, 20 and the second, 25 in the third; and there are 12 syllables in the first, 14 in the second, and 16 in the third.

Similar in its threefold structure is Jacob's blessing near the end of Genesis:

> 'May the **God** before whom my fathers
> Abraham and Isaac walked faithfully,
> the **God** who has been my shepherd
> all my life to this day,
> the **Angel** who has delivered me from all harm
> – may he bless these boys.'
> (Gen. 48:15-16 NIV)

In outline this is not unlike that of the blessing at the end of Paul's second letter to the Corinthians:

> May the grace of the **Lord Jesus Christ**,
> and the love of **God**, and the fellowship of the **Holy Spirit** be with you all.
> (2 Cor. 13:14 NIV)

Elsewhere in the Old Testament we encounter a number of similar threefold patterns, such as these:

> "Yahweh, the God of your ancestors —
> the **God** of Abraham,
> the **God** of Isaac, and
> the **God** of Jacob —
> has sent me to you."
> (Ex. 3:15 NLT)

> All you Israelites, trust in the **Lord** –
> he is their help and shield.
> House of Aaron, trust in the **Lord** –
> he is their help and shield.
> You who fear him, trust in the **Lord** –
> he is their help and shield.
> (Ps. 115:9-11 NIV)

> "The right hand of the **Lord** does valiantly,
> the right hand of the **Lord** exalts,
> the right hand of the **Lord** does valiantly!"
> (Ps. 118:15-16)

> "**Holy**, **holy**, **holy** is the Lord of hosts;
> the whole earth is full of his glory!" (Is. 6:3)

> For the **Lord** is our judge;
> the **Lord** is our lawgiver;
> the **Lord** is our king; he will save us.
> (Is. 33:22)

> Then the **Lord** will appear over them,
> and his arrow will go forth like lightning;
> the Lord **God** will sound the trumpet
> and will march forth in the whirlwinds of the south.
> The **Lord** of hosts will protect them,
> (Zech. 9:14-15)

Indeed, it is interesting to note that one of the principal words for God in the Old Testament, *'elohim*, is actually a plural noun. The significance here is that since Hebrew nouns also have a dual form, ending in *-aim* (יִם), the ending *-im* on its own normally only refers to three or more persons (compare 'seraphim' and 'cherubim'). Yet, almost invariably, *'elohim* takes a singular verb; thus Genesis 1:1 reads, literally, 'In the beginning God [plural] created [singular] the heavens and the earth.'

Finally, we should notice that there are NINE (3 × 3) special names for YHWH or Jehovah in the Bible, as follows:

Bees and Threes

- There are 3 kinds of bees in a hive: workers, drones and the queen
- A bee consists of 3 sections: a head and two stomachs
- Underneath the body are 6 (2×3) wax scales
- It has 6 (2×3) legs, each composed of 3 sections
- The foot is formed of 3 triangular sections
- The antennae consist of 9 (3×3) sections
- The sting has 9 (3×3) barbs on each side
- Worker bees have 12 antennae (4×3)
- A bee larva consists of 15 segments (5×3)
- The queens's egg hatches in 3 days
- It is fed for 9 days (3×3)
- It matures in 15 days (5×3)
- The worker larva matures in 21 days (7×3)
- It begins work 3 days after leaving its cell
- The drone matures in 24 days (8×3)
- It eats 3 times more food than a worker
- The cells of a honeycomb have 6 sides (2×3)

The decrees of the LORD are firm ... they are sweeter than honey... (Ps. 19:9-10 NIV)

The Nine Names of Yahweh

1. Yahweh Jireh
   (The LORD Will Provide: Gen. 22:14)
2. Yahweh Rapha
   (The LORD, Your Healer: Ex. 15:26)
3. Yahweh Nissi
   (The LORD Is My Banner: Ex. 17:15)
4. Yahweh Mekoddishkem
   (The LORD Who Makes You Holy: Ex. 31:13)
5. Yahweh Shalom
   (The LORD Is Peace: Judges 6:24)
6. Yahweh Raah
   (The LORD Is My Shepherd: Ps. 23:1)
7. Yahweh Sabaoth
   (The LORD of Hosts: Is. 6:1-3)
8. Yahweh Tsidkenu
   (The LORD Is Our Righteousness: Jer. 23:6)
9. Yahweh Shammah
   (The LORD Is There: Ezek. 48:35)

Jewish Perspectives on the Trinity

For most observant Jews, the idea of the Trinity is offensive and even blasphemous, undermining the absolute centrality and uniqueness of the one God. This is despite the many suggestive hints in the Old Testament.

Yet Jewish writers have sometimes appeared to use ideas which are at least outwardly similar to the Trinity in their understanding of God. Philo of Alexandria, for example, speculates in such terms when he comments in *de Abrahamo* on the 'three men' who appear to Abraham in Genesis 18 and who are described as 'the LORD':

The one in the middle is **the Father of the universe**, who in the sacred scriptures is called by his proper name, I am that I am; and **the beings on each side** are those most ancient powers which are always close to the living God, one of which is called his creative power [which Philo describes as 'God'] and the other his royal power [which he describes as 'Lord'] ... But that which is seen is in reality **a threefold appearance of one subject** is plain .... For when the wise man entreats those persons who are in the guise of travellers to come and lodge in his house, he speaks to them **not as three persons, but as one**.

Philo, *de Abrahamo*, 121-2; 131-2.

Very occasionally we also find Trinitarian patterns in later Rabbinical literature. A possible example of this can be found in a passage attributed to Rabbi Levi in Song of Songs Rabba 8:14:

When the nations of heathendom eat and drink, and blaspheme God, and provoke Him to anger by their immoral talk, then **God** thinks of destroying the whole of creation. Thereupon enters **the Torah** [effectively, the Word of God] and speaking in defence of Israel it says, 'Sovereign of the universe, instead of looking at these who blaspheme and provoke thee to indignation, look at thy people Israel, who praise and bless and adore thy great Name by the Torah, and with Psalms and Hymns.' After the Torah there enters **the Holy Spirit** and says, 'Flee away, O my beloved God, flee from the heathens and attach thyself to Israel only.'

Likewise we see passages such as the following in a later Jewish compilation called the *Zohar*:

"Hear, O Israel, *Adonai Eloheinu Adonai* is one." **These three are one**.... The mystery of the audible voice is similar to this, for though it is one yet it consists of three elements—fire, air, and water.... Even so it is with the mystery of the **threefold Divine manifestations** designated by *Adonai Eloheinu Adonai*—three modes which yet form one unity. II:43b

The Ancient One is described as being **three**: because the other lights emanating from him are included in the three. But how can three names be one? Are they really one because we call them one? **How three can be one can only be known through the revelation of the Holy Spirit**. II:43b

The Ancient of Days has **three** heads. He reveals himself in **three** archetypes, all **three forming but one**. He is thus symbolized by the number **Three**. They are revealed in one another. III:288b

It is striking that one of the translators of the English edition of the Zohar, Feivel Levertoff, came to believe in God as Trinity and Jesus as his Messiah through parallels he found between the Zohar and the New Testament, as others had done before him.

For many others, the quest continues. Commenting on the apparent overlap between the angel of the LORD and God himself in Ex. 23:20-21 and 33:18-23, the Jewish scholar Alan Segal once remarked that:

Yahweh himself, the angel of God, and his Glory are peculiarly melded together, suggesting a deep secret about the ways God manifested himself to humanity.[5]

"Listen to me, O Jacob, and Israel, whom I called! I am he; I am the first, and I am the last. ... from the beginning I have not spoken in secret, from the time it came to be I have been there." **And now the Lord GOD has sent me, and his Spirit.** (Is. 48:12,16)

The Trinity in the New Testament

The interlocking relationship between Father, Son and Holy Spirit is apparent in many ways in the New Testament. For example:

We are in the Father (1 John 2:24) but the Father is also in us (1 John 4:15)
We are in Christ (1 Cor. 1:30) but Christ is also in us (Col. 1:27)
We are in the Spirit (Rom. 8:9) but the Spirit is also in us (1 Cor. 3:16)

Likewise, we find such parallels as

> the God of glory (Acts 7:2); the Lord of glory (1 Cor. 2:8); and the Spirit of glory (1 Pet. 4:14)
>
> the living Father (John 6:57); the living bread of the Son (John 6:51); and the living water of the Spirit (John 7:38-9)
>
> the Holy Father (John 17:11); the Holy One [Jesus] (John 6:69); and the Holy Spirit (Matt. 1:18)
>
> the eternal Father (1 Tim. 1:17); the eternal Son (Heb. 13:8); and the eternal Spirit (Heb. 9:14)
>
> the life-giving Father (1 Tim. 6:13); the life-giving Son (1 Cor. 15:45); and the life-giving Spirit (John 6:63)
>
> the Only True God (John 17:3); Christ is Truth (John 14:6); and the Spirit is Truth (1 John 5:6)

Sometimes an activity said to be performed by one is actually done by all three. For example,

Who did Jesus promise would assist believers who are arrested for their faith? Is it the Father (Matt. 10:20), the Son (Luke 21:15), or the Spirit (Mark 13:11)?

Who is Peter addressing as 'Lord' in Acts 10:14-15? Is it the Father (v. 28), the Son (v. 36), or the Spirit (v. 19-20)?

Who is directing Paul's missionary activities in Acts 16:6-10? Is it the Father (v. 10), the Son (v. 7), or the Spirit (v. 6)?

Who raised Christ from the dead? Is it the Father (Acts 2:24), the Son (John 2:19-21), or the Spirit (1 Pet. 3:18)?

Even though as a general rule, the New Testament preserves a clear distinction between Father, Son and Spirit, as at Jesus' baptism, where they are performing very different functions, there are other instances where the opposite seems to be the case: in Matthew 28:19, for example, they are different aspects of a single unity, **one** name embracing **three** distinct persons:

> Go therefore and make disciples of all nations, baptizing them in the name of the **Father** and of the **Son** and of the **Holy Spirit** …

There are also passages where we can see them act in ways which are both distinct and yet closely co-ordinated at the same time. This is illustrated particularly well, for example, in 1 Corinthians 12:

> There are different kinds of gifts, but the same **Spirit** distributes them.
> There are different kinds of service, but the same **Lord**.
> There are different kinds of working, but … it is the same **God** at work. (v. 4-6 NIV)

Such verses remind us that the church, as the community of believers, is a microcosm of the Trinity and needs a full understanding of all three members of the Godhead in order to operate effectively.

---

*I therefore, a prisoner for the Lord, urge you .to … maintain the unity of the Spirit in the bond of peace. There is one body and **one Spirit** — just as you were called to the one hope that belongs to your call—**one Lord**, one faith, one baptism, **one God and Father of all**, who is over all and through all and in all. (Eph. 4:1-6)*

2. **Three** as a reflection of God's being

One image sometimes used to describe the Trinity is the **three** states of matter. Water, for example, can exist as a vapour, or in liquid or solid form. Although this is an imperfect example, clouds, flowing water and ice are all used in scripture as pictures of the way God acts in the world (see Ex. 13:21-22, Is. 55:10-11, John 7:37-39 and Job 37:10).

It is perhaps not surprising, therefore, to see the pattern of the Trinity reflected in the very makeup of a water molecule, the most fundamental necessity of life:

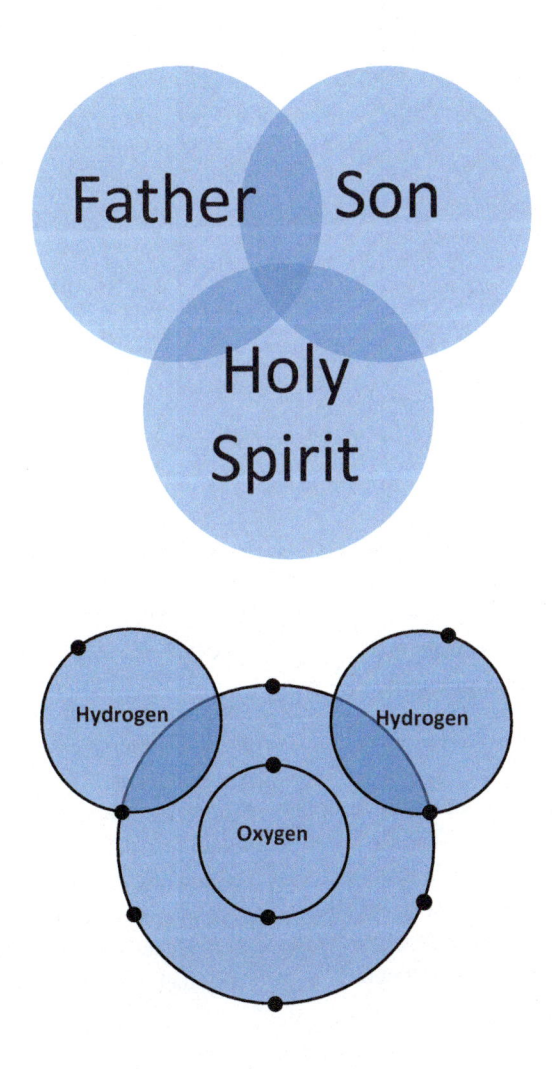

But as we burrow down even further into the microscopic world, these threefold patterns continue to manifest. Atoms, for example, consist of **three** kinds of elementary particles: electrons, protons and neutrons. Oxygen, the essential element of the air we breathe, and the central constituent of water, consists of **8** electrons, **8** protons and **8** neutrons.

Such elementary particles belong to a larger family of **three** weight classes: light, medium, and heavy, known technically as leptons, mesons, and baryons.

Inside a molecule, an electron can have **three** degrees of freedom (charge, spin, orbital) which are associated with **three** quasiparticles (the holon, the spinon, and the orbiton).

Neutrons and protons, which make up everything we see around us, meanwhile, are themselves made up of **three** other elementary particles called 'quarks'. 'Up' quarks have a charge of $+\frac{2}{3}$, while 'down' quarks have a charge of $-\frac{1}{3}$.

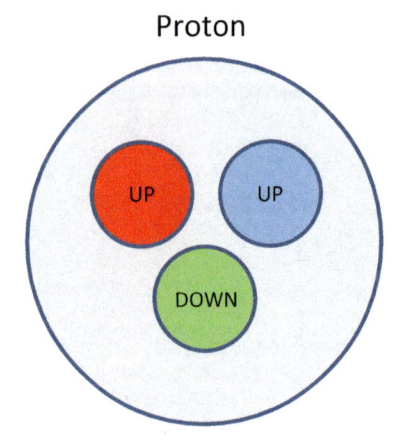

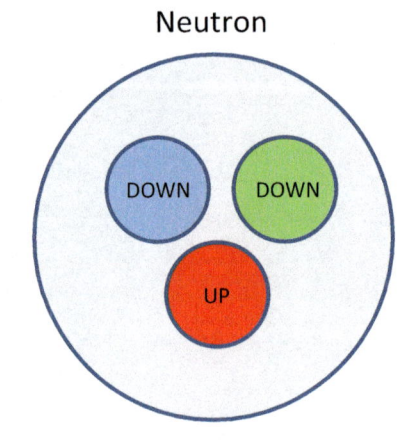

Proton

Neutron

The same fundamental proportions play a particular role in the Book of Revelation: a third of the grass and trees are burnt up (8:7), a third of the waters are contaminated (8:8-11), a third of the angels rebel (12:4), and so on.

These proportions also have an impact on Biblical history and geography. Firstly we should notice the significant role that the number three plays in the Flood story. Noah was 600 years old when entering the ark with his **three** sons. The ark was **three** hundred cubits long and 30 cubits high and had **three** storeys. The core part of the flood lasted for exactly **three** hundred days (150 x 2).

They also appear in the Genesis 10 genealogy where people spread out from the site of the Ark from Noah's three sons to **three** different continents. Much later these three directions became associated with the propagation of **three** world religions, each tracing its roots back to Abraham and staking a claim on Jerusalem, and rooted in an original group of 12 forefathers (4 × 3):

THREE: THE NUMBER OF FULFILMENT

Europe and Turkey

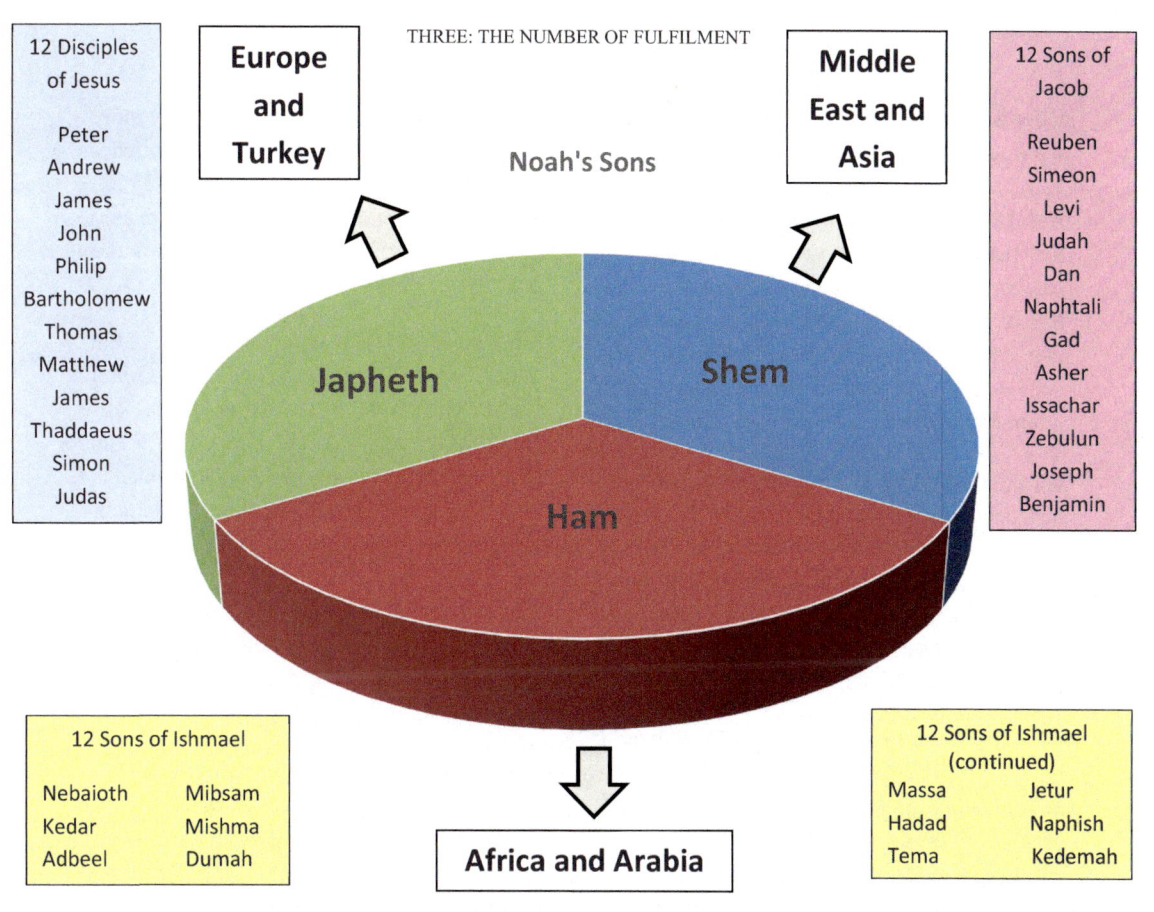

Middle East and Asia

Noah's Sons

Japheth | Shem | Ham

12 Disciples of Jesus

Peter
Andrew
James
John
Philip
Bartholomew
Thomas
Matthew
James
Thaddaeus
Simon
Judas

12 Sons of Jacob

Reuben
Simeon
Levi
Judah
Dan
Naphtali
Gad
Asher
Issachar
Zebulun
Joseph
Benjamin

12 Sons of Ishmael

Nebaioth   Mibsam
Kedar   Mishma
Adbeel   Dumah

Africa and Arabia

12 Sons of Ishmael (continued)

Massa   Jetur
Hadad   Naphish
Tema   Kedemah

In Acts also the gospel goes out from Jerusalem to these same three continents - Asia, Europe and Africa – propagated through the three concentric circles we observed earlier in the Menorah: from Judea, to Samaria, to the ends of the earth (Acts 1:8):

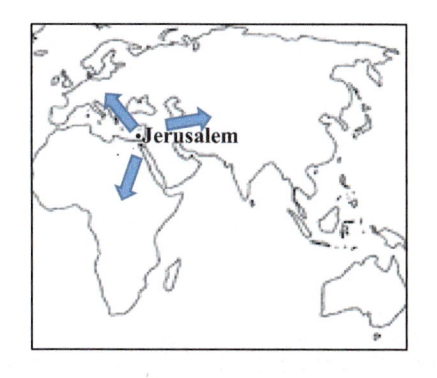

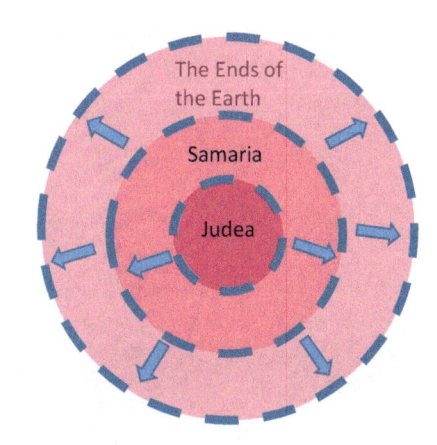

The Ends of the Earth
Samaria
Judea

79

If Jerusalem is at the centre of Biblical geography, it is also at the centre of Biblical history, as we saw in the chart at the end of the last chapter, which marks out **three** consecutive periods of around two thousand years, reaching the central point of the arch with the rule of King David, who established Jerusalem as Israel's capital in around 1000 BC, and culminating with the arrival of the *New* Jerusalem on the earth.

Indeed, the number three is central to Bible's understanding of time. God is the Lord of past, present and future, the God of Abraham, Isaac and Jacob, who **is** and who **was** and who **is to come** (Rev. 1:8). Jesus Christ, as we noted earlier, is 'the same **yesterday, today** and **forever**' (Heb. 13.8).

All Israel were to appear before God **three** times a year (Ex 23:17); Matthew divides Israel's history in **three** periods of fourteen generations (Matt. 1-17); Revelation also sets out **three** periods of sevenfold judgement. Israel returned to the Promised Land **three** times from exile: first from Egypt, secondly from Babylon (itself a **three**fold return, under Zerubbabel in 536 BC, under Ezra in 458 BC and under Nehemiah in 458 BC), and thirdly in recent times from the diaspora across the world.

Finally, we should note the prevalence of the number three in the arrangement of God's Word. The Bible is written in **three** languages (Hebrew, Aramaic and Greek). The Old Testament consists of 39 books, which is $(3^3) + (3^2) + (3^1)$, and the New Testament contains 27 ($3\times3\times3$). As we pointed out in the last chapter, this order is reflected in miniature in the book of Isaiah ($39 + 27$ [$3\times3 + 3\times3 + 3\times3$]), where the exact centre point of the second section points directly to the crucifixion of Jesus.

We also drew attention to the Bible Wheel in Chapter One, where some fascinating insights are gained by arranging the 66 books into three concentric rings, corresponding with the 22 letters of the Hebrew alphabet:

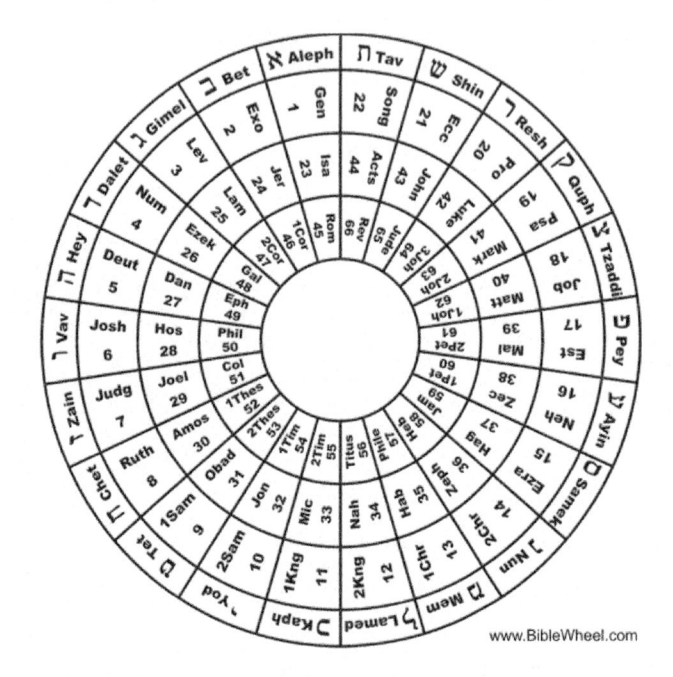

www.BibleWheel.com

The Jewish arrangement of the Old Testament, summarised by Jesus as 'Law, Prophets, and Psalms' (Luke 24:44) also forms a symmetrical threefold pattern as follows:

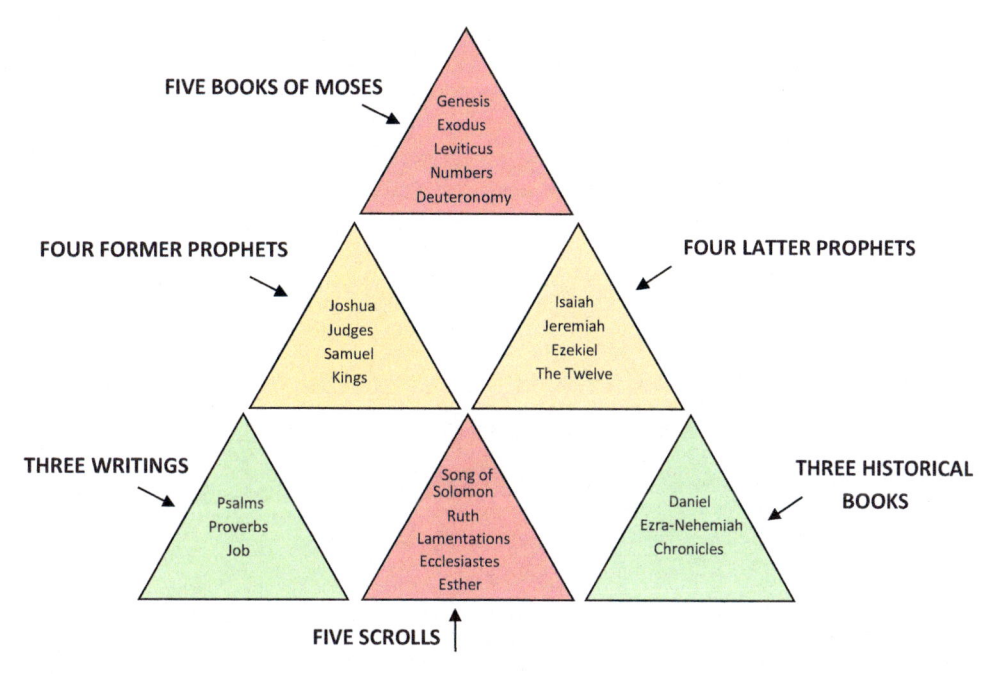

FIVE BOOKS OF MOSES → Genesis, Exodus, Leviticus, Numbers, Deuteronomy

FOUR FORMER PROPHETS → Joshua, Judges, Samuel, Kings

FOUR LATTER PROPHETS → Isaiah, Jeremiah, Ezekiel, The Twelve

THREE WRITINGS → Psalms, Proverbs, Job

FIVE SCROLLS ↑ Song of Solomon, Ruth, Lamentations, Ecclesiastes, Esther

THREE HISTORICAL BOOKS → Daniel, Ezra-Nehemiah, Chronicles

It seems, then, from whatever vantage-point we look, that the number three is woven into the divine ordering of time, space, history, geography and scripture. We can therefore move on to consider its implications for the human race, created to reflect God's nature, and see how it has become completely embedded within our culture.

3. Three expressed in humanity

The number three seems to be foundational to every aspect of human life. Most people structure their day around **three** meals: breakfast, lunch and dinner. We perceive **three** spatial dimensions (length, height and breadth) and **three** primary colours. Artists use a 'rule of **three**' to arrange their pictures. **Three** notes make up the triads that form the basis of Western music. We count to three before lifting and we use 'ready, steady, go!' as a signal for starting a race. We reward achievement with gold, silver and bronze.

Human language preserves **three** gender categories: masculine, feminine and neuter (he, she and it) **three** main tenses (past, present and future), and **three** subjects of a verb (1st, 2nd and 3rd persons). In some hunter/gatherer cultures even today **three** is the apex of the counting system, beyond which a word for 'many' is used.

Three is a common literary device ('Three Men in a Boat', 'Three Little Pigs', 'Three Bears', 'Three Musketeers'). Many classic jokes rely on a **threefold** construction for the punchline (of the Englishman, Irishman, Scotsman variety) and some of Jesus' parables work this way too (Priest, Levite, Samaritan being a familiar example) which makes them easy to remember after just one hearing. Many preachers still aim to deliver a **three-point** sermon each Sunday.

Elsewhere in the Bible the number three implies a completed action in the human sphere. **Three** days' journey into the wilderness signified a complete separation from Egypt (Ex. 5:3); **three** days' search for Elijah established beyond doubt that he could not be found (2 Kings 2:17); **three** years of seeking fruit testified to the completeness of Israel's failure (Luke 13:7). More than **three** days in the grave for Lazarus meant, according to Jewish tradition, that his spirit had already left his body (John 11:17, 39).

Three is also used as a definite confirmation. We see this, for example, in the **threefold** call of Samuel (1 Sam 3:1-10) and the **threefold** call of Peter (John 21:15-19; Acts 10:9-16). In each case it is the third prompt which seems decisive in moving things forward. On Peter's part it is particularly touching, given that he has previously denied Jesus **three** times (Matt. 26:69-75).

> 'A threefold cord is not quickly broken'
> (Ecclesiastes 4.12)

The number three also marks the Bible's witness to Jesus. Through the lens of the Old Testament he is shown to be prophet, priest, and king (Deut. 18:15; Ps. 110:4; Ps. 2:6). In the New Testament 'the Spirit, the water, and the blood' provide further confirmation of his completed work (1 John 5:7). **Three** times a voice from heaven confirms his eternal calling (Matt 3:17; 17:5; John 12:28). **Three** resurrections (Jairus' daughter, the widow's son in Nain and Lazarus) testify to his infinite power. Inscriptions on the cross in **three** languages underline his complete rejection by man (John 19:20).

Three is also a number that God uses to foil the ill-conceived schemes of men. **Three** lots of messengers sent to capture David all end up prophesying instead (1 Sam. 19:20-21); **three** consignments of soldiers sent to capture Elisha meet with varying fates (2 Kings 1:9-15). **Three** times God interrupts Balaam's journey to put a curse on Israel (Num. 22:22-28); **three** times his curses are turned into blessings (Num. 23:1-24:10). **Three** times in Acts we read of Paul's similarly ill-conceived journey to Damascus which results in **three** days of blindness (Acts 9:3-9; 22:6-11; 26:12-18).

Three also plays a significant role in prayer: Daniel prayed **three** times a day, and engages in **three** weeks of prayer and fasting (Dan. 6:10; 10:2-3). Elijah stretches himself out **three** times over the widow's son in Zarephath to revive him (1 Kings 17:21).

Above: Depiction of Three Wise Men at the Basilica of Sant'Apollinare Nuovo in Ravenna, dating from around 526 AD (photo taken by Nina Aldin Thune).

Below: Three Crosses depicted in the window of Florence Avenue Foursquare Church, Santa Fe Springs, California.

The same is true in the New Testament: Jesus asks the Father **three** times in the garden of Gethsemane for his cup to be taken away from him (Mark 14:32-42). Paul makes a similar **threefold** entreaty in prayer, and like Jesus receives the assurance of divine strength to sustain him, in the absence of immediate relief (2 Cor. 12:8-9). And Jesus promises to be present in a special way when **two or three** are gathered in his name (Matt. 18:20).

We also find several distinctive sets of names grouped in threes:

- Shem, Ham, and Japheth (Gen. 5:32)
- Abraham, Isaac, and Jacob (Gen. 50:24)
- Gershom, Kohath, and Merari (1 Chron. 6:16)
- Noah, Daniel, and Job (Ezek. 14:14)
- Shadrach, Meshach, and Abednego (Dan. 3:12)
- Peter, James, and John (Mark 9:2)

For the Jews, the number three also plays a significant role. Apart from the **three** divisions of Scripture that we saw earlier, they have **three** daily prayers: *Shacharit*, *Mincha* and *Maariv*; **three** Pilgrimage Festivals: Passover, Shavuot, Sukkot; **three** matzos on the Passover table; **three** Shabbat meals; and **three** stars that need to appear in the sky to signal the end of Shabbat.

Also, a *Beth Din* (Rabbinical court) is composed of **three** members; and those wanting to convert to Judaism are traditionally turned away **three** times to test how sincere they are. And just as there were **three** major branches of Judaism in the time of Jesus (Pharisees, Sadducees and Essenes), so there are **three** major branches of Judaism today: Orthodox, Conservative and Reform.

Spirit, Soul and Body

Since mankind is created in God's image (Gen. 1:26: Let US make man in OUR image), it is no surprise that we are also made up of **three** parts, as Paul explains:

> Now may the God of peace himself sanctify you completely, and may your whole **spirit** and **soul** and **body** be kept blameless at the coming of our Lord Jesus Christ. He who calls you is faithful; he will surely do it.
> (1 Thess. 5:23-24)

Of these the body is the purely physical part of us. The soul consists of mind, emotions, conscience, wisdom, intellect and imagination. The spirit, which is the Godward part of our being, remains largely inactivated until we come to faith in Christ, and this creates the sense of emptiness and futility that sadly mars the lives of so many people, since we were designed to live in communion with God:

> The spirit of man is the lamp of the LORD, searching all his innermost parts.
> (Prov. 20:27)

Body and soul acting together in rebellion or indifference to God are described as 'the flesh' in the New Testament. Without God filling our spirit with his Spirit we can never fully become the people we were meant to be, but remain a shadow of our true selves.

It is vitally important, therefore, to establish a correct alignment with respect to God. Our spirit should rule over our soul and body, keeping their incessant demands in check, and in turn be fully submitted to God's Spirit. A healthy chain of command, with a correct line of submission to God, enables his life to flow through us unimpeded, and for us to fully reflect his image within ourselves, as we abide in his unending love:

Life of God constantly replenishes

Body
submits to
Soul
submits to
Spirit
submits
through the Holy Spirit
and
in the Son
to
God the Father

This flow of life can be all too easily be interrupted, however. The Bible warns of the danger from **three** main sources of temptation: the sinful nature within us, the ungodly world around us, and the invisible forces of darkness that attempt to control it (or, in Biblical shorthand, the flesh, the world and the devil). These three avenues of temptation seem to correspond broadly to the threefold division of man into body, soul and spirit that we have just discussed, as John implies in his first letter:

> ಏಂಬ
>
> Do not love the world or anything in the world. If anyone loves the world, love for the Father is not in them. For everything in the world—the **lust of the flesh**, the **lust of the eyes**, and **the pride of life**—comes not from the Father but from the world. The world and its desires pass away, but whoever does the will of God lives forever.
> (1 John 2:15-17 NIV)
>
> ಏಂಬ

We can see a clear parallel here with the original temptation in the Garden of Eden, where Eve noticed that the tree of knowledge of good and evil was

- 'good for food'
- 'a delight to the eyes'
- 'to be desired to make one wise'

(Gen. 3:6)

The same pattern can be seen in the **three** temptations which Jesus faced (in the order that they appear in Luke's gospel) which also seem to fit the same body/soul/spirit model of John's first letter:

- to turn stones into bread
- to take a short cut to earthly dominion
- to jump off the pinnacle of the temple

We should notice that each time Jesus counters these temptations successfully by quoting the Word of God. This is an example of how we ourselves need to act when the hour of temptation strikes. Peter, by contrast, fails miserably when he is tempted **three** times to deny Jesus, because he is relying on his own strength.

Jesus did far more, however, than simply stand up to Satan. Through his perfect obedience he was able to put Adam's original act of disobedience into reverse and to begin restoring everything that Adam lost. For this reason the Bible calls him the 'second Adam'. Only by entering into death and taking the curse of sin onto himself at the cross could Jesus return us back to God's original purpose for our lives. In doing so he has turned history around.

The background, consequences and reversal of the Fall can be expressed in a series of threefold patterns which are shown on the chart on the next page:

THREE: THE NUMBER OF FULFILMENT

God's Original Purpose for Man:

Relationship	Dominion	Fruitfulness
SONSHIP 'In our image' (Gen. 1:26)	VICTORY 'Subdue it' (Gen. 1:28)	PURPOSE 'Be fruitful' (Gen. 1:28)
UNITY 'One flesh' (Gen. 2:24)	AUTHORITY 'That was its name' (Gen. 2:19)	ASSIGNMENT 'Care for it' (Gen. 2:15 NCV)
INNOCENCE 'Not ashamed' (Gen. 2:25)	FREEDOM 'Every tree' (Gen. 2:16)	BLESSING 'Fill the earth' (Gen. 1:28)

⇓ **Lost through the Disobedience of Man:** ⇓

Broken Relationship	Reversed Dominion	Unfruitfulness
SEPARATION Banishment (Gen. 3:23)	STRUGGLE 'Sweat of your face' (Gen. 3:19)	FRUSTRATION 'Thorns and thistles' (Gen. 3:18)
BLAME Broken relationships (Gen. 3:12)	DEATH 'Return to the ground' (Gen. 3:19)	FUTILITY Cut off from tree of life (3:22-24)
SHAME Fig leaves (Gen 3:7)	DEFEAT 'Rule over you' (Gen. 3:16)	SUFFERING Pain in childbearing (3:16)

⇓ **Regained through the Cross of Christ:** ⇓

Restored Relationship	Restored Dominion	Restored Fruitfulness
SONSHIP 'Children of God' (John 1:12)	VICTORY 'More than conquerors' (Rom. 8:37)	PURPOSE 'Make disciples' (Matt. 28:19)
UNITY 'Perfectly one' (John 17:23)	AUTHORITY 'Reign in life' (Rom. 5:17)	ASSIGNMENT 'Teach them to obey' (Matt. 28:20)
INNOCENCE 'Born again' (John. 3:3)	FREEDOM 'Free indeed' (John 8:36)	BLESSING 'Bear much fruit' (John 15:8)

Biblically, these phases in human history are called 'dispensations' and the number three plays a significant role in each one. For example, while **three** thousand died when the law was first given to Moses at Mount Sinai, **three** thousand were saved when the Spirit was poured out at Pentecost (on exactly the same date in the Jewish calendar) many centuries later.

As a result, the number three figures prominently at both the biggest and the smallest levels of the Bible. From a bird's eye view the Old Testament, the Gospels and the remaining books of the New Testament successively proclaim the **threefold** witness, 'Christ is coming' (Is. 42:1-4), 'Christ has come' (Luke 2:29-32) and 'Christ will come again' (Rev. 22:12); they reveal God *for* us (Neh. 4:20), God *with* us (Matt. 1:23) and God *in* us (Col. 1:27); they declare, 'Where is the Lamb?' (Gen. 22:7); 'Here is the Lamb' (John 1:29 NRSV); and 'Worthy is the Lamb!' (Rev. 5:12).

At the other end of the scale we might notice that it was at the **third** hour that Jesus was crucified; and it was for **three** hours (from the sixth to the ninth hour) that the sky turned black. At 33.3 years of age he had served exactly **one third** of what Isaiah 65:20 implies is a full ideal span of human existence (100 years). He was also raised to life on the **third** day. Jesus likened this to the experience of Jonah, who was in the belly of a whale for **three** days and three nights (Jonah 1:17; Matt. 12:39, 40).

This three-day pattern, in fact, seems to represent a 'deep structure' running throughout scripture, as we can see by considering a series of instances involving the number three or the 'third day', as set out on the next page:

Judgement/Death	Humbling/Waiting	Life
Cupbearer's dream in prison (Gen. 40:8-11)	Promise (Gen. 40:12-13)	Restoration (on 3rd day) (Gen. 40:20-21)
Wilderness (Ex. 19:1-2)	Consecration (Ex. 19:10-15)	Giving of law (on 3rd day) (Ex. 19:16-25)
Hezekiah's fatal illness (2 Kings 20:1)	Hezekiah's prayer (2 Kings 20:2-3)	Recovery (on 3rd day) (2 Kings 20:5-6)
Jonah thrown in sea (Jonah 1:15)	In whale's belly (for 3 days) (Jonah 1:17)	Salvation proclaimed to Nineveh (Jonah 3:1-10)
Haman's genocide order (Esther 3:12-15)	Fasting (for 3 days) (Esther 4:16)	Esther intervenes to save Jews (on 3rd day) (Esther 5:1; 7:1-10)
Israel abandoned (Hos. 5:15)	Repentance (Hos. 6:1)	Restoration (on 3rd day) (Hos. 6:2)
Jesus goes missing (Luke 2:43)	Searching for Jesus (Luke 2:44)	Jesus rediscovered (after 3 days) (Luke 2:46)
Jesus' death on the cross (Matt. 27:50)	Burial (Matt. 27:59-60)	Resurrection (on 3rd day) (Matt. 28:1-7)
Peter's threefold denial (Luke 22:54-62)	Peter's threefold vision (Acts 10:11-16)	Gospel reaches Gentiles (on 3rd day) (Acts 10:23-48)
Paul's vision (Acts 9:3-6)	Blind (for 3 days) (Acts 9:8-9)	Sight restored and baptised (Acts 9:17-18)
Witnesses killed (Rev. 11:7)	Left unburied (Rev. 11:9)	Raised to life (after 3½ days) (Rev. 11:11)

It is fascinating to consider some of the details of these stories. In Acts 10, for example, Cornelius has a vision at **three** o'clock in the afternoon (v.3). He sends **three** men to Peter (v.19) who has just had **three** identical visions (v.16) with the same **three** instructions ('Rise, Kill, and Eat') to which he replies **three** times 'Surely not, Lord!'. He arrives in Caesarea on the **third** day from this taking place (v.23-24), taking **six** other Christian brothers with him (11:12). We might even assume he stayed around **three** days (10:48)!

The salvation message that Peter preached brings us through a three-stage process similar to that outlined above. He told us to **repent**, to **be baptised**, and to **receive the gift of the Holy Spirit** (Acts 2:38). In baptism into the **threefold** divine name, we enter into Christ's **death**, **burial** and **resurrection**. The adventure that we begin in Christ takes us in turn through **three** progressive stages in our Christian walk, as we see below and on the next page:

Three Steps to Glory

- We are **justified**, where God declares us righteous because of Christ's death on our behalf
- We are **sanctified**, where God sets us apart for himself, working on our character over time
- We are **glorified**, where we get to share in the heavenly glory of Jesus himself

Justification

Justification is God's free gift which we do not deserve and could never earn. Three vital aspects are:

- God's sovereign call on our lives
- Our willing response to his righteous call
- His full declaration of pardon over our past and blessing over our future

This is another instance of the 'divine exchange' discussed in Chapter One: not only are all our sins transferred onto Jesus, but all his righteousness is transferred onto us!

*Therefore, since we have been **justified** by faith, we have peace with God through our Lord Jesus Christ. (Rom. 5.1)*

Sanctification

A beautiful threefold picture of **sanctification** appears in the Old Testament. When the priest was consecrated under the Old Covenant in Exodus 29:20, blood and oil were placed

- on the tip of his right ear, preparing him to be sensitive to God's voice
- on the thumb of his right hand, preparing him for a life of service to God
- on the big toe of his right foot, preparing him to walk in obedience to God and in conformity with his laws

We too have been called to be set apart for God to serve as part of his royal priesthood (1 Peter 2:9).

*Keep my statutes and do them; I am the LORD who **sanctifies** you. (Lev. 20.8)*

Glorification

Paul talks about how, as God's children, we suffer with Christ in order to be **glorified** with him (Rom. 8:16-17). He then goes on to list **three** stages through which God builds on his purpose for our lives:

- those whom he predestined he also called
- those whom he called he also justified
- those whom he justified he also glorified (Rom. 8:30)

Ultimately Jesus will 'transform our lowly body to be like his glorious body' (Phil. 3:21). John reminds us that 'when he appears we shall be like him, because we shall see him as he is' (1 John 3:2).

*I consider that the sufferings of this present time are not worth comparing with the **glory** that is to be revealed to us. For the creation waits with eager longing for the revealing of the sons of God. (Rom. 8:18-19)*

When we pull together the way Jesus links salvation to conception and birth (John 3:3), and the way Paul connects God's original creation with the *new* creation within a believer's spirit (2 Cor. 4:6), deeper patterns emerge based on the number three. These help to paint a 'big picture' connecting together the different stages of speech, creation, conception and redemption with the progressive revelation and activity of the different persons of the Godhead. There is a possible representation of this in the chart below:

Stage of Revelation	Stage of Expression	Stage of Creation	Stage of Conception	Stage of New Birth
TRIUNE GOD: Preparing	Infinitive (potential)	Earth in Darkness	Unfertilised Egg	Sinner in Darkness
FATHER: Revealing	I AM (Ex. 3:14)	DAY ONE - Light: Revelation	Sperm reaches egg	Illumination, conviction
SON: Redeeming	YOU ARE (Ps. 2:7)	DAY TWO - Firmament: Covering	Sperm penetrates egg; protective membrane forms	Receiving Christ; sins covered and forgiven
SPIRIT: Outworking	HE IS (John 14:17)	DAY THREE - Ground giving rise to life: Fruitfulness	Cells divide and differentiate	Growth in sanctification and fruitfulness

4. **Three** in One: The Living Trinity

In this chapter we have seen that the relationship between Father, Son and Holy Spirit provides a blueprint for everything that exists. In this sense church has always existed throughout continuous aeons of time in the form of the constant, never-ending fellowship and communion of the eternal Triune God.

Indeed, the whole human race was meant to be a reflection of this, as we can see back in the first chapter of Genesis. Here, after God says, 'Let US make man in OUR image, in OUR likeness', we are reminded that mankind is similarly made to be both **one** and **more than one**:

> ಸಿಂಡಿ
> So God created man in his own image, in the image of God he created **him**; male and female he created **them**.
> (Gen. 1:27)
> ಸಿಂಡಿ

If this diversity within humanity reflects God's own nature, it should guide us in the way we treat each other and our need to respect each other's God-given differences. The Trinity provides a perfect model for a loving Christian community, as Jesus himself shows us:

> ❧☙
>
> "I do not ask for these only, but also for those who will believe in me through their word, that they may all be *one*, just as you, Father, are in me, and I in you, that they also may be in *us*, so that the world may believe that you have sent me."
> (John 17:20-21)
>
> ❧☙

For this reason, the Trinity shows us how we can hold unity and diversity in balance within the church. For example, Paul uses the **threefold** pattern in 1 Corinthians 12:4-6 ('the same Spirit ... the same Lord ... the same God') to introduce a discussion of the church as 'many parts, yet *one* body' (12:20); he introduces the **triple** blessing at the end of 2 Corinthians to follow his instruction to be 'of *one* mind' (2 Cor. 13:11 NIV); and he proclaims the oneness of the **three** persons in Ephesians 4:4-6 ('*one* Spirit ... *one* Lord ... *one* God and Father of all') to back up his plea to 'keep the *unity* of the Spirit in the bond of peace' (4:3).

The Trinity is also a source of growth and multiplication. Just as God's revelation of himself as 'many-in-one' in Genesis 1:26-8 ('Let **us** make man in **our** image') results in a blessing on mankind to fill the earth, so the first complete unfolding of that 'us' in Scripture at Matthew 28:19 ("baptizing them in the **name** [singular] of the **Father**, and of the **Son**, and of the **Holy Spirit**") comes as part of Jesus' commission to the church to go forth and multiply.

This 'many-in-one', explosive principle of life contained within the Trinity underlines the fact that, throughout the Old Testament, Yahweh, the God of Israel, proclaims himself to be the 'living God.' It is not, in other words, that he is simply alive, but he embodies the very essence of life itself: that of potentially limitless expansion. Not surprisingly, when he touches things, they increase! As Isaiah 51:2 says,

> ❧☙
>
> Look to Abraham, your father,
> and to Sarah, who gave you birth.
> When I called him he was only one man,
> and I blessed him and made him many.
> (Is. 51:2 NIV)
>
> ❧☙

Considered in these terms, the 'many-in-one' aspect of God's nature provides the very driving force behind every living thing around us. This should encourage us not to view the Trinity as some kind of static triangle, but a picture of how God as 'one' and God as 'more than one' stand in creative tension with each other. Such tension is apparent in the way that God's name, Yahweh, can mean both '*I am*' and '*I will be*': it is, in other words, both Alpha and Omega, being and becoming.

In particular, the eternal communion of the three divine persons reminds us of the need to cultivate a vibrant relationship with the Holy Spirit. Without this our Christian walk can become weary, our worship can remain cold and colourless, and efforts to reach out to others reluctant and half-hearted. The difference between today's church and the church in Acts shows how much we need the Holy Spirit again to ignite us in power, as happened on the day of Pentecost, and for us to filled afresh with the Spirit of God each day.

For many today, such as Jews and Muslims, the idea of one God in three persons remains almost impossible to accept. Indeed, many Christians struggle to come to terms with the idea. But we must avoid the temptation of thinking that we can have neatly worked-out answers to every single question! Ultimately, we must admit that we are confronted by an unfathomable mystery far beyond human reason; like Job, we can only confess that, in the end, our thoughts and arguments amount to nothing more than futile speculation (Job 40:4-5).

Reason, therefore, is hardly an adequate response to the mystery of the Trinity. Rather, it is God's Spirit, working in our spirit, which inspires us to join in with countless saints throughout history the unending hymn of praise to our extraordinary Triune God, whose image we reflect:

༺༻

Holy, Holy, Holy! Lord God Almighty!
Early in the morning our song shall rise to Thee;
Holy, Holy, Holy! Merciful and Mighty!
God in Three Persons, blessed Trinity!

Holy, Holy, Holy! All the saints adore Thee,
Casting down their golden crowns around the glassy sea;
Cherubim and seraphim falling down before Thee,
Which wert, and art, and evermore shalt be.

Holy, Holy, Holy! though the darkness hide Thee,
Though the eye of sinful man, thy glory may not see:
Only Thou art holy, there is none beside Thee,
Perfect in power in love, and purity.

Holy, holy, holy! Lord God Almighty!
All thy works shall praise thy name in earth, and sky, and sea;
Holy, Holy, Holy! merciful and mighty,
God in Three Persons, blessed Trinity!

༺༻

Chapter Four

Four

The Number of Life

1. **Four** as a symbol of created life

The number **four** pictures God communicating his being to the entire creation, through every direction and dimension. It points to the universal reach of the outpoured life from God's throne, and in particular to the cross of Christ, through which a broken universe is reconciled to its Creator (Eph:1:6-10; Col. 1:20). If the number **one** directs us primarily to the Father's love, **two** to that between Father and Son, and **three** to that of the whole Trinity, then **four** reminds us that we, too, are bound up in this unending symphony of life that flows out from the very heart of God.

First and foremost, we should notice **four** letters in the divine covenant name, **YHWH** (probably pronounced 'Yahweh'). Originally introduced in the story of the creation of man in Genesis 2, it is used especially to highlight God's dealings with mankind, and in particular with his covenant people Israel. However, it is never revealed to them until the dramatic divine encounter of Moses at the burning bush, where it is linked to a **fourfold** repetition of the word *Elohim* ('God'):

> "Say this to the Israelites: Yahweh, the **God** of your fathers, the **God** of Abraham, the **God** of Isaac, and the **God** of Jacob, has sent me to you. This is My name forever ; this is how I am to be remembered in every generation." (Ex. 3:15 HCSB)

As we shall see, the whole created realm reverberates with this fourfold glory. Around God's throne in heaven, for example, are **four** living creatures who continually worship God (Rev. 4:6-8). These living creatures represent the fullness and the created order: the first living creature is like a lion, the second like an ox, the third has a man's face, and the fourth like a flying eagle.

Below these in the lower heavenlies is a hierarchy of **four** further spiritual powers which Paul calls 'thrones', 'dominions', 'rulers' and 'authorities' (Col. 1:16), possibly shadowed by the **four** fallen powers described in Ephesians 6:12 as 'rulers', 'authorities', 'cosmic powers over this present darkness', and 'spiritual forces of evil in the heavenly places'.

In the earthly realm we see in Daniel 7:2-7 **four** other spiritual authorities, appearing in the form of different beasts, which govern a succession of **four** human empires: a lion with wings of an eagle; a bear raised up on one side; a leopard with **four** heads and **four** wings; and a terrifying creature with iron teeth with many horns.

In addition, Revelation 7 describes **four** further angelic powers on earth who exercise authority over living things on earth:

> After this I saw **four** angels standing at the **four** corners of the earth, holding back the **four** winds of the earth, that no wind might blow on earth or sea or against any tree. (Rev. 7:1)

This fourfold structure of angelic and demonic powers has a physical parallel. The use of such phrases as 'four winds' and 'four corners of the earth' reminds us that in the earthly realm we have **four** compass points governing space. We also have **four** seasons governing time, which determine agriculture, plant growth, and religious festivals, established on the **fourth** day of creation (Gen.

1:14, 19). These in turn influence the rhythms of life on earth.

When we turn our eyes to the wider natural realm, we see **four** invisible fundamental forces which work to hold matter together: these are gravity, electromagnetism, the weak nuclear force and the strong nuclear force. Together they act in the **four** (or more) known dimensions of space and time.

The number four also seems to play a central role in living things. Carbon, the basic building-block of life, has **four** electrons in its outer shell. These enable it to combine as one of the **four** elements (along with nitrogen, hydrogen and oxygen) necessary to form the amino acids required to make up proteins. Proteins in turn are one of **four** macromolecules essential for metabolism (the others being lipids, complex carbohydrates and nucleic acids); while **four** of these nucleic acids (cytosine, guanine, adenine and thymine) make up our DNA. This copies information to enable cell division, where subsequent separation into **four**, eight and sixteen becomes the next stepping-stone towards development and growth. Biological processes follow the **four** mathematical operations of multiplication, division, addition and subtraction, and the **four** laws of thermodynamics.

It is also noticeable that most larger land animals have **four** limbs; most species of insects (barring flies and mosquitoes) have **four** wings; a mammalian heart has **four** chambers. Tests have shown that human beings can hold up to **four** pieces of information clearly in our short-term memory.[6] **Four** has also been shown to be the maximum limit to which other creatures such as honeybees can count accurately.[7]

The number **four** is also prominent in the way that the Bible categorises living things. In Genesis 1:26 **four** kinds of animal (fish, birds, livestock and 'every creeping thing') are represented as being under the dominion of Adam, and these **four** basic groupings reappear in the renewed commission to Noah after the flood (Gen. 9:2).

In Leviticus 11, describing clean and unclean foods, **four** examples of unclean mammals are given, **twenty** examples of unclean birds (5×4), and **eight** examples of unclean creeping things. In addition, *all* **four**-winged insects are forbidden as food (with **four** named exceptions). **Four** animals are described as 'exceedingly wise' in Proverbs 30:24-28.

In Revelation we see, furthermore, a **fourfold** description of the entire created order crying out in a **fourfold** hymn of praise:

> And I heard every creature **in heaven** and **on earth** and **under the earth** and **in the sea**, and all that is in them, saying, "To him who sits on the throne and to the Lamb be **blessing** and **honour** and **glory** and **might** for ever and ever!"
> (Rev. 5:13)

Four also appears as a symbol of humanity. In Daniel 2 the statue in Nebuchadnezzar's dream consisting of **four** metals appears to represent the whole of human history. Likewise, Revelation 20:8 talks about 'the nations that are at the **four** corners of the earth' as a totality of the human race. Repeatedly they are described elsewhere in the book in **fourfold** terms, although no two descriptions are the same:

> 5:9 every **tribe** and **language** and **people** and **nation**
> 7:9 every **nation**, from all **tribes** and **peoples** and **languages**
> 10:11 many **peoples** and **nations** and **languages** and **kings**
> 11:9 the **peoples** and **tribes** and **languages** and **nations**
> 13:7 every **tribe** and **people** and **language** and **nation**
> 14:6 every **nation** and **tribe** and **language** and **people**
> 17:15 **peoples** and **multitudes** and **nations** and **languages**

Finally, we should note that just as four is a symbol of life, it also provides a symbol of **new** life. For example, there were **four** pairs of humans on the ark; **four** cups of wine are drunk at Passover to celebrate deliverance from slavery and from the angel of death; Shadrach, Meshach and Abednego are saved by a **fourth** person with them in the furnace; Jesus, whose **four** divine titles are listed in Isaiah 9:6, prophesied his resurrection **four** times in Matthew's Gospel (16:21; 17:22-23; 20:17-19; 26:32); and raised Lazarus to life after **four** days (John 11:39-44).

The same is true of its multiple eight. In the Old Testament **eight** persons were saved in the ark; circumcision took place on the **eighth** day as a picture of new creation (Gen. 17:12; Col. 2:11); priests began their work on the **eighth** day after consecration (Lev. 8:33, 9:1-2); those with healed sores were cleansed by the priest on the **eighth** day after self-isolation (Lev. 14:10-20); David, who brought Israel into a new era in its history, was the **eighth** son of Jesse; Elijah is recorded as performing **eight** miracles, and Elisha exactly twice that number.

In the New Testament Jesus was revealed in glory about **eight** days after revealing his Messiahship (Luke 9:28-36); revealed himself as the spring of living water on the **eighth** day of the Feast of Dedication (John 7:37); rose from the dead on the **eighth** day (John 20:1) and appeared to Thomas **eight** days later (20:26).

Outside the future events outlined in the book of Revelation, **eight** people apart from Jesus himself and the resurrected saints in Matthew 27:52-53 are named as having been raised from the dead:

Eight Resurrections in the Bible

The widow's son in Zarephath (1 Kings 17:17-24)
The Shunammite's son (2 Kings 4:32-35)
The corpse which touched Elijah's bones (2 Kings 13:21)
The widow's son in Nain (Luke 7:11-15)
Jairus' daughter (Luke 8:49-56)
Lazarus (John 11:38-44)
Dorcas (Acts 9:40-41)
Eutychus (Acts 20:9-10)

Finally, an interesting result may be obtained from the use of *gematria*, where the numerical value of names is calculated on the basis that every letter has a number value of its own. It is striking that adding the letters of many of the titles of Jesus in Greek in the New Testament produces multiples of 8, as follows:

Jesus = 888 (8×111)   Christ = 1,480 (8×185)
Lord = 800 (8×100)   King = 848 (8×106)
Lord Jesus Christ = 3,168 (8×396)
Messiah = 656 (8×82)   Saviour = 1,408 (8×8×8×4)
Bridegroom = 1160 (8×145)   Son = 680 (8×85)
Son of Man = 2,960 (8×370)   Son of God = 1,256 (8×157)

The Power of Squares

Square numbers play an important role in the Bible:

- The number 1 maps onto itself (1×1), denoting the unity of God (Deut. 6:4)
- The number 4 is the next square number (2×2), denoting fullness (Gen. 2:10; Ezek. 1:4-21).
- The number 9 (3×3) yields 9 gifts of the Spirit and 9 fruits of the Spirit (1 Cor. 12:8-10; Gal. 5:22-23)
- Four kings either began their reign at 16 (4×4) or reigned for 16 years (2 Kings 13:10; 14:21; 15:33; 16:2)
- Five kings either began their reign at 25 (5×5) or reigned for 25 years (1 Kings 22:42; 2 Kings 14:2; 15:33; 18:2; 23:36)
- 49 years (7×7) had to elapse before the Year of Jubilee (Lev. 25:8)
- The number 100 (10×10) is a description of fruitfulness (Gen. 26:12; Matt. 13:23; 19:29)
- The New Jerusalem is 144 (12×12) cubits thick (Rev. 21:17)
- In Daniel 10,000 × 10,000 stand before the throne of God (7:10) - now considered to be an accurate estimate of world population at that time.
- Sir Isaac Newton, who helped to discover the inverse-square law and a method for working out square roots still in use today, spent many years studying the square ground plan of the temple.

I heard ... the voice of many angels, numbering myriads of myriads and thousands of thousands (Rev. 5.11)

FOUR: THE NUMBER OF LIFE

Above: The design on the octagonal mosaic ceiling inside the Baptistry of St. John, Florence, dates back to the 13th century, and depicts scenes from the final judgement (photo by Ricardo André Frantz). St. Ambrose wrote that fonts and baptistries were octagonal 'because on the eighth day, by rising, Christ loosens the bondage of death and receives the dead from their graves.'

2. **Four** as a symbol of outpoured life

The number four also plays a particularly significant role in the outer sections of the book of Ezekiel. The book begins with a vision, similar to that in Revelation, with **four** living creatures alongside **four** wheels on the **four** sides of the heavenly throne, each with **four** faces and **four** wings, moving together in co-ordinated right angles. Above them God is enthroned in dazzling glory:

> And from the midst of it came the likeness of **four** living creatures. And this was their appearance: they had a human likeness, but each had **four** faces, and each of them had **four** wings. ... Under their wings on their **four** sides they had human hands. And the **four** had their faces and their wings thus: their wings touched one another. Each one of them went straight forward, without turning as they went. As for the likeness of their faces, each had a human face. The **four** had the face of a lion on the right side, the **four** had the face of an ox on the left side, and the **four** had the face of an eagle. (Ezek. 1:5-10)

These living creatures, or *cherubim*, have an interesting history in scripture. Although they first appear in Genesis 3 guarding the way to the tree of life when Adam and Eve were thrown out of the Garden of Eden, they come particularly into prominence as carved figures above the Ark of the Covenant in the tabernacle, which was intended as an earthly representation of God's throne in heaven.

When we compare the design of the ark with Ezekiel's heavenly vision, many striking parallels appear. Like the living creatures with their **four** faces and **four** wheels, the ark had **four** feet (Ex. 25:12) to which **four** gold rings were attached. Inside the ark **four** objects were placed (the gold jar of manna, Aaron's rod which had budded, and the two stone tablets). It was situated in a room of **four** equal sides, the Holy of Holies.

In addition, the ark was one of **four** holy objects which had rings attached at each of their **four** corners (the others being the altar of incense, the altar of burnt offering and the table which carried the bread of the presence). Poles of acacia wood were inserted into these, to enable them to be transported easily through the wilderness. We might remember here that in Ezekiel's vision, one of the purposes of the four living creatures was to *transport* the glory of God throughout the earth (Ezek. 10:15-19).

Figures of cherubim were also woven into the curtain which separated the ark from the rest of the tabernacle. This curtain was made up of **four** materials (finely twisted linen and blue, purple and scarlet yarn), and was hung using gold clasps on **four** posts of acacia wood mounted on **four** silver bases. This material was also one of **four** layers of coverings protecting the tabernacle (the others being made of goat hair, ram skins and sea cows).

If the vision at the beginning of Ezekiel reflects the fourfold patterning of the tabernacle, the description at the end of the book of a future temple does so much more extensively.

What is striking here is that the *shape* and *measurements* of the building are not just laid out to make a beautiful design, but to teach Israel the difference between right and wrong:

> ଓଃ
>
> "As for you, son of man, describe to the house of Israel the temple, that they may be ashamed of their iniquities; and they shall *measure* the plan. And if they are ashamed of all that they have done, make known to them the *design* of the temple, its arrangement, its exits and its entrances, that is, *its whole design*; and make known to them as well all its statutes and its whole *design* and all its laws, and write it down in their sight, so that they may observe all its laws and all its statutes and carry them out.
> (Ezek. 43:10-11)
>
> ଓଃ

When we look at the design, the connection with the first chapter of Ezekiel becomes immediately apparent. Where in the original vision he sees 'wheels within wheels', he is now confronted by 'squares within squares', with the altar set at the very heart of it:

Groundplan of Ezekiel's Temple (as sketched by Isaac Newton):

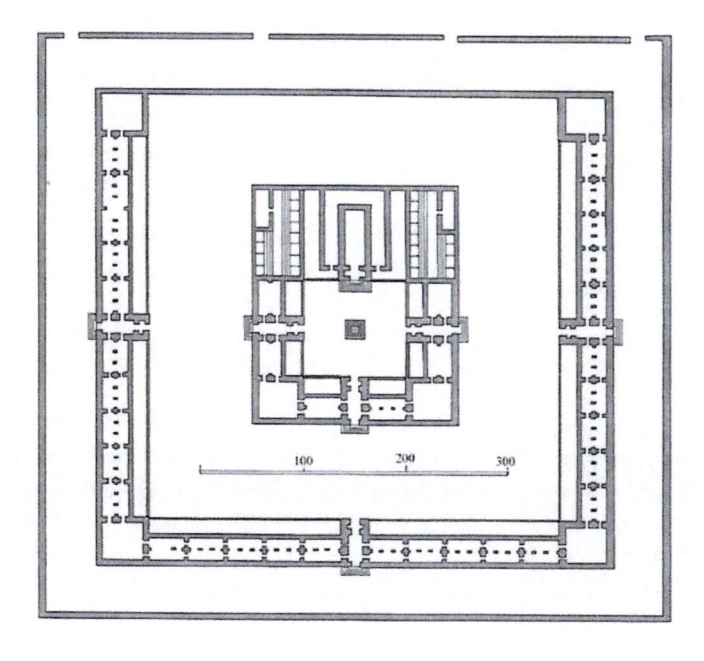

There are several aspects this groundplan which really stand out. Firstly, we should notice its universal significance. The temple, and the altar set at its heart, is *facing outwards in every direction*. Jesus insisted that 'my house shall be a house of prayer for all the nations' (Mark 11:17). The design was meant to be a declaration not just to Israel, but to the whole world, of the goodness and glory of God. Insofar as it speaks to us today, it should remind us that our lives ought to have this same outward focus.

Secondly, we should notice that the lengths of the temple walls and the altar at its centre are *identical on each side*. These interlocking squares seem to be telling us something about the nature of God. He is utterly consistent and unwavering from whichever angle we look at him. Indeed, the inner sanctuary of the Temple, the place where God himself was supposed to dwell, was not just a perfect square but a perfect cube (as is the New Jerusalem in Revelation). As we saw in Chapter One, Paul reminds us that the new covenant brings equal access to all, regardless of race, background or social class:

> For as many of you as were baptized into Christ have put on Christ. There is neither Jew nor Greek, there is neither slave nor free, there is no male and female, for you are all **one** in Christ Jesus. (Gal 3:27-28)

Thirdly, we should note that the temple, like the New Jerusalem, is set in a perfect north-south-east-west alignment. In many ways it acts as a spiritual compass, reminding us of the importance of remaining completely in alignment with God's will.

This helps to underline a primary characteristic of God, that he is straight and upright in every respect, and that all his qualities are equal and absolute. Even in the English language, the words *right*-angle and *right*eousness share a

---

An Altar in Sound

Much of the design of Ezekiel's temple reflects geometrical proportions and the ratios between whole numbers. Such symmetries can touch our deep subconscious in the same way that music does. Some Greek philosophers such as Pythagoras thought that whole number ratios were important and that music, which is largely based on these ratios, reflected the harmony of the universe.

Given that the temple was intended to offer the earthly equivalent of the endless praise to God that we encounter in Revelation, in which the **four** living creatures play a leading part, it should not escape our notice that much worship music today is built on a set of **four** chords played over **four** beats in a bar, which themselves extend into larger symmetries based on **four**-bar units.

A life of worship helps our lives reflect this heavenly proportion and balance that can bring harmony to the discordant world around us, and draw others towards God's indescribable beauty.

*And I heard a voice from heaven like the roar of many waters and like the sound of loud thunder. The voice I heard was like the sound of harpists playing on their harps, and they were singing a new song before the throne and before the **four** living creatures and before the elders.* (Rev. 14:2-3)

common root and a common set of associations. God uses a plumbline in the Old Testament to demonstrate that his Word alone determines absolute truth and justice (Amos 7:8).

In this connection, we should notice that the Hebrew character for 'four' (ר) is made up of two strokes at right angles to each other. Just as the living creatures in Ezekiel only move in straight lines or right-angles (Ezek. 1:9, 12, 17), so we too need to line up with God's purposes if we are to live in harmony with him. In Proverbs we are told:

> ಬ)ಲ
> Let your eyes look directly forwards,
> and your gaze be straight before you.
> Ponder the path of your feet;
> then all your ways will be sure.
> Do not swerve to the right or to the left;
> turn your foot away from evil.
> (Prov. 4:25-27)
> ಬ)ಲ

Comparing these two visions at the beginning and ending of Ezekiel leads us to a remarkable conclusion. At the start of the book we see a throne surrounded on four sides by angelic beings. Yet by the end of the book this central throne has been transformed into an altar, the place of sacrifice and bloodshed. It is here, not the Holy of Holies, that marks the exact centre of the temple design.

This might lead us to consider the extraordinary thought that the ultimate expression of the reign of God is not the throne of majesty in heaven, but the cross of Jesus on earth, towards which every altar in the Old Testament was merely a pointer. Let us not forget that John, in his vision of heaven in Revelation, sees a slain Lamb at the very heart of the throne, in whose spilt blood the heavenly saints have washed their robes (7:14,17).

There seems to be a remarkable irony here. At his 'coronation' as King of the Jews, Jesus' throne is a wooden torture-stake, his crown woven together from thorns, and his royal robe gambled away, while his 'courtiers' mock and jeer. And yet, what seems to be the moment of greatest defeat is actually the moment of supreme victory.

Jesus cries triumphantly, 'It is finished!' (John 19:30). This was not a cry of defeat but a shout of triumph! The Greek word *tetelesthai* was an accounting word written across bills to indicate 'paid in full' (see page 164). The curse of sin and death had finally been broken forever.

It is striking that, in Ezekiel's end-time temple, no veil is mentioned inside: this is because, after Jesus' death, the veil in the temple tore in two from top to bottom, symbolising that the barrier between God and man had been removed once and for all. Also, unlike Herod's temple, there is no separate 'Court of Women' or 'Court of the Gentiles'. Now all are brought near through the shed blood of the Messiah on behalf of all mankind, as Paul writes:

> ಬ)ಲ
> But now in Christ Jesus you who once were far off have been brought near by the blood of Christ. (Eph. 2:13)
> ಬ)ಲ

It is hard, then, to escape the conclusion that the temple design is basically a huge visual pointer to Jesus' finished work on the cross, as might be suggested in the diagram below:

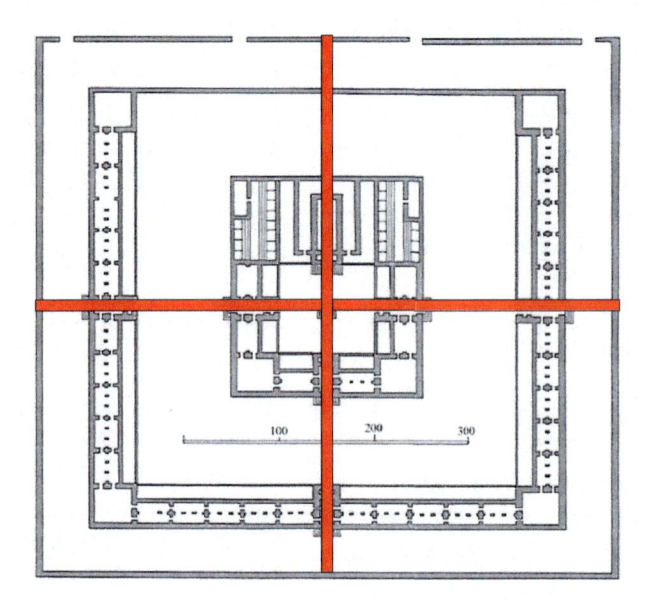

The design of the altar itself at the centre of the structure (Ezek. 43:13-17) underlines this further. On the one hand the **four** horns on each corner might remind us of the **four** living creatures around God's throne (a voice from the horns of God's heavenly altar instructs **four** earthly angels in Revelation 9:13-15). But they also point to sacrifice: the very first mention of 'horns' in scripture appears in Genesis 22:13 where a lamb, caught in a thicket by its horns, is sacrificed in place of Isaac. It was on the horns of the altar that the blood of the sin offering was applied (Lev. 4:18, 25, 30, 34), and they acted as a place of refuge where a condemned man could seek sanctuary (1 Kings 1:50-51; 2:28).

There may be a link, therefore, between the altar at the exact centre of the temple and a verse from the Psalm which, as we saw on page 63, appears next to the very midpoint of the Bible:

> ℘℧
> Bind the festal sacrifice with cords,
> up to the horns of the altar! (Ps. 118:27)
> ℘℧

It is hard to avoid the conclusion that these horns point us to the outstretched limbs of Jesus on the cross:

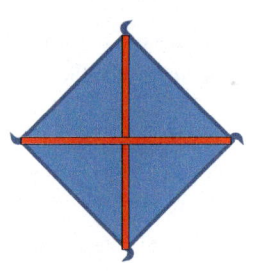

102

The layout of Ezekiel's temple with its central focus on the altar is just one among many possible visual pointers to the cross in the Old Testament. We might remember, for example, Moses holding up his staff in the air to ensure victory over the Amalekites (Ex. 17:8-13); Aaron lifting up his arms to bless the Israelites (Lev. 9:22); the bronze serpent on a pole (Num. 21:8-9); or Samson pushing out the pillars of the temple with both arms to achieve victory through his death (Judges 16:29-30). To this we might add Joseph crossing his arms to switch the blessing of the firstborn from Manasseh to Ephraim (Gen. 48:14); the mark on the foreheads of the faithful in Ezekiel 9.4, which as an old Hebrew *tau* would have taken the form of a cross; and the gallows built by Haman for Mordecai which becomes the instrument of his own destruction (Esther 7:9-10).

A final picture comes in the structure of the tabernacle, the place of sacrifice, which was supported by vertical wooden poles with horizontal crossbars on either side, extending the entire length of the structure:

> "Make upright frames of acacia wood for the tabernacle. Each frame is to be ten cubits long and a cubit and a half wide. ... Also make crossbars of acacia wood: five for the frames on one side of the tabernacle, five for those on the other side, and five for the frames on the west, at the far end of the tabernacle. The centre crossbar is to extend from end to end at the middle of the frames."
> (Ex. 26:15-16; 26-28 NIV)

In effect, the entire tabernacle was completely surrounded by a construction resembling the form of a cross!

Life on the Edge

The four horns of the altar may have a parallel in the four tassels or *tzitzit* on the corners of the Jewish prayer shawl, the *tallit katan*, a four-cornered garment which was made in following the instruction in Numbers 15:37-38:

The LORD said to Moses, "Speak to the people of Israel, and tell them to make tassels on the corners of their garments throughout their generations, and to put a cord of blue on the tassel of each corner."

When the gospels tell us of the woman with the flow of blood who is healed by touching the hem of Jesus' garment, it is possible that she was holding onto one of these four tassels, since the Greek word for 'hem' here was the specific word used for the *tzitzit* in later writings. In this sense, it may have been a New Testament equivalent of Adonijah seeking refuge by clinging to the horns of the altar in Solomon's time (1 Kings 1:50-51), reminding us again of the redemptive power symbolised by the number four.

Jesus turned, and seeing her he said, "Take heart, daughter; your faith has made you well." And instantly the woman was made well. (Matt. 9:22)

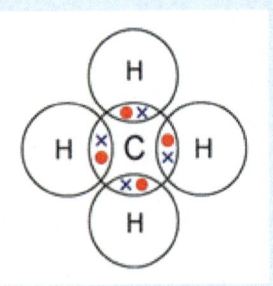

methane (CH₄)

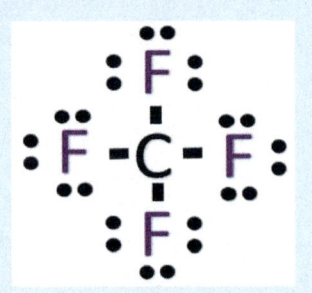

carbon tetrafluoride (CF₄)

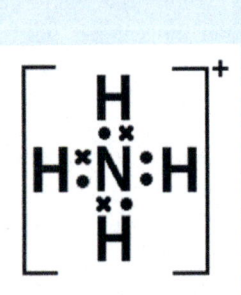

ammonium ion (NH₄⁺)

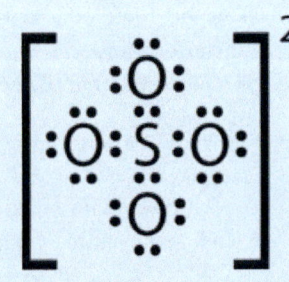

sulphate ion (SO₄²⁻)

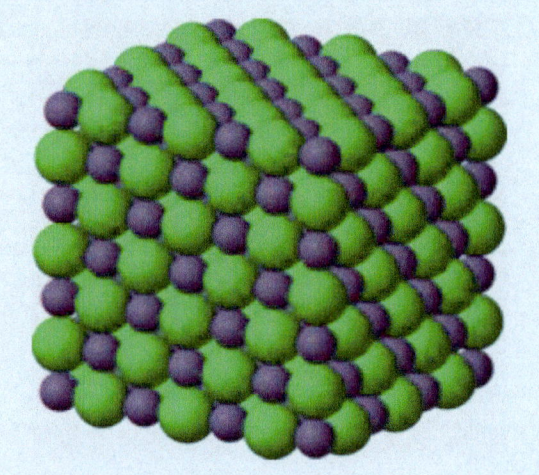

sodium chloride (NaCl)

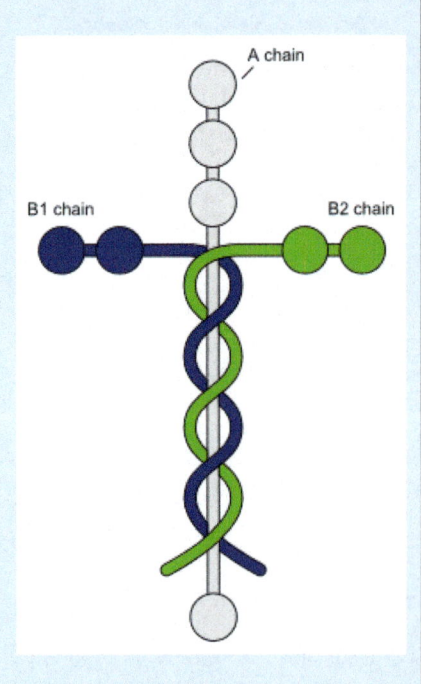

Above left: Many naturally occurring molecules are arranged in modified cruciform shapes.

Above right: The protein laminin forms a cross-shaped 'glue' which binds to cell membranes and holds the human body together

Left: In sodium chloride (better known to us as table salt) the two constituent atoms are arranged in a cross-shaped lattice worked out in three dimensions. Salt recurs in the Bible as a significant symbol pointing to the power and presence of God (see page 118).

One further anticipation of the cross can be seen in the way in which God instructed the Israelite tribes to encamp round the tabernacle in the wilderness, as we see laid out below:

The Alignment of Tribes in the Wilderness:

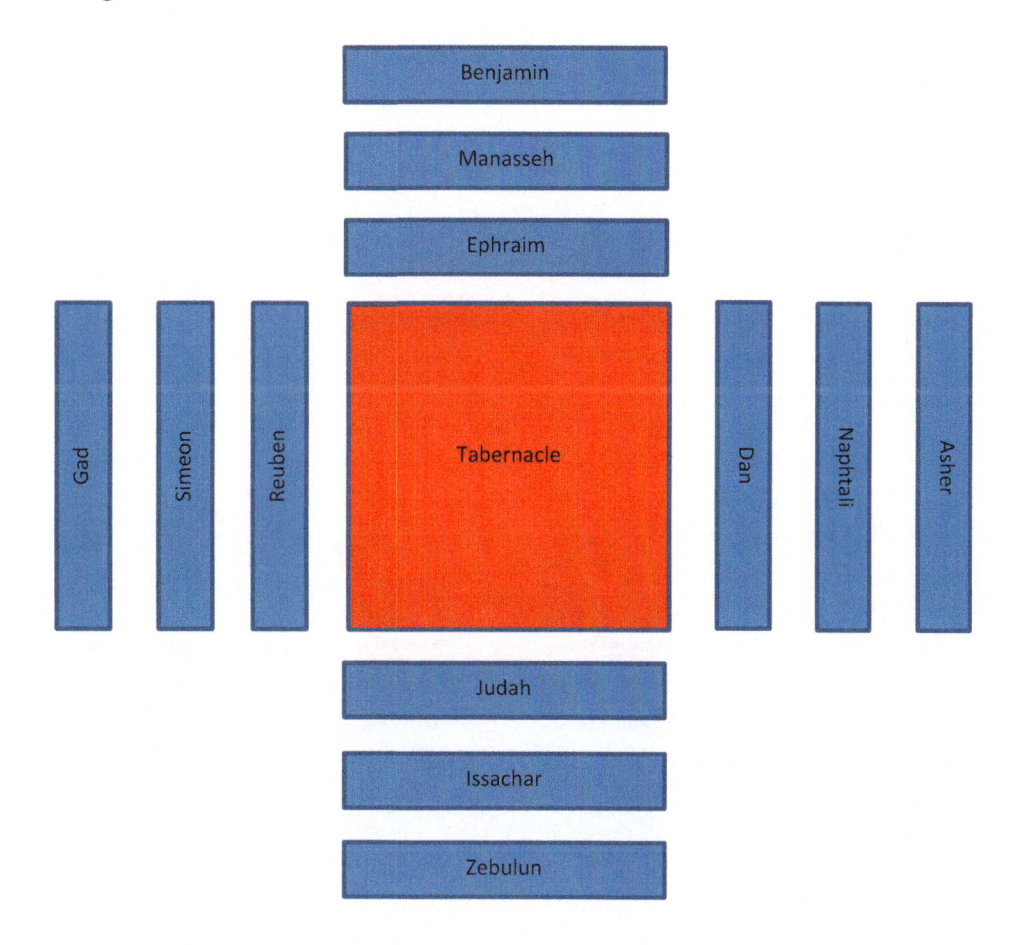

```
                    Benjamin
                    Manasseh
                    Ephraim
  Gad  Simeon  Reuben  [Tabernacle]  Dan  Naphtali  Asher
                    Judah
                    Issachar
                    Zebulun
```

Jewish tradition as recounted in the Talmud assigns each of these four groups a logo on their banners corresponding to the four living creatures in Ezekiel 1: the standard of Judah represented by a lion, that of Reuben by a man, that of Ephraim by an ox, and that of Dan by an eagle. This acts as a reminder to us that the four living creatures are themselves arranged in a cross formation, as we can see overleaf:

In a broader sense, the symbolism of the cross seems to picture the meeting-point between vertical and horizontal dimensions, the heavenly and the earthly. There are several verses in the Old Testament which seem to trace this outward cross-shape in the meeting of these two intersecting realms:

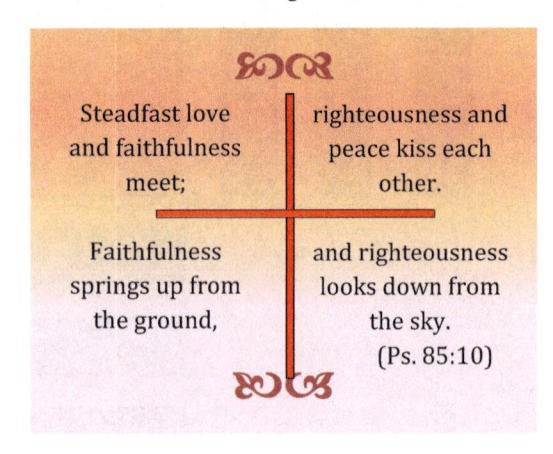

"Can you find out the deep things of God? Can you find out the limit of the Almighty?

It is higher than heaven—
what can you do?

Deeper than Sheol—
what can you know?

Its measure is longer than the earth

and broader than the sea."
(Job 11:7-9 ESV)

Steadfast love and faithfulness meet;

righteousness and peace kiss each other.

Faithfulness springs up from the ground,

and righteousness looks down from the sky.
(Ps. 85:10)

These verses provide a foretaste of Paul's **four**-dimensional description of love in Ephesians:

For this reason I bow my knees before the Father ... that you, being rooted and grounded in love, may have strength to comprehend with all the saints what is the **breadth** and **length** and **height** and **depth**, and to know the love of Christ that surpasses knowledge, that you may be filled with all the fullness of God. (Eph. 3:14, 17-19)

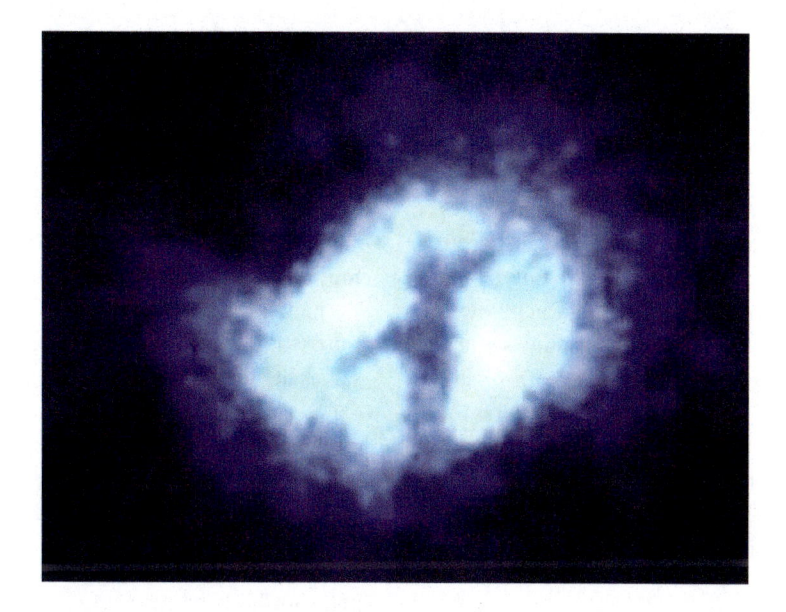

Above: A cross-shaped formation at the centre of the Whirlpool Galaxy, taken by the Hubble Space Telescope in 1992. The 'cross' in the centre is thought to be 100 light years in diameter.

Below: The X- Chromosome spans about 155 million DNA building blocks and represents approximately one twentieth of the total DNA in cells. It carries around 1,000 genes.

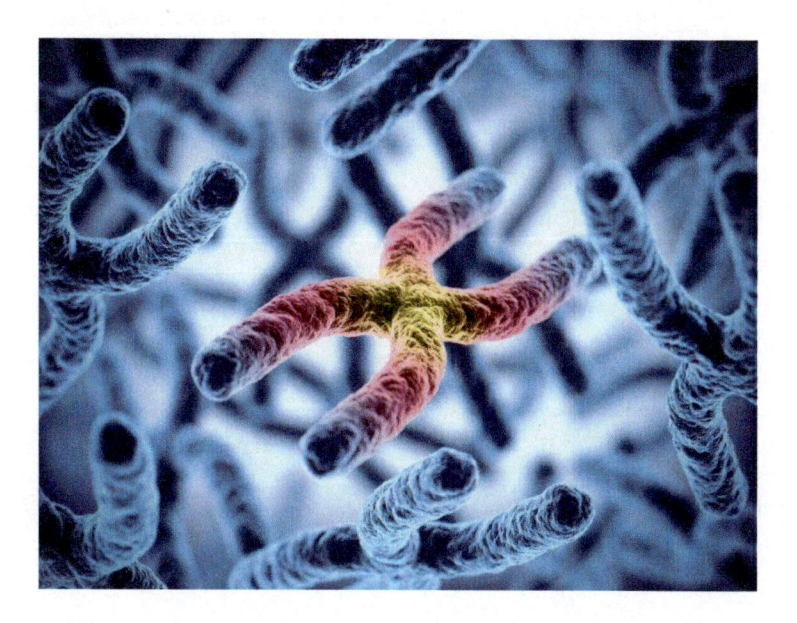

3. **Four** as a symbol of renewed life

If the cross speaks of ultimate sacrifice, it also reminds us of the new life that results. It is striking, therefore, that from the altar at the heart of Ezekiel's temple, the place of death and brokenness, a river flows out (Ezek. 47:1). This river recalls the one which flowed out of Eden, which divided into **four** streams (Gen. 2:10). Ezekiel sees the depth of this river being measured **four** times until it is too deep to cross. As the river flows into the Dead Sea, a place that is barren and inhospitable to life, it begins to teem with fish (Ezek. 47:8-9) and trees bringing healing grow along its banks (verse 12).

This river is mentioned again twice by Zechariah (Zech. 13:1 and 14:8), shortly after the extraordinary verse which looks directly ahead to the cross of Calvary:

> "When they look on **me**, on him whom they have pierced, they shall mourn for **him**, as one mourns for an only child, and weep bitterly over him, as one weeps over a firstborn." (Zech. 12:10)

This reminds us that, after Jesus died on the cross, blood and water flowed out from his side (John 19:34, 37). In Revelation the faithful martyrs are those who have washed their robes in the blood of the Lamb and drink from springs of living water (7:14, 17; John 7:37-38).

In this regard, the cross might also remind us of the **four** compass points to which the outpoured life of Christ flows. Just as we read about **four** streams in Eden, the Bible talks of **four** winds that communicate the life of God: Zechariah sees **four** chariots going out to the **four** winds of heaven after presenting themselves before the LORD of all the earth (Zech. 6:1-5). In Ezekiel it is **four** winds which blow on the dry bones of Israel to bring them back to life (37:9). Jesus talked of gathering his elect from the same **four** winds (Matt. 24:31).

Indeed, throughout scripture, four seems to point to the good news of salvation. As we have already mentioned, **four** couples were saved on the ark. It is **four** lepers in 2 Kings 7 who bring the good news of the end of the siege of Samaria (the word used for 'good news' in the Greek translation of the Old Testament in verse 9, *euangelion*, is the very word used for 'gospel' in the New).

In the New Testament, it is **four** friends who lower the stretcher carrying the paralysed man by its **four** corners in front of Jesus, who pronounces those **four** liberating words, 'your sins are forgiven' (Mark 2:1-5). Jesus gives **four** instructions to the twelve before sending them out: 'Heal the sick, raise the dead, cleanse lepers, cast out demons' (Matt. 10:8). There are **four** kinds of soil listed in the parable of the sower, describing the varying outcomes of the gospel message (Matt. 13:3-8). Jesus' garments are divided into **four** parts at the cross (John 19:23).

In Acts **sixteen** (4x4) locations are referred to in the first gospel message preached after Jesus's ascension to heaven (Acts 2:9-11). And it is the sailsheet full of 'unclean' **four**-footed animals, lowered by its **four** corners in Acts 10:11-12, which convinces Peter to preach the gospel to the Gentiles. Hebrews 2:4 tells us that God provided **four** witnesses to the truth of the gospel message: signs, wonders, miracles, and gifts of the Holy Spirit.

After the scattering resulting from the stoning of Stephen, we see the gospel witness sent out in **four** directions: north-west to Samaria, south-west towards Gaza (*en route* to Africa), north-east to Damascus, and then west to Lydda and Joppa, as a backdrop for Peter's first outreach to the Gentiles in Caesarea.

This might be seen as a partial fulfilment of God's instruction to Abraham two thousand years earlier to walk through the **length** and **breadth** of the land (Gen. 13:17) after saying to him,

> "Lift up your eyes and look from the place where you are, **north**wards and **south**wards and **east**wards and **west**wards for all the land that you see I will give to you and to your offspring for ever."
> (verses 14-15)

Similarly, the 'great commission' that Jesus gives his disciples in Matthew 28 echoes the promise given to Jacob in Genesis, when he sees a ladder stretching up to heaven:

> Your offspring shall be like the dust of the earth, and you shall spread abroad to the **west** and to the **east** and to the **north** and to the **south**, and in you and your offspring shall all the families of the earth be blessed. (Genesis 28:14)

Likewise, Jesus' promise of an ingathering of Gentile believers echoes the promise in Psalm 107 about the regathering of Israel:

> "And people will come from **east** and **west**, and from **north** and **south**, and recline at table in the kingdom of God."
> (Luke 13:29)

> Let the redeemed of the Lord say so, whom he has redeemed from trouble and gathered in from the lands, from the **east** and from the **west**, from the **north** and from the **south**.
> (Psalm 107:2-4)

Another striking pointer of the spread of the gospel is the bronze laver used to purify the temple priests so that they could enter the presence of God without fear of death. This is another powerful symbol of the gospel message of reconciliation. We are told that:

> ❧☙
> It stood on twelve oxen, three facing **north**, three facing **west**, three facing **south**, and three facing **east**. The sea was set on them, and all their rear parts were inward.
> (1 Kings 7:25)
> ❧☙

Given that this arrangement looks ahead to the twelve gates facing outwards from the New Jerusalem, whose foundations bore the names of the twelve apostles (Rev. 21:10-14), we might again see a foretaste of way that Jesus' companions went on to share his message across the earth.

Biblically, the symbol of an ox reminds us both of strength and yet servanthood: a beast of burden that also made a prime candidate for a sacrificial offering. We might be reminded how the Twelve carried the living water of the gospel to different parts of the earth, where many of them suffered martyrdom. Although there are many conflicting traditions often based on scant evidence, there are suggestions that

- John, Bartholomew and Matthias travelled north to minister in Asia Minor and Armenia
- Peter, Andrew, and (in some traditions) James went west to Europe
- Matthew, Philip and James son of Alphaeus went south to Africa
- Simon the Zealot, Thaddaeus and Thomas went east to Persia and India

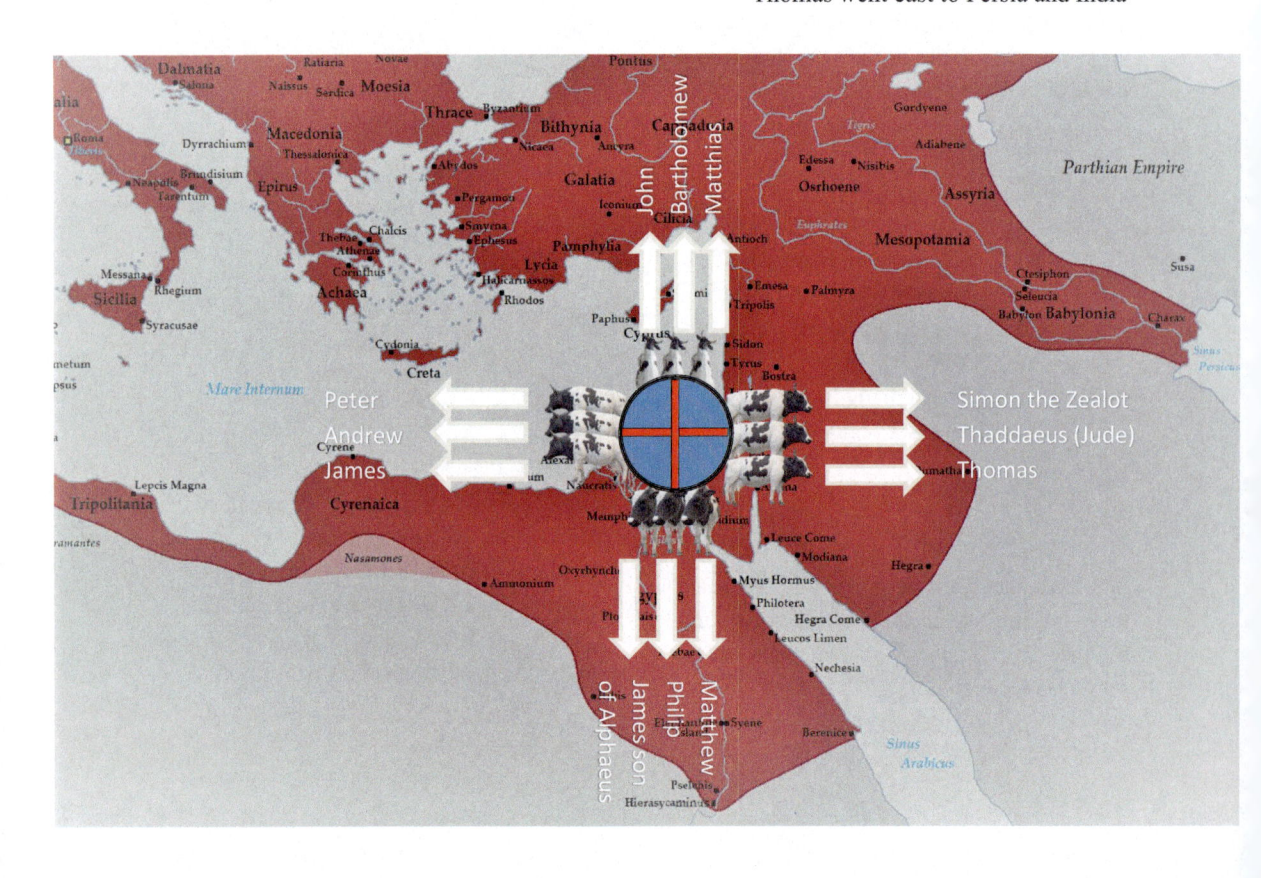

Finally we should remember that there are not just one but **four** gospels testifying to the life, teaching, death and resurrection of Jesus. The Church Father Irenaeus, writing in *Adversus Haereses*, comments that:

> The gospels could not possibly be more or less than they are in number. Since there are **four** zones in the world in which we live, and **four** principal winds, it is fitting that the church, spread out across the earth, whose pillar and foundation is the gospel and the Spirit of life, has **four** pillars, breathing out immortality everywhere and bringing life to mankind. It is clear therefore that the Word, the maker of all things, in being revealed to mankind, gave us the gospel in a **fourfold** form but held together by **one** Spirit.
> Irenaeus, *Adversus Haereses* (3.11.8)

He goes on to link these with the four cherubim in Revelation:

> For the cherubim have **four** faces, and their faces reflect the activity of the Son of God. For the first living creature, we are told, was like a lion, showing its active, princely and royal character; the second was like an ox, showing its sacrificial and priestly role; the third had the face of a man, indicating very clearly his coming in human form; and the fourth was like a flying eagle, revealing the giving of the Spirit who broods over the church. Now the gospels, in which Christ is enthroned, are like these.

Various attempts have been made at correlating the various living creatures with the different gospel writers, but probably the most satisfying solution is to take the order that the creatures appear in the book of Revelation (lion, ox, man, and flying eagle) as pictures of each of the four successive gospels:

Matthew, as the lion, is supremely the gospel to Israel. Jesus is described as the 'Lion of the tribe of Judah' in Revelation 5:5 (recalling Genesis 49:9), and Matthew presents Jesus as the King of the Jews, the fulfilment of Old Testament prophecy, and the culmination of Jewish history.

Mark, by contrast, draws attention to Jesus as the obedient suffering servant. The ox is a very fitting image here: powerful and strong, yet also a beast of burden being prepared for sacrifice. Its focus is on Jesus' actions, more than his words, and a large proportion of the gospel is devoted to the final week of Jesus' life.

For **Luke**, the image of a man seems appropriate given the attention given to Jesus' compassion, mercy and concern for the downtrodden and the outcast. The shepherds who spread the good news of Jesus' birth, the unnamed sinner who washes Jesus' feet with her hair and the thief on the cross, and innumerable other participants, are all beautifully delineated in his gospel.

John's gospel has a very different atmosphere from the others and begins in timeless eternity. A sense of awe and majesty pervades the whole gospel which is well suited to the picture of an eagle in flight, with Jesus' divine nature very clearly expressed. It makes a fitting climax to the greatest story ever told.

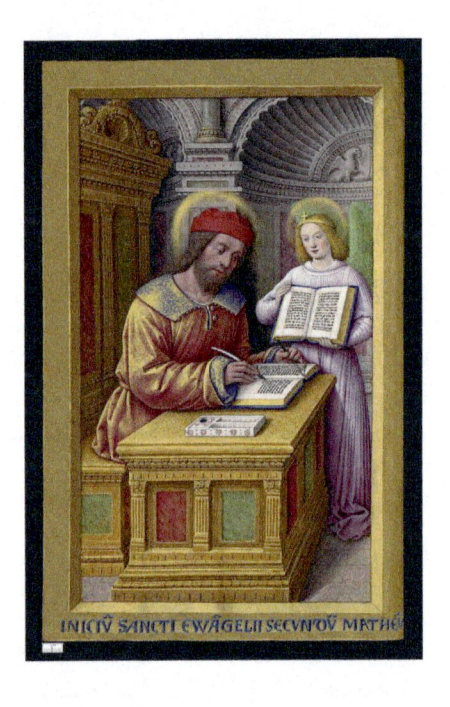

Above and below: Miniatures from the *Grandes Heures* of Anne of Brittany, Queen Consort of France (1477–1514), depicting the writers of the four gospels. Photo taken by Jean Bourdichon – Bibliothèque Nationale de France.

A Lost Christian Symbol?

Scattered across the Roman world is an intriguing inscription which appears in various forms, with examples spread as far apart as Manchester and Cirencester in England and Dura-Europos in Syria. The words are SATOR (the sower); AREPO (a proper name unknown in Latin literature); TENET (he holds); OPERA (labours, or with effort); and ROTAS (the wheels, or he causes to turn). A loose translation might be 'Arepo the sower sustains the wheels with effort'. The same words read down, across, backwards and forwards in **four** directions:

```
S A T O R
A R E P O
T E N E T
O P E R A
R O T A S
```

Associations with known Christian sites have led many to believe that it originated as a covert Christian symbol, possibly to communicate faith during times of intense state persecution. The image of a sower is a familiar reference to Jesus in the gospels; Arepo may be a cypher for Christ (A and O are the first and last letters of the Greek alphabet, used to describe him in Revelation); while the image of TENET ('he holds'), lined up in a cross shape, might have offered powerful comfort to believers in times of hardship:

```
S A T O R
A R E P O
T E N E T
O P E R A
R O T A S
```

Two other intriguing features may also link the word square with scripture. Firstly, two of the words appear (one in a slightly altered form) in the Latin Vulgate translation of Ezekiel 1:16. This is the passage about the four living creatures that we considered earlier in this chapter, which as we noticed were also arranged in a cross shape. In addition, the mysterious name Arepo seems to be partly spelt out at the opening of the verse:

ET ASPECTUS ROTARUM ET OPUS EARUM QUASI VISIO MARIS ET UNA SIMILITUDO IPSARUM QUATTUOR ET ASPECTUS EARUM ET OPERA QUASI SIT ROTA IN MEDIO ROTAE

And the appearance of the wheels, and the work of them was like the appearance of the sea: and the four had all one likeness: and their appearance and their work was as it were a wheel in the midst of a wheel. (Ezek. 1:16 Douay-Rheims)

Secondly, by arranging the letters around the central 'N' of TENET, the words PATER NOSTER ('Our Father'), the opening words of the Lord's prayer, can be formed vertically and horizontally, again in a cross formation. The four remaining letters – two each of 'A' and 'O' - might refer again to 'Alpha and Omega', a title applied *both* to Jesus *and* to the Father in Revelation:

```
            P
            A
            T
            E
       A    R         O
            
P A T E R N O S T E R
            O
            S
            T
       A    E         O
            R
```

And he is before all things, and in him all things **hold together***... making peace by the blood of his cross* (Col. 1.17, 20)

4. **Four** as a symbol of upturned life

Up to now, the number four has been uniformly positive in its associations. Yet, in symbolising the righteousness of God, which can come into collision with a sinful world, it can also express judgement and calamity. In Exodus 34:7 Moses is told that God's judgement on sin extends for up to **four** generations. Moreover, various nations are described as being scattered to the **four** winds of heaven through God's judgement (Jer. 49:36, Dan. 11:4, Zech. 2:6).

In Job chapter 1 **four** catastrophes of progressively increasing severity act to test his faith:

- loss of cattle and donkeys
- loss of sheep
- loss of camels
- loss of children

In Jeremiah 15:3, God appoints **four** kinds of destroyers against Jerusalem:

- the sword
- the dogs
- the birds of the air
- the beasts of the earth

In Ezekiel 14:21 God again decrees **four** acts of judgement against Jerusalem:

- sword
- famine
- wild beasts
- pestilence

Daniel chapter 2 describes the destruction of the **four** great kingdoms of the earth, represented by **four** metals in a great statue:

- the head of gold (Babylon)
- the chest of silver (Medo-Persia)
- the thighs of bronze (Greece)
- the legs of iron (Rome)

In Luke's gospel (6:24-26) Jesus pronounces **four** warnings aimed at

- the fortunate
- the fully-fed
- the frivolous
- the famous

In Revelation 6 the **four** horsemen successively bring a series of convulsions to the world, the **fourth** exercising authority over a **quarter** of the earth:

- white horse (totalitarian rule)
- red horse (military conflict)
- black horse (economic collapse)
- pale horse (disease and environmental catastrophe)

In addition, **four** angels are given the power to harm the earth and the sea (Rev. 7:2) and **four** angels are released to kill a third of mankind (9:14-15).

The number **forty** also contains a similar set of associations, both positive and negative, as we see on the next three pages:

Four, Forty, and the Division of Time

If four is a significant unit in the structuring of space in the Bible, it also plays an important role in the organisation of time. There are **four** weeks in a month and **four** seasons in a year. Jesus walked out to his disciples in the **fourth** watch of the night; Lazarus was dead for **four** days; Jesus spoke of **four** months until the harvest.

The number **forty** (4x10) plays an even greater role in the structuring of Biblical time. Isaac and Esau both got married at **forty** years old (Gen. 25:20; 26:34); Joseph was embalmed for **forty** days (Gen. 50:2-3); Moses' life of 120 years was divided into three periods of **forty** years each, marking the three main periods of his life (Egypt, desert, wilderness: Acts 7:23; 30; 36). Joshua was **forty** years old when he was sent out to spy the Promised Land for **forty** days (Num. 13:25; Josh. 14:7). A human pregnancy reaches its climax at **forty** weeks.

This standard yardstick of **forty** years marks the length of rule of the following judges and kings in Israel:

Othniel (Judges 3:11)
Barak (Judges 5:31)
Gideon (Judges 8:28)
Eli (1 Sam. 4:18)
Saul (Acts 13:21)

David (2 Sam. 5:4; 1 Chron. 29:27)
Solomon (1 Kings 11:42; 2 Chron. 9:30)
Jehoash (2 Kings 12:1)
Joash (2 Chron. 24:1)

It is also noteworthy that:

- Moses was on the mount Sinai for **forty** days and **forty** nights to receive the Law (Ex. 24:18)
- Elijah travelled for **forty** days and **forty** nights to Mount Horeb (1 Kings 19:8)
- Jesus was tempted in the wilderness for **forty** days and **forty** nights (Matt. 4:2)
- Jesus spent **forty** days after his resurrection teaching his disciples on the kingdom of God (Acts 1:3)

We should also note that the Bible was written by **forty** authors covering **four** thousand years from Adam to Christ; it includes **four** hundred years of slavery in Egypt and **four** hundred years of silence between the two Testaments.

The number **forty** also acts as an amplified symbol of hardship and judgement in scripture:

- In the flood rain fell upon the earth for forty days and forty nights (Gen. 7:4).
- Disobedience after forty days of spying the land (Num. 13:25; 14:34) led to forty years wandering in the wilderness (Deut. 8:2-5; Ps. 95:10; Acts 13:18)
- Moses had to intercede for Israel forty days and forty nights on Mount Sinai after the sin of the Golden Calf (Deut. 9:18; 25; 10:10)
- Israel suffered under the Philistines forty years for its disobedience (Judges 13:1)
- Goliath threatened Israel for forty days (1 Sam. 17:16)
- Ezekiel has to lie on his right side for forty days to embody the forty years of Judah's rebellion (Ezek. 4:6).
- Egypt has to reap God's judgement for forty years (Ezek. 29:11-12)
- Nineveh was to be destroyed after forty days if it did not repent (Jonah 3:4)
- Jesus followed Moses' example and fasted forty days and forty nights in the wilderness, where he was tempted by Satan (Matt. 4:2)
- Forty years after the crucifixion of Jesus, Jerusalem was destroyed by the Romans (see next page).

*"And you shall remember the whole way that the LORD your God has led you these **forty** years in the wilderness, that he might humble you, testing you to know what was in your heart, whether you would keep his commandments or not." (Deut. 8:2)*

Forty Years after the Cross

The gospels recount that, when Jesus died in the cross, the veil in the temple tore in half from top to bottom, symbolising that the way through into God's presence was now open. This is one of **four** supernatural signs that accompanied the death of Jesus (the others being the darkening of the sun from the sixth to the ninth hour, the resurrection of dead saints from their tombs, and the earthquake).

Although there is no independent Jewish account of these events, the Talmud tells of **four** further strange happenings that occurred in the **forty years** between 30 AD (the probable date of Jesus' crucifixion) and 70 AD (the date of the destruction of the temple by the Romans).

Jesus left the temple and was going away, when his disciples came to point out to him the buildings of the temple. But he answered them, "You see all these, do you not? Truly, I say to you, there will not be left here one stone upon another that will not be thrown down." (Matt. 24:1-2)

The Evidence of the Talmud

Here is what Jerusalem Talmud says:

Forty years before the destruction of the Temple, the western light went out, the crimson thread remained crimson, and the lot for the Lord always came up in the left hand. They would close the gates of the Temple by night and get up in the morning and find them wide open.

A similar passage appears in the Babylonian Talmud:

Our rabbis taught: During the last **forty years** before the destruction of the Temple the lot ['for the Lord'] did not come up in the right hand; nor did the crimson-coloured strap become white; nor did the western most light shine; and the doors of the Temple would open by themselves."

*"You shall bear your iniquity for **forty** years, and you shall know my displeasure." (Num. 14:34)*

The Disappearing Light

The Menorah, the seven-branched candlestick pictured in Chapter Two, was one of the most recognisable symbols of temple worship. Leviticus 24:1-3 stresses the critical importance of keeping the central flame of the lampstand burning continuously, as it was from this that the other lights on the Menorah were lit.

However, in the **forty years** from AD 30, the light kept going out of its own accord, despite the careful precautions kept in place to prevent this from happening. 1 Samuel 3:3 hints that extinguishing the 'lamp of God' anticipates the end of the entire sacrificial system. Several events in Jesus' final week, such as the withered fig tree, seem to point to the end of an old dispensation.

"The light is among you for a little while longer. Walk while you have the light, lest darkness overtake you. The one who walks in the darkness does not know where he is going." (John 12:35)

The Crimson Thread

On the Day of Atonement it was the custom to tie a crimson thread of cloth (symbolising the sins of the nation) to the scapegoat (onto which the people's sin was to be confessed). Part of this thread was also tied to the Temple door.

On many occasions the red thread on the Temple door had turned white miraculously as a sign to Israel that its sins had been taken way and its guilt pardoned. This was seen as a fulfilment of the promise in Isaiah 1:18 ("though your sins are like scarlet, they shall be as white as snow"). However, in the **forty years** from AD 30 onwards the thread *never* turned white, suggesting that the traditional sacrificial system had ceased to be effective.

Consequently, when Christ came into the world, he said, "Sacrifices and offerings you have not desired, but a body have you prepared for me"... He does away with the first in order to establish the second. (Heb. 10.5, 9)

The Black Stone

On the Day of Atonement the High Priest would cast lots to determine which of two goats would be sacrificed for the sin of the nation and which would be the 'scapegoat' that carried the sins away (Lev. 16:8). This was done by a 'heads-or-tails' choice of either a black stone in the left hand or a white stone in the right.

In the two centuries previously, white and black stones were selected with equal frequency. But for **forty years** in a row, beginning in 30 AD, it was only the black stone that was ever picked. It has been calculated that the odds of this happening by chance are about one in 5.5 billion.

What happened to the white stone? A possible hint appears in the book of Revelation.

*'To the one who conquers I will give some of the hidden manna, and I will give him a **white stone**, with a new name written on the stone that no one knows except the one who receives it.'* (Rev. 2:17)

The Temple Doors

For **forty years** from 30 AD the Talmud declares that the temple doors would swing open of their own accord during the night. The Roman historian Tacitus also records an event of this kind (*Histories* 5.13), as does the Jewish historian Josephus, who identifies it as the massively heavy eastern gate of the inner temple, built of brass on an iron base, with bolts fastened deep into the floor, which twenty men could only shut with difficulty (*Jewish War* 6.5.3-4).

In many ways this is the closest recorded equivalent outside the Bible of the tearing of the temple curtain, signalling that access into God's presence was now open to all through the shed blood of Jesus.

"Behold, I stand at the door and knock. If anyone hears my voice and opens the door, I will come in to him and eat with him, and he with me." (Rev. 3:20)

5. **Four** in the life of the church

In considering the ground plan of Ezekiel's idealized temple, we identified **four** features which are still relevant to the church today.

Firstly, we noticed that it was *outward-facing*. God had told Ezekiel that he had placed Jerusalem 'in the centre of the nations, with countries all around her' (5:5). Moreover, the temple was to be set, like the New Jerusalem, on a very high mountain, far bigger than the Temple Mount today (Ezek. 40:2; Rev. 21:10). From here the temple was to look outwards in all **four** directions. Today's church is called to have this outward focus: to the community, to the nation, and to the world. As Jesus said,

> "You are the light of the world. A city set on a hill cannot be hidden. Nor do people light a lamp and put it under a basket, but on a stand, and it gives light to all in the house." (Matt. 5:14-15)

It is worth remembering that immediately before these verses Jesus describes the church as the 'salt of the earth'. As well as bringing out flavour, salt is used preserve, to disinfect, and to prevent ice from forming, all pictures of ways in which Christians can bring transformation to society. Intriguingly, like the Holy of Holies in the temple and the New Jerusalem, salt crystals are also shaped as perfect cubes, with their sides facing in every direction. The church needs to have the same outward focus, and to restore flavour to a valueless world.

Secondly, we pointed out that the temple was to be *equal in dimension* on all **four** sides. One lesson from this is that there is no place for prejudice or racism of any kind in the church. Jesus treated every human being with equal dignity and respect, regardless of their social standing. James warns us that:

> My brothers, show no partiality as you hold the faith in our Lord Jesus Christ, the Lord of glory. For if a man wearing a gold ring and fine clothing comes into your assembly, and a poor man in shabby clothing also comes in, and if you pay attention to the one who wears the fine clothing and say, "You sit here in a good place", while you say to the poor man, "You stand over there", or, "Sit down at my feet", have you not then made distinctions among yourselves and become judges with evil thoughts? Listen, my beloved brothers, has not God chosen those who are poor in the world to be rich in faith and heirs of the kingdom? (James 2:1-5)

By the same token, while the church needs to give equal honour to all when looking outwards, it also needs to present the same face when others look in at it. Integrity and transparency are at the centre of its calling. Nothing brings more disrepute to the gospel than yet another scandal where church leaders are caught out preaching one thing but practising another. Jesus presents a stark warning to the religious leaders of his own time:

> ಸಃಬ
>
> "Woe to you, scribes and Pharisees, hypocrites! For you are like whitewashed tombs, which outwardly appear beautiful, but within are full of dead people's bones and all uncleanness. So you also outwardly appear righteous to others, but within you are full of hypocrisy and lawlessness." (Matt. 23:27-28)
>
> ಸಃಬ

> ಸಃಬ
>
> "Behold, I am the one who has laid as a foundation in Zion,
> a stone, a tested stone,
> a precious cornerstone, of a sure foundation:
> 'Whoever believes will not be in haste.'
> And I will make justice the line,
> and righteousness the plumb line;
> and hail will sweep away the refuge of lies,
> and waters will overwhelm the shelter." (Is. 28:16-17)
>
> ಸಃಬ

Thirdly, we saw that the design of Ezekiel's temple was *set in alignment* with a north-south-east-west axis. Just as the **four** living creatures encircle the heavenly throne, and the tribes of Israel gathered in a cross shape around the tabernacle in the wilderness, so there is a treasured place around God's throne for every Christian denomination and tradition that truly reflects his glory. But within this place of security comes the added responsibility for us all to line ourselves up with God's purposes as expressed through the Bible, rather than each of us slanting off on our own course. God has set his Word as a plumbline by which he measures everything else.

Just as Ezekiel's temple is set on a high and immovable mountain, the church needs to set its foundations on the mountain of God's Word. The following message, given to Isaiah, sets the background to Jesus' famous parable about the wise and foolish builders:

Like the wise man who built his house on the rock, the church will only be ready for the inevitable storm that comes its way if it has set itself on solid and immovable foundations.

Here we can also learn from the four living creatures. They consistently move in a straight line, without changing course (Ezek. 1:17). This too, should be a template for us to follow. As Paul forcefully declares,

> ಸಃಬ
>
> Forgetting what lies behind and straining forward to what lies ahead, I press on towards the goal for the prize of the upward call of God in Christ Jesus.
> (Phil. 3:13-14)
>
> ಸಃಬ

Finally, we observed *the centrality of the cross* in God's scheme. As we noted earlier, the beating heart of Ezekiel's temple was not the Holy of Holies, but the altar, the place of sacrifice. Given that Jerusalem was placed 'at the centre of the nations', this pinpoints the altar at the very heart of world geography. Moreover, Ezekiel's description of this altar comes *exactly halfway* through the seven chapters devoted to the temple, just as the 'suffering servant' prophecy of Isaiah 53 appears *at the exact midpoint* of the second half of Isaiah's book.

This is a stark reminder to the church that there is no way it can bypass the cross and yet remain faithful to the gospel. In an age of short cuts, quick fixes and instant gratification, it is all too easy to present a crossless Christianity based on success, prosperity and happiness. There is no way around the cross, or over it or under it: we just have to go *through* it. Ezekiel was told that worshippers had to go out the opposite entrance that they came in (46:9). There was no way of avoiding the altar, and, as with the living creatures in the first chapter, no turning back (1:17)!

But we should also remember that it is from the altar, the place of sacrifice, that a river bursts out, bringing life to the Dead Sea, and trees with healing fruits on its banks. This may well be the river Jesus referred to when he declared,

> "If anyone thirsts, let him come to me and drink. Whoever believes in me, as the Scripture has said, 'Out of his heart will flow rivers of living water.'"
> (John 7:37-38)

As we noted earlier, blood and water flowed out from Jesus' side after he was struck with a spear on the cross, just as water gushed out from the rock in the wilderness after Moses struck it.

But the same river also flows from the broken places within each one of us. Just as the stream in Eden broke into **four** headwaters which watered the garden, so we in turn can be conduits for the life of God. He has a purpose in the trials and tribulations we go through, which is in part that life and healing should flow out for others. As the Psalmist reminds us,

> He who goes out weeping, bearing the seed for sowing, shall come home with shouts of joy, bringing his sheaves with him. (Ps. 126:6)

The challenge to take up our cross daily is not an easy one for us to obey. But it is the only way to bring hope to a dying world. As Jesus laid down his life completely for us, so we in turn should be ready to lay or lives down for him. As in so many things, the way up is down, and the way of sacrifice is also the path to glory.

Chapter Five

Five

The Number of Order

1. **Five** as representing the hand of God

At first sight five might seem to be a rather unpromising number. It lacks the obvious charisma of 3, the geometric beauty of 4, the mathematical elegance of 6, or the divine mystery of 7. Yet in the end this rather modest and unassuming number is the key which opens up the door to hundreds, thousands, millions, billions and trillions, and all the large numbers used in scripture and in our everyday lives.

In the last chapter we saw that the number four points to the entirety of the created order, and the life of God which animates every part of it. In many ways it could be argued that five portrays that same order with God in the centre. In heaven, for example, the four living creatures stand with the throne of God in their midst:

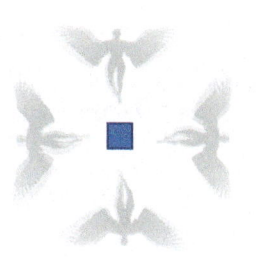

In the wilderness we also saw a similar arrangement, with the tabernacle, the earthly throne of God, at the heart of the encampment and the tribes of Israel arranged around each of the four sides. Likewise, in the temple, the upper face of the altar symbolises the Godward side of the sacrifice, and the four horns in each corner the manward side, distributing the blessing in every direction to the four corners of the earth:

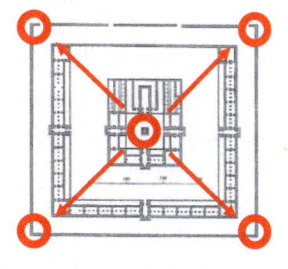

If four represents life and the entire created order, therefore, **five** stands for creation from God's perspective, centred on him as the focal point of worship and adoration.

Our hands represent a helpful visual picture of these universal patterns. The middle finger in the centre is the longest, and the others spread out from it, a telling reminder of the critical importance of keeping God at the centre of our lives. And these hands, made in God's image, are the root of our counting system in multiples of five and ten. Indeed, it is likely that the Roman numeral V started as the symbol for an open hand, with X (V combined with its reflection underneath) being a picture of twice that quantity. Today we use the word 'digit' (from the Latin for 'finger') for numbers, and 'digital' for devices that can navigate vast quantities of information.

While other numbers like twelve subdivide far more easily than five or ten, it is this simple arrangement of our hands which determines the way we group large quantities, and this seems to be broadly true of cultures the world over. Indeed, almost all amphibians, reptiles, and mammals which have fingers or toes have **five** of them on each extremity.

Beyond this, the number five appears around us in many different guises. **Fivefold** symmetry is found in the echinoderms, the group that includes starfish, sea urchins, and sea lilies, and in many families of flowers. There are **five** regular polyhedra (the tetrahedron, cube, octahedron, dodecahedron and icosahedron), **five** oceans (Atlantic, Pacific, Indian, Arctic and Antarctic), **five** kingdoms of living things (animals, plants, fungi, and two microbial kingdoms) and **five** planets visible to the naked eye (Mercury, Venus, Mars, Jupiter and Saturn).

In addition, the number five plays an important role in music. Western music is written on a musical staff made of **five** horizontal lines, and bases its key system and tuning system on the interval of a **fifth**, which plays an important organisational role, akin to a right angle in architecture or painting. A chain of **five** of these **fifths** when rearranged in order produces the **five**-note *pentatonic scale* that is the basis of a great many musical systems the world over, appearing in the folk music of a range of cultures scattered across the globe.

Five is also the number with which we interact with the world around us. We have **five** physical senses (sight, hearing, touch, smell and taste) and **five** tastes (sweet, salty, sour, bitter, and umami). With our **five** senses we perceive the world, just as with the **five** fingers of each hand we attempt to manipulate and control it.

This may help to explain why hands in the Bible represent order and authority. This can clearly be seen, for example, in Exodus 15:6, which states that:

> Who has measured the waters in the hollow of his **hand** and marked off the heavens with a span? (Is. 40.12)

> Your right **hand**, O LORD, glorious in power,
> your right **hand**, O LORD, shatters the enemy.

Above: Primroses appear on grassy slopes across much of Europe in the early spring. Like many other plants from the order *Ericales*, they are characterised by distinctive fivefold floral shapes.

Below: The African red knob sea starfish, which lives in the Indian Ocean and can grow up to twelve inches in diameter, is notable for its attractive colouring.

We might take this into account when attempting to understand the pivotal role played in the Old Testament by the Ten Commandments. As the only part of the Bible written directly by God without any human intermediary (described as the work of the 'finger of God' in Exodus 31:18), they might be described as his divine 'signature' upon the whole. It is striking that, in being inscribed on two tablets in two groups of five, they correspond directly to the number of fingers on each hand. The same God who designed perfect laws also designed perfect bodies to accomplish them on his behalf.

Given the importance of the human hand in the way we relate to the world, therefore, we should not be surprised to see the integral role it plays in Biblical measurements. The diagram on the facing page shows how the ratio between the numbers 2, 3 and 5 (the last being the sum of the other two) is fundamental both to the proportions of our hands, and to many dimensions in the Old Testament. For example, the standard unit of Hebrew measurement, the cubit (the distance from the elbow to the tip of the finger) was equal to **two** spans, which in turn was equivalent to **three** handbreadths. As we noticed in the introduction to this book, 1, 2, 3 and 5 are the first degrees of the Fibonacci series, which is created by adding successive numbers together to create a larger number.

Just as these simple ratios between such whole numbers crop up again and again in music, chemistry and biology, so too we find them occurring repeatedly in the Bible. Proportions based in two of these numbers are prominent, for example, in the design of Noah's ark, where we discover that the dimensions of 300 x 50 x 30 cubits produce a structure that is virtually unsinkable in water (the measurements of Brunel's SS Great Britain were, by comparison, 322ft × 50ft × 30ft). This stands in complete contrast to the completely unseaworthy cube-shaped vessel in the Babylonian version of the flood story.

Another striking instance of these number combinations can be seen in a very different context, when Jesus warns us about the effects of his coming:

> For from now on in one house there will be **five** divided, **three** against **two** and **two** against **three**. (Luke 12:52)

The numbers 2, 3 and 5 also played an important part in the sacrificial system. Even as far back as Genesis 15, long before that system was formally established, God told Abraham to choose **three** domestic animals, each **three** years old, along with **two** birds, to make a complete sacrifice with **five** creatures in total:

> He said to him, "Bring me a heifer three years old, a female goat three years old, a ram three years old, a turtle-dove, and a young pigeon. (Gen. 15:9)

FIVE: THE NUMBER OF ORDER

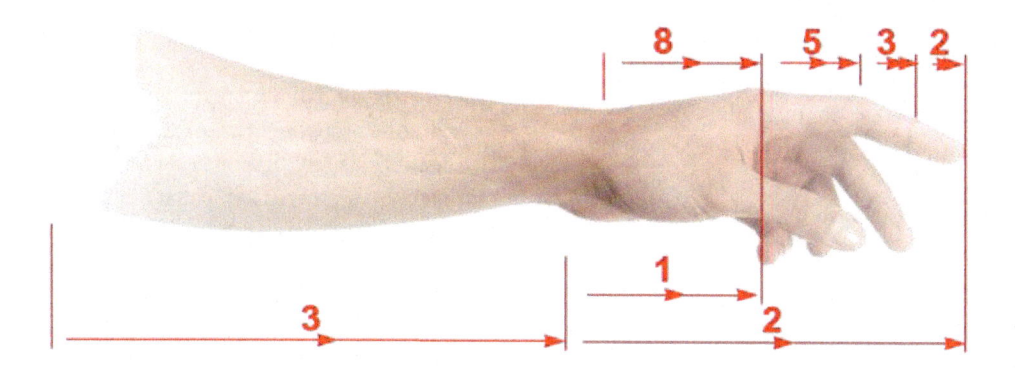

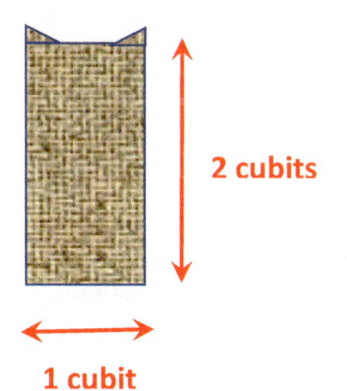

A comparison between the relative proportions in the tabernacle of the altar of incense (left) and the altar of burnt offering (below). These ratios are similar to the dimensions of the human forearm and hand (above) from which the cubit measurement was originally taken. It should be noticed that these ratios appear to correspond to the lower degrees of the Fibonacci series, described in the introduction to this book, which governs the structure of many things in the natural world.

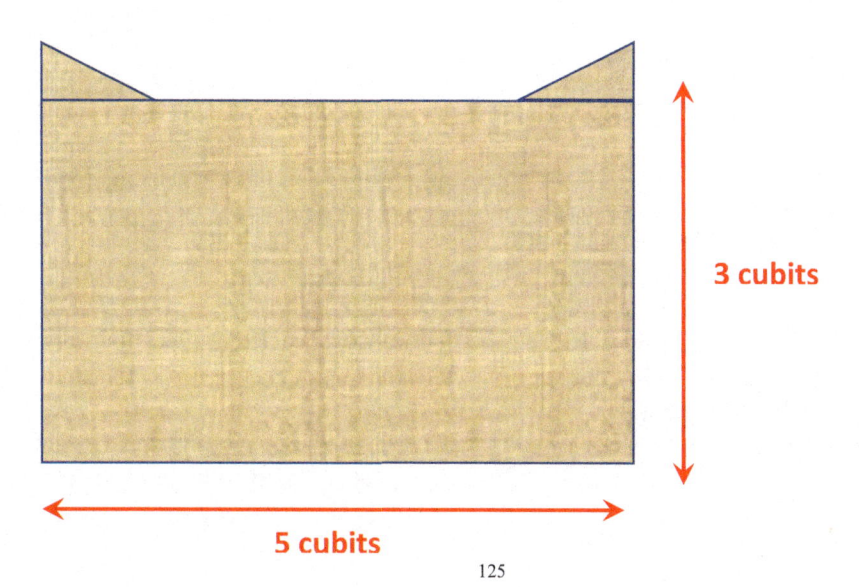

These five creatures became the standard five used in the Levitical system, and the number five seems to penetrate every possible aspect of it. There were, for example, **five** kinds of offerings: burnt offerings, grain offerings, peace offerings, sin offerings and guilt offerings. The **fifth** offering, the guilt offering, adds a **fifth** of the value to what was being sacrificed.

These numbers were also important in the design of the tabernacle itself. As we have suggested already, they may have been a reflection of the fact that at its heart was the ark which contained two tablets, each with **five** commandments written on.

Reflecting this, almost every measurement in the tabernacle was a multiple of **five**. It was **10** cubits high, **10** cubits wide, and **30** cubits long with **10** linen curtains, **five** linked on either side, with **50** loops and **50** gold clasps to attach the end curtains together. These were overlaid by another layer of curtains made of goat's hair, attached together with **50** loops and **50** bronze clasps. The entrance was supported by **five** posts of acacia wood over **five** bronze bases.

The altar of burnt offering was **five** cubits long and **five** cubits wide and three cubits high, while the Most Holy Place that lay behind it was a perfect cube (**10×10×10**) and the remainder of the tabernacle twice that length. The curtains dividing these different sections were each hung on **five** pillars. The outer court was **100** cubits long and **50** cubits wide (**five** times the breadth of the tabernacle itself). On either side were **20** upright frames on **20** bronze bases, and along each end were **10** upright frames mounted on **10** bases, each one **five** cubits apart, with **five** horizontal crossbars on either side.

For the dedication of the tabernacle a member of each tribe brought in two oxen, **five** rams, **five** male goats, and **five** male lambs a year old. The Levites served in the tent of meeting for **twenty-five** years, from the age of **twenty-five** and upwards (Num. 8:24-25).

Moreover, every item in the tabernacle was anointed by sacred anointing oil consisting of **five** ingredients:

1. Myrrh, 500 shekels (5×100).
2. Sweet cinnamon, 250 shekels (5×50).
3. Aromatic cane, 250 shekels (5×50).
4. Cassia, 500 shekels (5×100).
5. One hin of olive oil.

Likewise the incense offered consisted of **five** components: stacte, onycha, galbanum, pure frankincense, all in equal quantities, along with salt (see pages 104, 118 and 156-7).

Many of these proportions were carried through into the design of the temple which succeeded the tabernacle, which was twice its overall dimensions. Again many of the details reflect the presence inside the ark of the two tablets, both with **five** commandments written on. This is apparent, for instance, in the measurements of the cherubim above it:

> In the inner sanctuary he made two cherubim of olive wood, each ten cubits high. **Five** cubits was the length of one wing of the cherub, and **five** cubits the length of the other wing of the cherub; it was ten cubits from the tip of one wing to the tip of the other. (1 Kings 6:23-24)

FIVE: THE NUMBER OF ORDER

The Structure of the Tabernacle

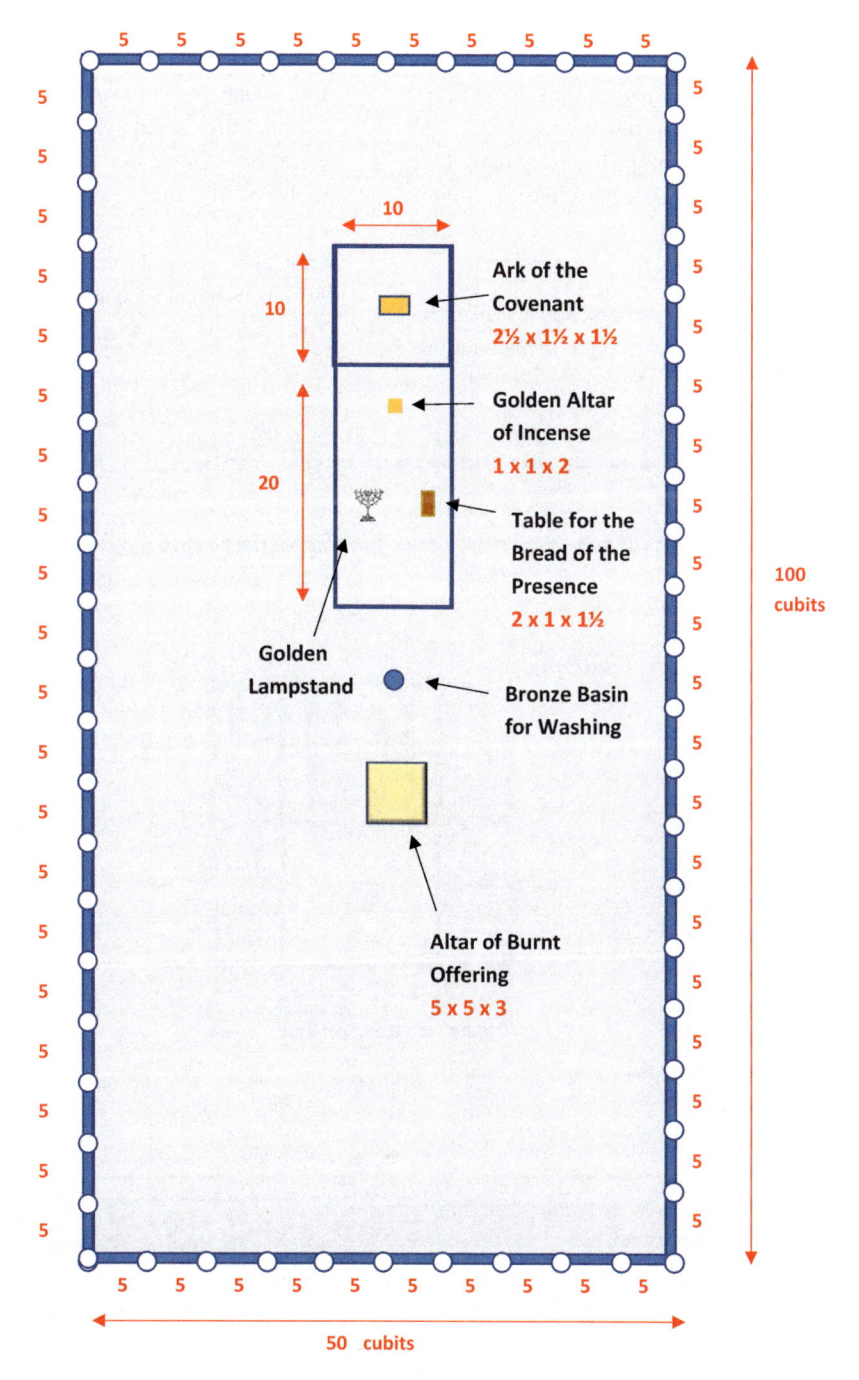

Ark of the Covenant
2½ x 1½ x 1½

Golden Altar of Incense
1 x 1 x 2

Table for the Bread of the Presence
2 x 1 x 1½

Golden Lampstand

Bronze Basin for Washing

Altar of Burnt Offering
5 x 5 x 3

100 cubits

50 cubits

Likewise the doorposts to the innermost sanctuary were five-sided, as was the lintel over the top. In the outer sanctuary **five** golden lampstands were set on either side, while **five** bronze basins were placed outside on either side of the temple on **five** bronze stands. The capitals on the top of the bronze pillars at the front of the temple were both **five** cubits high, as was the enormous Sea of cast metal at the south-eastern corner of the inner court.

Similar numerical relationships are also present in the millennial temple of Ezekiel that we considered in the last chapter. Here, however, the dimensions have mushroomed even beyond those of Solomon's temple: the total ground area is now **five** times longer than the original tabernacle, so that it could contain no less than **fifty** tabernacles within its grounds. Moreover, many of the key dimensions are in multiples of 25 (5^2) as we can see from the diagram below. The result is a picture of wholeness, integrity and balance, a demonstration to Israel of what a truly redeemed a God-centred life would look like (Ezek. 40:4):

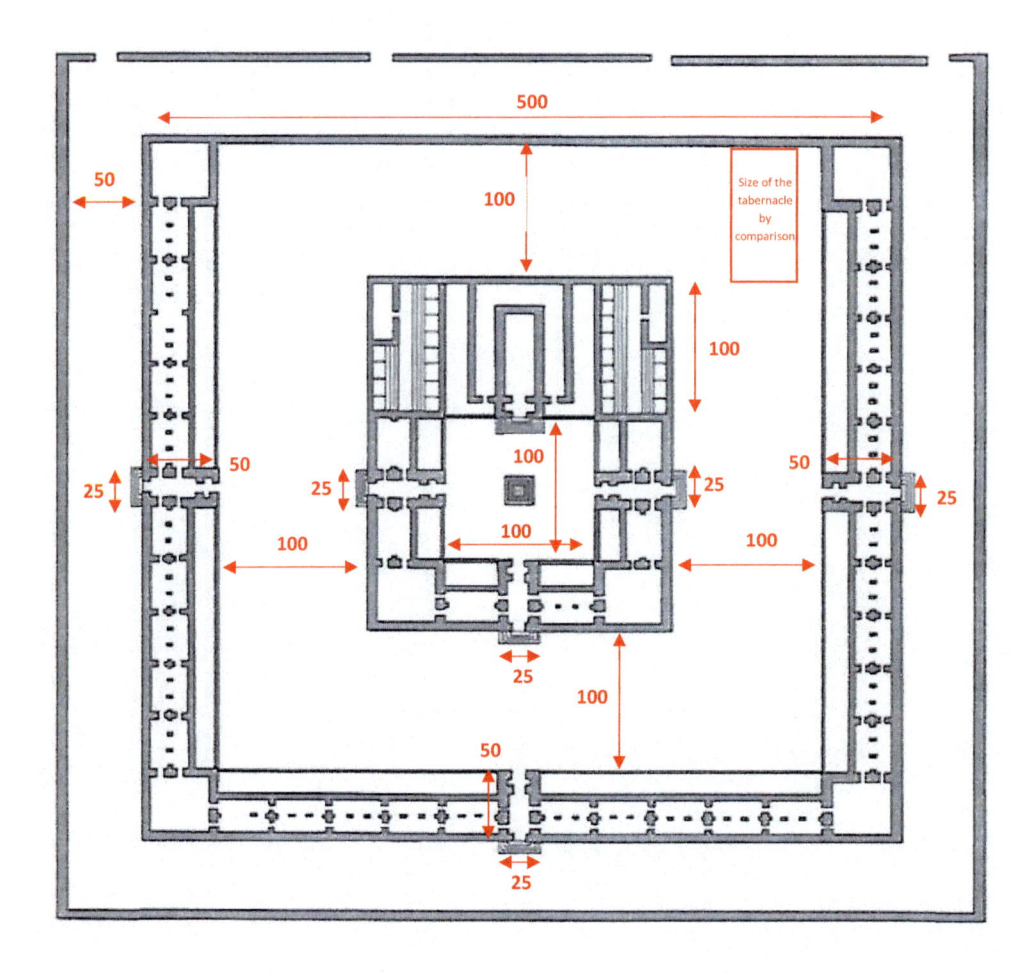

FIVE: THE NUMBER OF ORDER

The 16th century Rose Window of the north transept in Sens Cathedral in Burgundy, displaying a fivefold symmetry.

2. **Five** in the ordering of scripture

If the tabernacle and temple which followed it reflected the very hand of God on its construction, the same is true of scripture itself. The number five plays an integral part in its design and ordering. This can be seen clearly regardless of whether we are considering the books in their traditional Christian or older Jewish arrangement. Below is the format most of us will recognise from Protestant arrangements of the Old Testament:

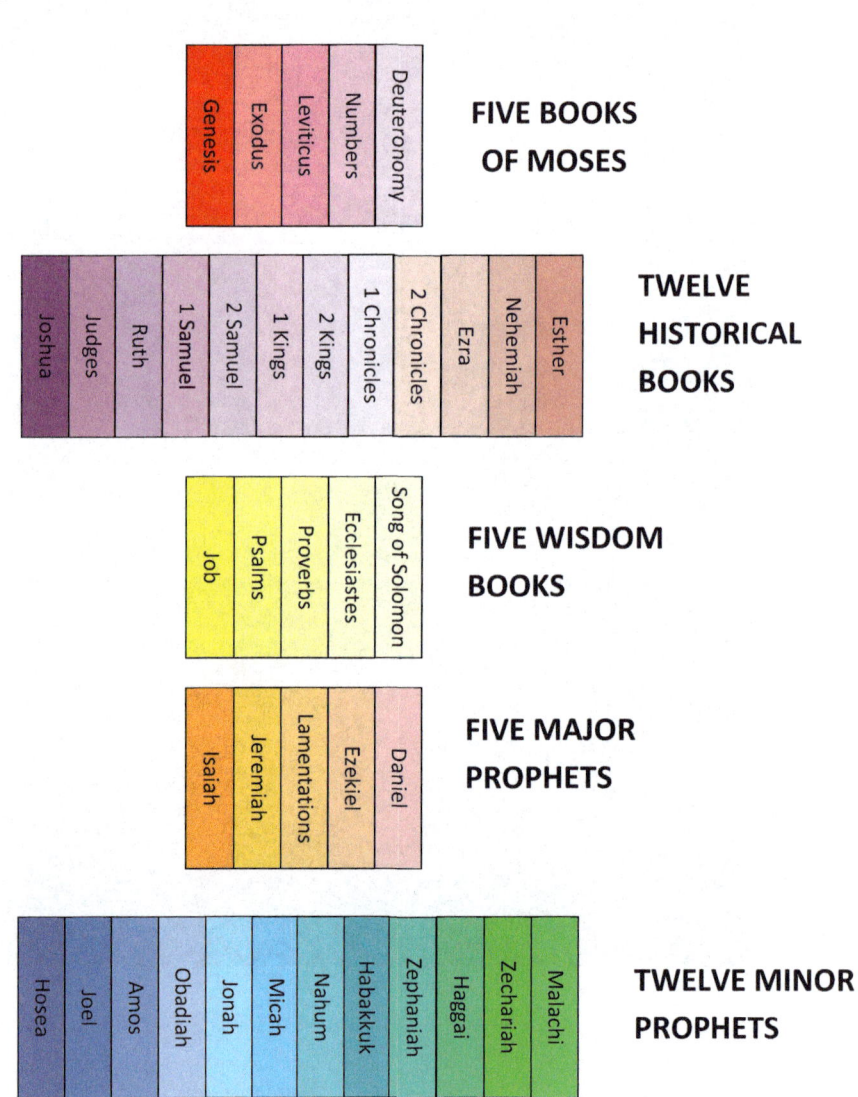

FIVE BOOKS OF MOSES
Genesis, Exodus, Leviticus, Numbers, Deuteronomy

TWELVE HISTORICAL BOOKS
Joshua, Judges, Ruth, 1 Samuel, 2 Samuel, 1 Kings, 2 Kings, 1 Chronicles, 2 Chronicles, Ezra, Nehemiah, Esther

FIVE WISDOM BOOKS
Job, Psalms, Proverbs, Ecclesiastes, Song of Solomon

FIVE MAJOR PROPHETS
Isaiah, Jeremiah, Lamentations, Ezekiel, Daniel

TWELVE MINOR PROPHETS
Hosea, Joel, Amos, Obadiah, Jonah, Micah, Nahum, Habakkuk, Zephaniah, Haggai, Zechariah, Malachi

FIVE: THE NUMBER OF ORDER

But if we consider the Jewish arrangement of the Old Testament that Jesus and his disciples would have been familiar with, it is apparent that the number five still plays a significant part, providing the centre of another symmetrical formation:

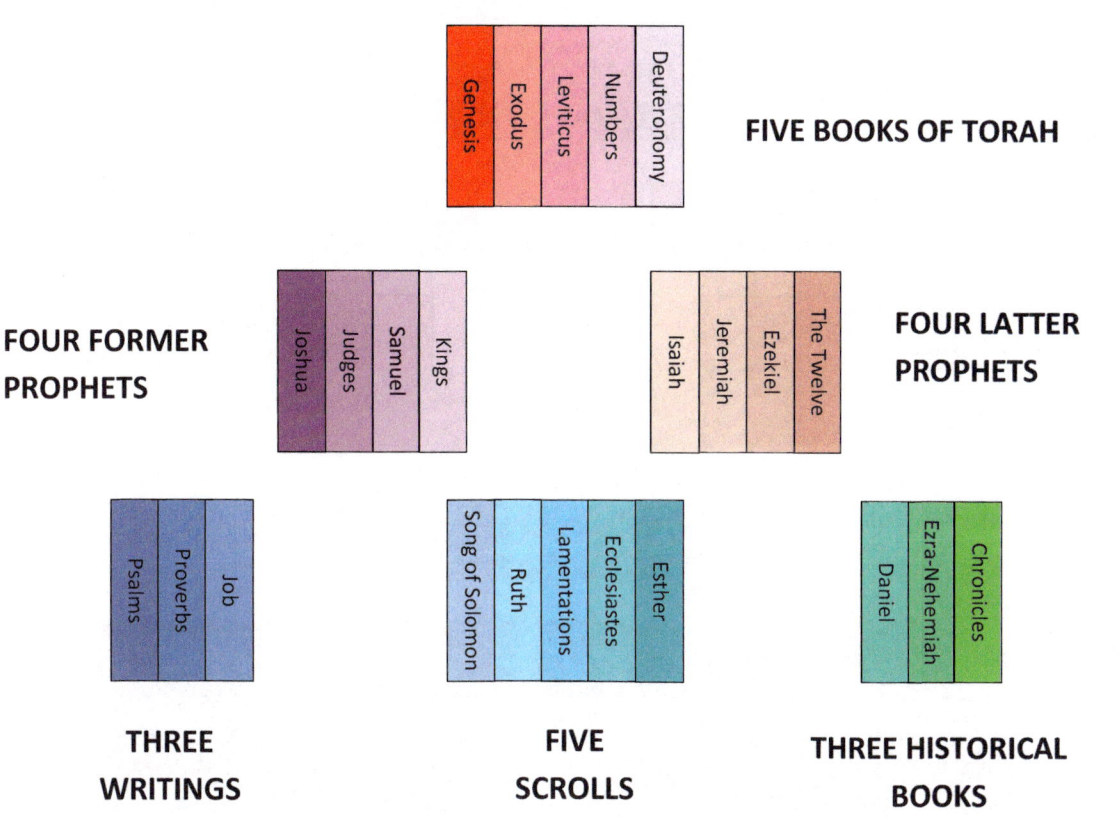

FIVE BOOKS OF TORAH: Genesis, Exodus, Leviticus, Numbers, Deuteronomy

FOUR FORMER PROPHETS: Joshua, Judges, Samuel, Kings

FOUR LATTER PROPHETS: Isaiah, Jeremiah, Ezekiel, The Twelve

THREE WRITINGS: Psalms, Proverbs, Job

FIVE SCROLLS: Song of Solomon, Ruth, Lamentations, Ecclesiastes, Esther

THREE HISTORICAL BOOKS: Daniel, Ezra-Nehemiah, Chronicles

At the centre of the upper layer, the Torah, (sometimes described as the 'Pentateuch', from the Greek for 'five scrolls') lies Leviticus, a book that might seem obscure for us today, but which played an absolutely key role for the people of Israel. At the midpoint of Leviticus are the instructions for the Day of Atonement in Chapter 16. At the heart of the Day of Atonement was the jaw-dropping moment when the High Priest entered the Holy of Holies and uttered, in a whisper, the sacred name YHWH or 'Yahweh': the only occasion in the whole year that the word could be spoken (and which even today Orthodox Jews will not pronounce). Such was the solemnity of the occasion that a rope had to be tied around the feet of the High Priest, in case he died in the presence of the Almighty. Almost like stepping into a highly radioactive chamber, the utmost precautions were taken so that the divine protocol would not be broken. The result, as we see on the next page, is a direct line of vision which ultimately points to the centrality of the cross:

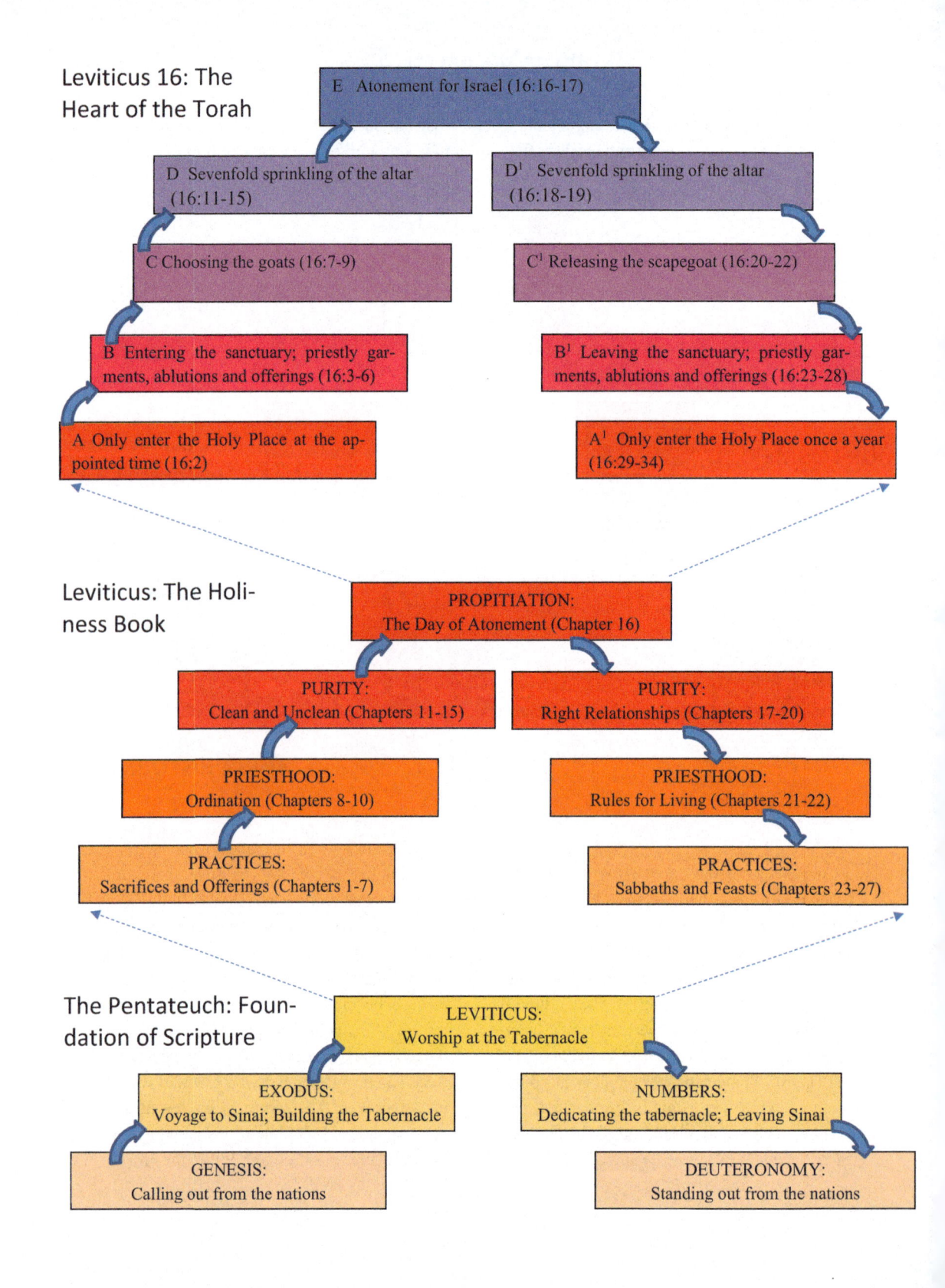

Leviticus 16: The Heart of the Torah

- **E** Atonement for Israel (16:16-17)
- **D** Sevenfold sprinkling of the altar (16:11-15)
- **D¹** Sevenfold sprinkling of the altar (16:18-19)
- **C** Choosing the goats (16:7-9)
- **C¹** Releasing the scapegoat (16:20-22)
- **B** Entering the sanctuary; priestly garments, ablutions and offerings (16:3-6)
- **B¹** Leaving the sanctuary; priestly garments, ablutions and offerings (16:23-28)
- **A** Only enter the Holy Place at the appointed time (16:2)
- **A¹** Only enter the Holy Place once a year (16:29-34)

Leviticus: The Holiness Book

- **PROPITIATION:** The Day of Atonement (Chapter 16)
- **PURITY:** Clean and Unclean (Chapters 11-15)
- **PURITY:** Right Relationships (Chapters 17-20)
- **PRIESTHOOD:** Ordination (Chapters 8-10)
- **PRIESTHOOD:** Rules for Living (Chapters 21-22)
- **PRACTICES:** Sacrifices and Offerings (Chapters 1-7)
- **PRACTICES:** Sabbaths and Feasts (Chapters 23-27)

The Pentateuch: Foundation of Scripture

- **LEVITICUS:** Worship at the Tabernacle
- **EXODUS:** Voyage to Sinai; Building the Tabernacle
- **NUMBERS:** Dedicating the tabernacle; Leaving Sinai
- **GENESIS:** Calling out from the nations
- **DEUTERONOMY:** Standing out from the nations

A monologue given to Rabbi Asrael in the play *The Dybbuk* written in 1914 by the Russian Jewish author S. Ansky, highlights the extraordinary importance in Jewish thought of this moment that the High Priest steps into the Holy of Holies:

> God's world is great and holy.
>
> The holiest land in the world is the land of Israel. In the land of Israel the holiest city is Jerusalem. In Jerusalem the holiest place was the Temple, and in the Temple the holiest spot was the Holy of Holies. ...
>
> There are seventy peoples in the world. The holiest among these is the people of Israel. The holiest of the people of Israel is the tribe of Levi. In the tribe of Levi the holiest are the priests. Among the priests, the holiest was the High Priest. ...
>
> There are 354 days in the year [according to the Hebrew lunar calendar]. Among these, the holidays are holy. Higher than these is the holiness of the Sabbath. Among Sabbaths, the holiest is the Day of Atonement, the Sabbath of Sabbaths. ...
>
> There are seventy languages in the world. The holiest is Hebrew. Holier than all else in this language is the holy Torah, and in the Torah the holiest part is the Ten Commandments. In the Ten Commandments the holiest of all words is the name of God. ...
>
> And once during the year, at a certain hour, these four supreme sanctities of the world were joined with one another. That was on the Day of Atonement, when the High Priest would enter the Holy of Holies and there utter the name of God. And because this hour was beyond measure holy and awesome, it was the time of utmost peril not only for the High Priest but for the whole of Israel. For if in this hour there had, God forbid, entered the mind of the High Priest a false or sinful thought, the entire world would have been destroyed.

In the New Testament the book of Hebrews shows how the solemnity of this moment points ahead to Christ's finished work on the cross:

> But when Christ came as high priest of the good things that are now already here, he went through the greater and more perfect tabernacle that is not made with human hands, that is to say, is not a part of this creation. He did not enter by means of the blood of goats and calves; but he entered the Most Holy Place once for all by his own blood, thus obtaining eternal redemption. (Heb. 9:11-12 NIV)

Later in the chapter we are reminded of the full significance of this:

> ❧❦
>
> For Christ did not enter a sanctuary made with human hands that was only a copy of the true one; he entered heaven itself, now to appear for us in God's presence. Nor did he enter heaven to offer himself again and again, the way the high priest enters the Most Holy Place every year with blood that is not his own. Otherwise Christ would have had to suffer many times since the creation of the world. But he has appeared once for all at the culmination of the ages to do away with sin by the sacrifice of himself.
> (Heb. 9:24-26 NIV)
>
> ❧❦

The core of the central chapter of Leviticus, standing at the very heart of the Torah, thus seems to point ahead to the 'culmination of the ages' as represented by the cross of Christ.

Intriguingly, another powerful pointer to the cross appears in the symmetry of the book of Lamentations, standing at the midpoint of the fourth rung of books in the Old Testament in its traditional Christian ordering and the centre of the third level in the Jewish ordering (the order alluded to by Jesus in Luke 24:44).

Given that the book appears at the heart of a **fivefold** structure in both cases, it is striking to see how it consists itself of **five** poems, themselves arranged with the longest poem in the middle. Just as the heart of Leviticus seems to point forward to Christ's offering of himself on the cross, so the poem in the centre of this 'arch' seems again to look beyond the sufferings of Jerusalem itself to anticipate the utter desolation of Calvary, where Jesus bore God's wrath against the sins of the whole world in his own body:

> ❧❦
>
> I am the man who has seen affliction
> under the rod of his wrath;
> he has driven and brought me
> into darkness without any light;
> surely against me he turns his hand
> again and again the whole day long.
> He has made my flesh and my skin waste away;
> he has broken my bones;
> he has besieged and enveloped me
> with bitterness and tribulation;
> he has made me dwell in darkness
> like the dead of long ago.
> He has walled me about so that I cannot escape;
> he has made my chains heavy;
> though I call and cry for help,
> he shuts out my prayer;
> he has blocked my ways with blocks of stones;
> he has made my paths crooked. ...
> I have become the laughing-stock of all peoples,
> the object of their taunts all day long.
> (Lam. 3:1-9, 14)
>
> ❧❦

The following verse from the next poem also seems to anticipate the total despair of the disciples in the immediate aftermath of Jesus' death (compare Luke 24:21):

> The breath of our nostrils, the LORD's anointed,
> was captured in their pits,
> of whom we said, "Under his shadow
> we shall live among the nations."
> (Lam. 4:20)

Two other things are worth noting about these poems. The first is that four out of the five are acrostics: in other words each successive section begins with the next letter of the Hebrew alphabet, implying an application which is universal and all-embracing. The other is that in the middle poem, with 66 verses (the same total as the number of books in whole of the Bible) there is a marked change of mood exactly a third of the way through, opening out from the unassailable gloom in the other poems to a much brighter outlook, which lasts for most of the central section of the poem. The ultimate sovereignty of God is highlighted in the midst of otherwise unrelieved tragedy, a powerful reminder of how we can encounter him at the bottom of life's deepest pits of despair. It is from this that the stirring chorus of one of our most-loved hymns is taken:

> Great is thy faithfulness!
> Great is thy faithfulness!
> Morning by morning new mercies I see
> All I have needed thy hand hath provided
> Great is thy faithfulness, Lord unto me!

The Major Prophets

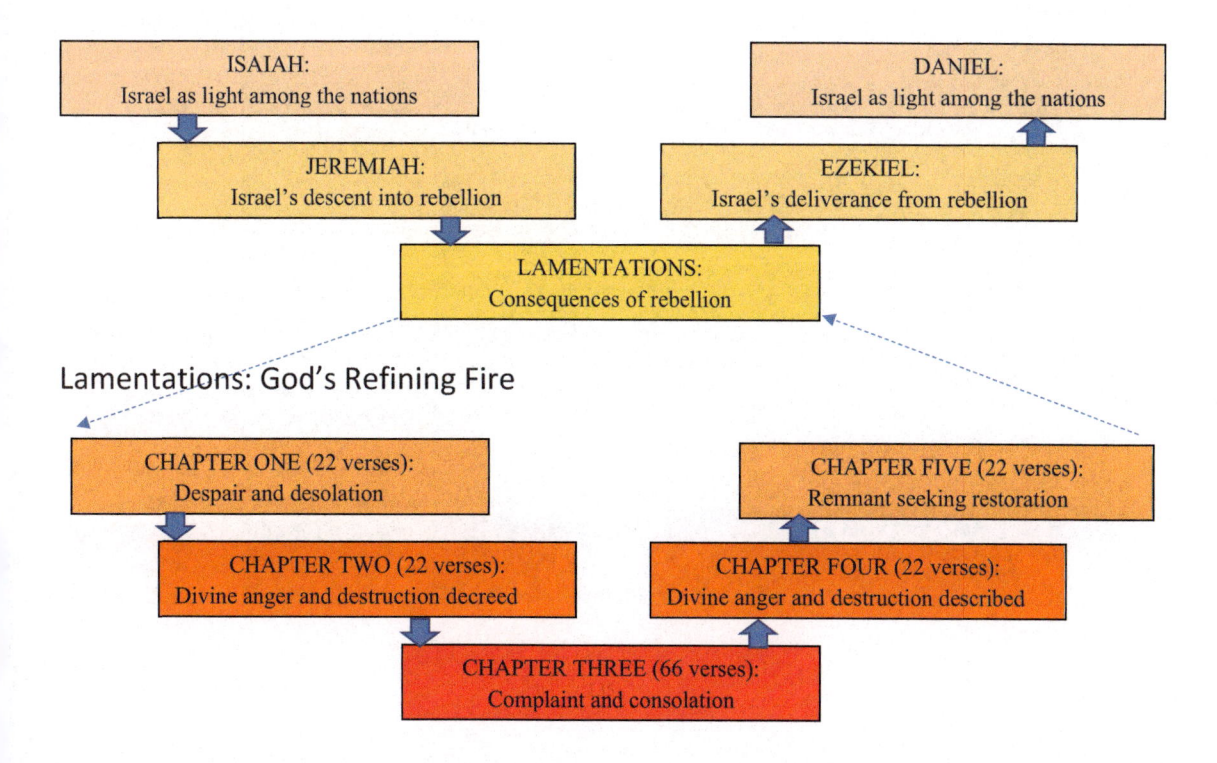

- **ISAIAH:** Israel as light among the nations
- **JEREMIAH:** Israel's descent into rebellion
- **LAMENTATIONS:** Consequences of rebellion
- **EZEKIEL:** Israel's deliverance from rebellion
- **DANIEL:** Israel as light among the nations

Lamentations: God's Refining Fire

- **CHAPTER ONE (22 verses):** Despair and desolation
- **CHAPTER TWO (22 verses):** Divine anger and destruction decreed
- **CHAPTER THREE (66 verses):** Complaint and consolation
- **CHAPTER FOUR (22 verses):** Divine anger and destruction described
- **CHAPTER FIVE (22 verses):** Remnant seeking restoration

This clear fivefold structure is also apparent in the Psalms, which are divided into **five** separate books, each of which (except for the last) finishes with a 'doxology' (an ascription of praise to God), beginning with the words 'Blessed be the Lord' and ending with 'Amen'. In Book 4, each of the three final Psalms ends with 'Hallelujah!' (or 'Praise the LORD!') and in Book 5 each of the last five Psalms begins and ends with 'Hallelujah'.

While the mood of each of these segments varies, we see in the first three books a landscape of troughs and valleys, birthed through the crucible of opposition and affliction, but with some glorious sunlit mountain peaks. A few of the deepest troughs anticipate the mood of Lamentations: some Psalms, such as 22, 69 and 88, provide a foretaste of the utter desolation of the cross, while Israel's despair at the apparent failure of the anointed ruler in Psalm 89 again anticipates the disciples' crisis of faith after the death of Jesus. But with Book 4 there is a significant change of direction and focus, and while the troughs continue to appear, there is an increasing focus on the sovereignty of God in the remaining Psalms, in the context of worship and hope:

PSALMS	BOOK ONE	BOOK TWO	BOOK THREE	BOOK FOUR	BOOK FIVE
PSALM NUMBERS:	Psalms 1-41	Psalms 42-72	Psalms 73-89	Psalms 90-106	Psalms 107-150
OVERARCHING THEME:	God beside us	God before us	God around us	God above us	God among us
AUTHORSHIP:	Mainly David	Mainly David and Korah	Mainly Asaph	Mainly anonymous	Mainly anonymous
PRINCIPAL DIVINE NAME:	Yahweh (LORD)	El/Elohim (God)	El/Elohim (God)	Yahweh (LORD)	Yahweh (LORD)
CONCLUDING STATEMENT:	Blessed be the LORD, the God of Israel, from everlasting to everlasting! Amen and Amen. (Ps. 41:13)	Blessed be his glorious name forever; may the whole earth be filled with his glory! Amen and Amen! (Ps. 72:19)	Blessed be the LORD forever! Amen and Amen. (Ps. 89:52)	Blessed be the LORD, the God of Israel, from everlasting to everlasting! And let all the people say, "Amen!" Praise the LORD! (Ps. 106:48)	Let everything that has breath praise the LORD! Praise the LORD! (Ps. 150:6)

The New Testament continues this pattern of fivefold grouping by arranging the four gospels and Acts together at its beginning, mirroring the Pentateuch at the start of the Old Testament. Within this template some clear fivefold patterns begin to emerge. These are most clearly marked in Matthew's Gospel, where **five** major blocks of teaching are clearly evident, marked off by the formula 'when Jesus finished these sayings' at 7:28 and similar phrases at 11:1, 13:53, 19:1 and 26:1. In the other books a variety of underlying structures have been plausibly suggested, but one possible interpretation might be to see a fivefold pattern lying behind all of them:

MATTHEW

Pattern of the Kingdom (5:1-7:27)
Preaching of the Kingdom (10:1-42)
Parables of the Kingdom (13:1-52)
Problems of the Kingdom (18:1-35)
Prelude to the Kingdom (23:1-25:46)

MARK

Prologue (1:1-14)
Galilee (1:15-9:50)
Judea (10:1-10:52)
Jerusalem (11:1-13:37)
Death and Resurrection (14:1-16:8)

LUKE

Birth and Childhood (1:1-2:52)
Preparation for Ministry (3:1-4:13)
Galilee (4:14-13:21)
Judea (13:22-19:27)
Jerusalem (19:28-24:53)

JOHN

Prologue (1:1-1:18)
Public Ministry (1:29-12:50)
Private Ministry (13:1-17:26)
Death and Resurrection (18:1-20:31)
Epilogue (21:1-21:25)

ACTS

Upper Room (Acts 1:1-1:26)
Jerusalem (2:1-8:3)
Judea and Samaria (8:4-12:25)
Asia and Europe (13:1-20:38)
Jerusalem to Rome (21:1-28:31)

Thus every major segment of scripture may be said to express the hands of its Creator.

3. **Five** as a key to limitless expansion

If our hands embody the number five, we might see its presence in scripture as a reflection of the human condition. On the one hand, out of communion with God, **five** might be viewed as a picture of shortcoming, inadequacy and lack.

For example, the **five** books of the law are unable to save (Gal. 2:16); the **five** husbands of the Samaritan woman unable to satisfy (John 4:18); and the **five** brothers of the rich man unable to save themselves (Luke 16:27-31). **Five** of the virgins have insufficient oil (Matt. 25:1-12); **five** loaves appear to the disciples insufficient for **five** thousand people (John 6:8-9); and even Jesus' appearance to **five** hundred people at once after his resurrection was insufficient to quell the doubts of some (Matt. 28:16-17; 1 Cor. 15:6).

However, with God at the centre, the number five changes to present a picture of breakthrough. Man is subject to the common laws of arithmetic, but with God in control **five** can chase a hundred (Lev 26:8). David's '**five** smooth stones' seemed insignificant in themselves, but were more than enough with God to slay Goliath (1 Sam. 17:40). Likewise, **five** loaves were insufficient in human terms to feed **five** thousand people in themselves, but with Jesus in charge they gave rise to a lavish banquet (John 6:11-13).

We might also note that, while **five** of the virgins are unprepared, the other five are ready (Matt. 25:4). And of the **five** hundred who saw the risen Jesus, some may have doubted the resurrection, but others believed (Matt. 28:17).

The same lesson that 'less is more' is also true in the dimension of speech: Paul writes as follows:

> I would rather speak **five** words with my mind in order to instruct others, than ten thousand words in a tongue. (1 Cor. 14:19)

The Five Ways

The 'Five Ways' are a series of five arguments for God's existence put forward by the 13th century theologian Thomas Aquinas in his book *Summa Theologica*. They are:

1. The Argument from Motion:

Every movement is set up by the action of something else. Ultimately the one who sets everything in motion is God.

2. The Argument from Efficient Cause:

Nothing can cause itself, and without a first cause, there would be no others. God is that first cause.

3. The Argument from Necessary Being:

Since nothing can come from nothing, something must exist at all times. This 'something' is God.

4. The Argument from Gradation:

Different things have different degrees of goodness, but the greatest form of good that can be conceived must be God himself.

5. The Argument from Design:

The amazing order of the universe shows it cannot be the result of chance, but must have an intelligent designer.

For his invisible attributes, namely, his eternal power and divine nature, have been clearly perceived, ever since the creation of the world, in the things that have been made.
(Rom. 1:20)

Above: The Wise and Foolish Virgins by Claes Brouwer from a Dutch illustrated Bible, (c. 1430)
Below: Parable of the Ten Virgins (c.1616) by Hieronymous Francken the Younger (1578-1623)

Five also appears as number of *restitution* and *redemption*. We have already noted that the **fifth** offering in Leviticus, the guilt offering, adds a **fifth** of the value to what was being sacrificed. To redeem land back you added a **fifth** to the value of the original (Lev. 27:30-31). Similarly, a thief caught stealing an ox had to make a **fivefold** restitution (Ex. 22:1), while **five** shekels was the redemption price for Levites (Num. 3:47, 18:16).

The same is true of the number **fifty**. Leviticus states that:

> The valuation of a male from twenty years old up to sixty years old shall be **fifty** shekels of silver, according to the shekel of the sanctuary.
> (Lev. 27:3)

Similarly Deuteronomy states that, in the case of rape:

> The man ... shall give to the father of the young woman **fifty** shekels of silver, and she shall be his wife, because he has violated her. He may not divorce her all his days.
> (Deut. 22:29)

The same number is present in the restitution that David needs to make to stop the plague that his own miscalculations have brought upon Israel. A price still has to be paid:

> But the king said to Araunah ... "I will not offer burnt offerings to the LORD my God that cost me nothing." So David bought the threshing floor and the oxen for **fifty** shekels of silver.
> (2 Sam. 24:24)

Beyond this, five and its progeny can be seen as a symbol of plenty. Joseph, during the years of abundance in Egypt, collected a **fifth** of the produce of the land to store for hard times ahead (Gen. 41:34), while later at a banquet for his brothers, Benjamin, his favourite, is given **five** times as much as the others (43:34), and subsequently **five** times as many changes of clothes on his return to Canaan (45.22). Fruit in the Promised Land was only to be eaten in the **fifth** year, to ensure abundant harvests (Lev. 19:25); while in the New Testament, the **fivefold** ministry of apostles, prophets, evangelists, pastors and teachers enables the church to multiply exponentially and to grow in depth (Eph. 4:11-12).

From such examples, we may see why **five** is the root of a whole series of numbers that point to limitless expansion. Indeed, it may be said to be a seed number that builds into mighty structures, ultimately far outstripping six and seven.

A clear example of how multiples of five acquire a kind of universal significance is the parable of the ten minas in Luke:

> Calling **ten** of his servants, he gave them **ten** minas, and said to them, 'Engage in business until I come.' ... When he returned ... the first came before him, saying, 'Lord, your mina has made **ten** minas more.' And he said to him, 'Well done, good servant! Because you have been faithful in a very little, you shall have authority over **ten** cities.' (Luke 19:13, 15-17)

The numbers 100 and 1,000 underline this 'seed number' principle even further:

> And Isaac sowed in that land and reaped in the same year a **hundredfold**. (Gen. 26:12)
>
> "And everyone who has left houses or brothers or sisters or father or mother or children or lands, for my name's sake, will receive a **hundredfold** and will inherit eternal life." (Matt. 19:29)
>
> "And some fell into good soil and grew and yielded a **hundredfold**." As he said these things, he called out, "He who has ears to hear, let him hear." (Luke 8:8)
>
> May the LORD, the God of your fathers, make you a **thousand** times as many as you are and bless you, as he has promised you! (Deut. 1:11)
>
> May our granaries be full, providing all kinds of produce; may our sheep bring forth **thousands** and **ten thousands** in our fields. (Ps. 144:13)

If the numbers 10, 100 and 1,000 suggest plenty and abundance, they also, like 5, represent a clear basis of *order* and *arrangement*. This can be seen, for example, in Jethro's advice to Moses to delegate his onerous responsibilities to a much wider circle of people:

> Moreover, look for able men from all the people, men who fear God, who are trustworthy and hate a bribe, and place such men over the people as chiefs of **thousands**, of **hundreds**, of **fifties**, and of **tens**. (Ex. 18:21)

These numbers also appear repeatedly in military contexts:

> And Moses was angry with the officers of the army, the commanders of **thousands** and the commanders of **hundreds**, who had come from service in the war. (Num. 31:14)

It is also striking that these numbers take on an organisational role in the account of Jesus feeding the five thousand, indicating a military-style operation:

> Then he commanded them all to sit down in groups on the green grass. So they sat down in groups, by **hundreds** and by **fifties**. (Mark 6:39-40)

> ### Ten Lost Books
>
> **Ten** books are mentioned in the Old Testament that are no longer extant:
>
> - The Book of the Wars of the LORD (Numbers 21:14)
> - The Book of Jashar (Joshua 10:13; 2 Samuel 1:18)
> - The Book of the Acts of Solomon (1 Kings 11:41)
> - The Book of Nathan the Prophet (1 Chronicles. 29:29; 2 Chron. 9:29)
> - The Book of Gad the Seer (1 Chron. 29:29)
> - The Prophecy of Ahijah the Shiloite (2 Chron. 9:29)
> - The Visions of Iddo the Seer (2 Chron. 9:29 and 12:15)
> - The Book of Shemaiah the Prophet (2 Chronicles 12:15)
> - The Book of Jehu the son of Hanani (2 Chronicles 20:34)
> - The Chronicles of the Seers (2 Chronicles 33:19)
>
> *And the vision of all this has become to you like the words of a book that is sealed.* (Is. 29:11)

The same rounded whole numbers also play a significant role in the mapping out of space:

> The pasture lands of the cities, which you shall give to the Levites, shall reach from the wall of the city outwards a **thousand** cubits all round. And you shall measure, outside the city, on the east side two **thousand** cubits, and on the south side two **thousand** cubits, and on the west side two **thousand** cubits, and on the north side two **thousand** cubits, the city being in the middle. This shall belong to them as pasture land for their cities. (Num. 35:4-5)

Most of all, we see these multiples of five, and particularly **ten**, used as a picture of totality or completeness. For example, the **ten** decrees given in Genesis 1 ('And God said …') were sufficient to create everything in existence. The **ten** plagues represented the complete cycle of God's judgments on Egypt (Ex. 9:14). The **Ten** Commandments were a comprehensive summary of the entire law (Deut. 5:6-22). Paying back a **tenth** of all the produce of the land as a tithe to God was an acknowledgement that *everything* in reality belongs to him (Mal. 3:8-12).

The **tenth generation** represented the whole existence of a family or nation. It was the **tenth** generation of mankind that was judged in the flood. Likewise Deuteronomy 23:3 says that:

> No Ammonite or Moabite may enter the assembly of the LORD. Even to the **tenth** generation, none of them may enter the assembly of the LORD for ever.

Ten is also a marker of sin. Israel's **ten** rebellions in the wilderness (Num. 14:22) symbolised the completeness of its unfaithfulness towards God, as did the **ten** spies who gave a bad report (Num. 13:31-33).

Likewise, the **ten** tribes who broke away from Judah under the reign of Solomon's son Rehoboam (1 Kings 11:31) symbolised the totality of God's judgement on the nation and ultimately became the **ten** lost tribes of Israel (2 Kings 17:21-23).

In scenes of judgement, such as we see in Daniel, these numbers are multiplied exponentially:

> A stream of fire issued and came out from before him; a **thousand thousand**s served him, and ten **thousand** times ten **thousand** stood before him; the court sat in judgement, and the books were opened.
> (Dan. 7:10)

The same is true in the New Testament. In the parable of the unforgiving servant (Matt. 18:23-35), **ten thousand** talents are symbolic of the incalculable amount we owe to God through failure and sin.

In Revelation **ten** kingdoms constitute the totality of the antichrist's global rule, equivalent to the **ten** toes on the feet of the statue in Nebuchadnezzar's dream (Dan. 2:41), and the **ten** horns of the fourth beast of Daniel's vision (Dan. 7:7, 20, 24; Rev. 17:3, 7, 12).

On the other hand, in the parables of Jesus in Luke 15, the numbers **ten** (as in the parable of the ten virgins in Matthew 25) and **one hundred** represent the entirety of the church:

> "Or what woman, having **ten** silver coins, if she loses one coin, does not light a lamp and sweep the house and seek diligently until she finds it?"
> (Luke 15:8)

> "What man of you, having a **hundred** sheep, if he has lost one of them, does not leave the ninety-nine in the open country, and go after the one that is lost, until he finds it?"
> (Luke 15:4)

Finally we should note the significance of the number **one thousand** as a pointer towards the infinite. In Deuteronomy, for example, 'a thousand generations' effectively means 'forever':

> Know therefore that the Lord your God is God, the faithful God who keeps covenant and steadfast love with those who love him and keep his commandments, to a **thousand** generations.
> (Deut. 7:9)

The same is true of the **thousand** year reign of Christ towards the end of Revelation. Though undoubtedly intended as a literal figure, it is also symbolic of the perfection and completeness of God's ultimate order, acting as a preview of the new heavens and the new earth which are to follow (Rev. 20:4-6).

FINGERPRINT

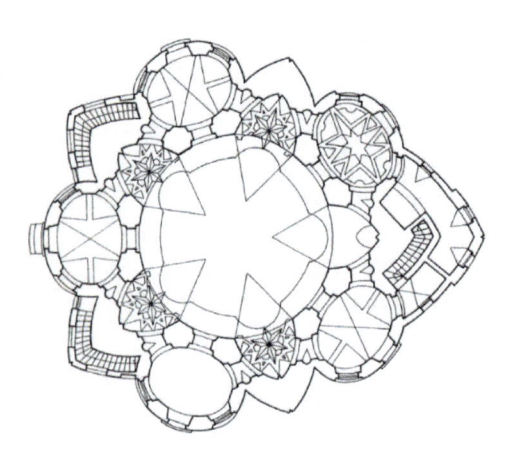

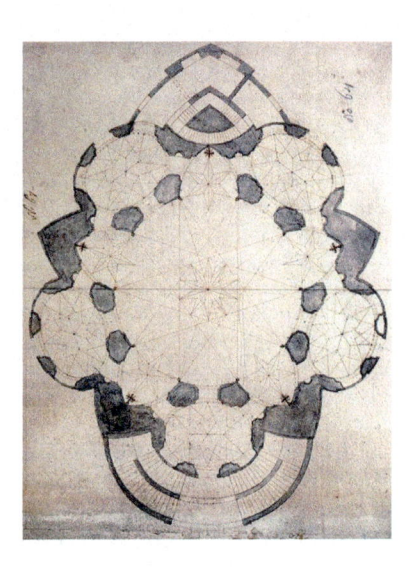

Above and Below: the 1721 Pilgrimage Church of St John of Nepomuk at Zelená Hora, near Žďár nad Sázavou in the Czech Republic, designed by Jan Blažej Santini Aichel (his original ground plan is shown above right). Around the circular central nave are five pairs of columns and five oval domes, five chapels and five altars. The church also has five gates (photo by Gampe).

4. **Five** in the purposes of God

In this chapter we have seen how the number five seems to be a reflection of the hand of God, as the ultimate source of authority in the universe. We have seen how, through its progeny of tens, hundreds and thousands, it provides a gateway to vast and potentially unlimited resources of power, amplified through the powers of multiplication. We have also observed its central role in the structuring of scripture.

Our hands, therefore, as pointers to the hands of our Creator, serve as a powerful reminder of the order built into God's word and the authority that it possesses. From a divine perspective, hands can create (Is. 45:12); bless (Luke 24:50); provide (Ps: 104:28); sustain (Ps. 139:5); deliver (Is. 11:11); heal (Mark 6:5); or transfer supernatural authority (Acts 13:3). From a human perspective, they are also used for worship (Ps. 134:2) and prayer (1 Tim. 2:8), and therefore carry an intercessory function for believers in expressing the power and authority of God.

A striking picture of what happens when we pray can be seen in Exodus 17, where Israel is fighting against the battlefield against the Amalekites. The default situation is that they are losing badly. Yet when Moses lifts up his hands to intercede, the balance tilts dramatically, and the authority of God overrules in an otherwise impossible situation:

> Whenever Moses held up his **hand**, Israel prevailed, and whenever he lowered his **hand**, Amalek prevailed. But Moses' **hands** grew weary, so they took a stone and put it under him, and he sat on it, while Aaron and Hur held up his **hands**, one on one side, and the other on the other side. So his **hands** were steady until the going down of the sun.
> (Ex. 17:11-12)

This account is a telling reminder of the victory over the powers of darkness won many centuries later by the outstretched hands of Jesus on the cross. Moses's hands were held up by those close to him; Jesus' hands with iron nails. As a modern hymn reminds us, 'hands that flung stars into space' were 'to cruel nails surrendered'.

God has given us tremendous power, therefore, in the way we use our hands. They can be used to create, order, and heal. Or they can be used to maim, abuse, and destroy. But with this heavy responsibility comes a huge opportunity: our hands can act as extensions of our Maker's hands, to reach out and serve those around us. Let us waste no opportunity, therefore, in being the hands of Jesus, to touch the people and situations that need his healing and restoring power, and to bring God's dynamic, life-giving order to a broken world.

Chapter Six

Six

The Number of Dominion

1. **Six** as a template for creation

In contrast with the glories of seven which we will read about in the next chapter, the number six often suffers from a bad press in Christian circles. It is not uncommon to hear that, because the Bible teaches that man was made on day **six** of creation, the number symbolises incompleteness, failure and rebellion, especially since six falls short of seven, the unique number of God.

While there may be elements of truth here, it presents an unreasonably negative view of what is, in both scripture and creation, a rich and beautiful number, as we shall see. It also misses the fact that man was introduced as the crowning pinnacle of all that God had made, intended to represent him in the world and to reflect his image in a unique way, the climax of a glorious process of creation accomplished in **six** successive stages:

> Then God said, "Let us make man in our image, after our likeness. And let them have dominion over the fish of the sea and over the birds of the heavens and over the livestock and over all the earth and over every creeping thing that creeps on the earth."
>
> So God created man in his own image, in the image of God he created him; male and female he created them. ...
>
> And God saw everything that he had made, and behold, it was very good. And there was evening and there was morning, the **sixth** day. (Gen. 1:26-7, 31)

SIX: THE NUMBER OF DOMINION

Above: Snowflakes form in distinctive six-pointed shapes, but every single one of them is unique.

Below: The hexagonal columns formed by cooling volcanic basalt at the Giant's Causeway in Northern Ireland. Again, no two columns are exactly identical (photo by Enric Moreu).

Moreover six, in addition to possessing many fascinating mathematical, natural and Biblical properties in its own right, is half of twelve, a number which plays an important symbolic and organisational role in scripture.

From a mathematical point of view six and its multiples have a rich and fertile pedigree. The series of numbers that arises from it has played a vital role in systems of human measurement throughout history. To begin with, six belongs, along with 12, 60, 120 and 360, to an elite group of numbers called 'superior highly composite numbers' and 'colossally abundant numbers' because of the numerous ways they can be divided up. We can see this if look at members of the 'family tree' of six:

$1 \times 2 \times 3 = 6$

$1 \times 2 \times 3 \times 4 = 24$

$1 \times 2 \times 3 \times 4 \times 5 = 120$

120 is a particularly rich number, being divisible by 1, 2, 3, 4, 5, 6, 8, 10, 12, 15, 20, 24, 30, 40 and 60.

Indeed, it turns out that when we multiply any four consecutive numbers, the result is always divisible by 6, 12 and 24. As we shall see, it is striking that all these numbers seem to be symbolic in scripture of the people of God.

Six is also a member of an even more elite group called 'perfect numbers' of which just over fifty are known to exist. These numbers are equal to all the smaller numbers that can divide into them. Thus $6 = 1 + 2 + 3$, while the next 'perfect' number, 28 is equal to the total of its divisors, $1 + 2 + 4 + 7 + 14$.

In his first-century book *On the Creation*, the Jewish writer Philo of Alexandria called six 'the most productive of all numbers, being the smallest perfect number.' He argued that the world was created in six days and the moon orbits in 28 days because 6 and 28 are perfect numbers. This argument is repeated by early Christian writers such as Origen (Commentary on the Gospel of John 28.1.1-4) and later by Augustine, who wrote as follows:

> **Six** is a number perfect in itself, and not because God created the world in **six** days; rather the contrary is true: God created the world in **six** days because this number is perfect, and it would remain perfect, even if the work of the **six** days did not exist.
> Augustine *The City of God* XI 30

The number **six** and its multiples also play a vital role in the natural world. In the realm of quarks, the very smallest constituents of matter, they appear in **six** types or 'flavours'.

> I will command my blessing on you in the **sixth** year, so that it will produce a crop sufficient for three years. (Lev. 25.21)

These flavours have the rather whimsical names of 'up', 'down', 'strange', 'charm', 'top', and 'bottom'. Each quark has a corresponding antiquark. Only up and down quarks are found inside atoms of normal matter:

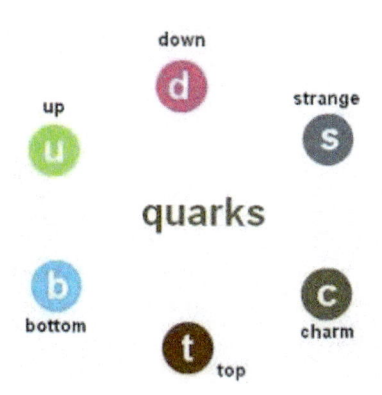

At a slightly higher level of scale, carbon (element number **six**), is a key component in the structure of almost everything around us on earth. Carbon-12 (or ^{12}C), which contains **six** protons, **six** neutrons, and **six** electrons, accounts for almost 99 per cent of all the carbon in the universe, and has an atomic weight of **twelve**.

Carbon is the **sixth** most plentiful element in existence and has an extraordinary ability to form a range of patterns and textures: if its atoms are arranged one way, they can make a soft material like graphite, used in pencils, but arranged differently can form a substance as hard as diamond.

Because of its ability to combine with other elements, carbon is one of most versatile members of the periodic table, providing the basis for all living things and of 95 per cent of known compounds in existence. The benzene molecule, for example, is a key component of natural gas and is arranged in a clear **sixfold** shape:

A more complex particle, C_{60}, was discovered in 1985 and named *Buckminsterfullerene* after the American designer of geodesic domes: it has sixty carbon atoms in each molecule, arranged in a truncated icosahedron. The shape was known to Archimedes with twelve regular pentagonal faces, twenty regular hexagonal faces, sixty vertices and ninety edges, and is immediately recognisable as being identical to the iconic new football shape introduced in the 1970 World Cup (which is 31 million times larger than the carbon molecule itself):

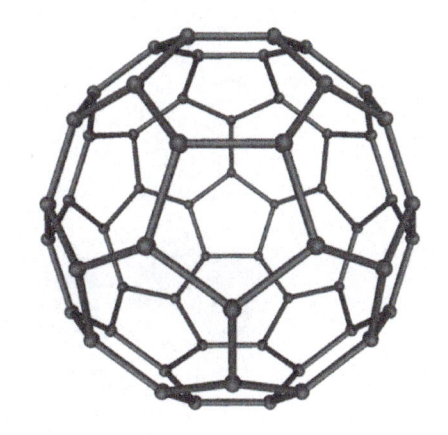

Above: In Salvador Dali's *The Sacrament of the Last Supper* (1955) Christ and his disciples are pictured inside a giant dodecahedron, a regular twelve-sided solid.

Below: In Revelation 21 every single one of the twelve different precious stones set aside for the walls of the New Jerusalem share distinctive properties not recognised until many centuries after the Bible was written, in that each one happens to be *anisotropic*, resulting in a dazzling array of colours when viewed under cross-polarised light.

Jasper (Quartz) — Sapphire — Chalcedony — Emerald

Sardonyx — Sardius (Carnelian) — Chrysolyte (Peridot) — Beryl (Aquamarine)

Topaz — Chrysoprasus — Jacinth (Zircon) — Amethyst

2. **Six** as a template of glory

The six days of creation outlined in Genesis chapter 1 have sometimes been compared to the building and consecration of a temple. Certainly the number six and its multiples play a significant role in the tabernacle itself, and the temple which replaced it.

For example, as we mentioned previously, the Holy of Holies was a perfect cube with **six** sides. There were **sixty** pillars around the tabernacle in all. The golden candlestick, or Menorah, had a central shaft with **six** branches going out of its sides, three on either side (Ex. 25:32). There were two onyx stones on the High Priest's ephod with **six** names of the tribes of Israel engraved on each (Ex. 28:10). The loaves for the bread of the presence were set out in two groups of **six** on the golden table (Lev. 24:6)

Moreover, Solomon's temple that replaced the tabernacle was **sixty** cubits in length, and twenty in breadth, with a vestibule **120** cubits high (2 Chron. 3:3-4) and the Holy Place was overlaid with **six hundred** talents of pure gold (3.8). At its dedication **120** priests played trumpets and **120 thousand** sheep were sacrificed (2 Chron. 5:12; 7:5). The temple that eventually replaced this under Ezra had foundations that were **sixty** cubits square (Ezra 6:3). And the reed used for measuring the dimensions of Ezekiel's temple was **six** long cubits in length, establishing walls **six** cubits thick (Ezek. 40:5).

In the dedication of the original tabernacle, multiples of six also played a central role:

> This was the dedication offering for the altar on the day when it was anointed, from the chiefs of Israel: **twelve** silver plates, **twelve** silver basins, **twelve** golden dishes, each silver plate weighing 130 shekels and each basin 70, all the silver of the vessels **2,400** shekels according to the shekel of the sanctuary, the twelve golden dishes, full of incense, weighing 10 shekels apiece according to the shekel of the sanctuary, all the gold of the dishes being **120** shekels; all the cattle for the burnt offering **twelve** bulls, **twelve** rams, **twelve** male lambs a year old, with their grain offering; and **twelve** male goats for a sin offering; and all the cattle for the sacrifice of peace offerings **twenty-four** bulls, the rams **sixty**, the male goats **sixty**, the male lambs a year old **sixty**. This was the dedication offering for the altar after it was anointed.
> (Num 7:84-88)

In this sense the number six might be described as a *preparation* for glory. Exodus 24:16 tells us how the glory of the LORD dwelt on Mount Sinai, and the cloud covered it for **six** days, before he called to Moses out of the midst of the cloud. Likewise, it is striking that the same timeline of **six** days leads up to the transfiguration of Jesus, where he appeared in glory in front of a select group of his disciples (Matt. 17:1-8).

Above: The north rose window of the Abbey of St Denis, Paris, showing God the Creator, surrounded by the days of creation, twelve constellations representing the order of the heavens, and twelve monthly human activities representing the order of the earth (photo by T. Taylor).

Right: The central rose window on the façade of the Basilica of Santa Maria di Collemaggio (1287) at l'Aquila in Italy, radiating out into twelve and then twenty-four segments (photo by Aquilanus).

The Six Trials of Jesus

Six stages appear in the lead-up to the sentence eventually passed on Jesus. These were, in order:

- Preliminary questioning by Annas, the previous High Priest (John 18:19-24)
- Further interrogation by Caiaphas, the current High Priest (John 18:24; Matt. 26:57; Mark 14:53)
- A hastily convened meeting of the whole Jewish Sanhedrin (Matt. 26:59-68; Mark 14:55-65; Luke 22:66-71)
- An initial interview before Pontius Pilate, the Roman governor (Matt. 27:11-14; Luke 23:1-7; John 18:28-40)
- An appearance before Herod, the ruler of Galilee (Luke 23:8-12)
- A final interview before Pilate (Luke 23:1-7; John 19:8-11) who reluctantly accedes to the wishes of the crowd, and sends Jesus off to be crucified.

Then Pilate said to the chief priests and the crowds, "I find no guilt in this man." (Luke 23:4)

This theme of *preparation* for glory is brought out in the story of the wedding at Cana in Galilee. When the guests run out of wine, Jesus orders the servants to fill up **six** stone jars (used for Jewish purification rites) to the brim with water. Miraculously the water becomes wine. The miracle helps to portray the change from outward cleansing under the Old Covenant to the glory of inward transformation in the New:

> This, the first of his signs, Jesus did at Cana in Galilee, and manifested his glory. And his disciples believed in him. (John 2:11)

This picture of preparation for glory can also be seen in the last week of Jesus' life. According to many Bible commentators, Jesus died on the **sixth** day of the week, which was a preparation for the special Sabbath to come (John 19:31). He had received **six** wounds in his body while still alive (his head, hands, feet, and back) but it was the seventh, a spear in his side, that proved he was actually dead (John 19:34). He had been on the cross for **six** hours, but at the start of the seventh he cried out 'It is finished' and breathed his last (19:30). He had gone through **six** trials, but at the final trial of all humanity, it is he who will sit as the judge (Matt. 25:31-46).

And in heaven these numbers will truly declare the glory of God. Isaiah talked of *seraphim* guarding the heavenly throne:

> Each had **six** wings: with two he covered his face, and with two he covered his feet, and with two he flew. And one called to another and said:
> "Holy, holy, holy is the LORD of hosts; the whole earth is full of his glory!"
> (Is. 6:2-3)

Above: Bees build hexagonal honeycombs to store honey and pollen and to hatch their larvae.

Below: Graphene, a sheet of carbon only one atom thick, spread out in two dimensions in a hexagonal lattice, is the strongest material ever created.

3. **Six** and **twelve** in the ordering of God's people

Each number has its own personality. If the odd numbers one, three, five and seven draw attention to those attributes of God unique to himself, the numbers two, four and six seem more to describe his relationship with redeemed humanity. While the number two underlines the relationship between Christ and his church, and the number four presents the universal scope of the gospel, the number **six**, and especially its multiples, highlights God's ultimate purposes for his children as a redeemed people.

Firstly we should note that **six**, representing the divine activity of creation in six days, which culminated in the creation of man on that day, provides the template for man's own labour:

> For **six** years you shall sow your field, and for **six** years you shall prune your vineyard and gather in its fruits ... I will command my blessing on you in the **sixth** year, so that it will produce a crop sufficient for three years.
> (Lev. 25:3,21)

Multiples of six are evident in the human body: for example, we have **twelve** pairs of ribs, and **twelve** paired nerves called cranial nerves that control senses and movements in the upper part of the body. In addition, blood cells last **120** days each, while there are **twelve** billion neurons in the human brain. Notwithstanding the long age-spans of the patriarchs, **120** became God's declared limit for a human lifespan (Genesis 6:3) and remains the upper maximum of life even to this day.

Because they divide up in so many possible ways, multiples of six have provided the basis of many human measuring systems. We thus have **twenty-four** hours in a day, **sixty** seconds in a minute and **sixty** minutes in an hour, along with **twelve** months in a year and **360** degrees in a circle. **Twelve** constellations appear in the zodiac used by ancient stargazers. **Twelve** years of age marked the passing into adulthood for a Jewish male, reflected by Jesus' trip to Jerusalem at that age, where he stayed behind in the temple instead of returning with his parents.

On a wider scale, the number twelve exerts a fascination across many cultures. In our own society, we counted **twelve** inches in a foot and **twelve** pence in a shilling for centuries, while we still retain **twenty-four** carats for measuring the purity of gold. In other fields of activity, **twelve** hues appear in the colour wheel used by artists, **twelve** notes in the chromatic scale used by musicians, and **twelve** degrees of wind speed in the Beaufort Scale used by meteorologists. A **twelve**-step programme provides the foundation for reform in Alcoholics' Anonymous and similar organisations. The practice of using **twelve** jurors in trials dates back to ancient Greece and has survived as standard in many English-speaking countries to this very day. Alongside Easter a cycle of **twelve** great feasts is celebrated in the Orthodox Church.

Multiples of **six** also play a significant part in the revelation of God's Word. The Bible the church possesses today has **sixty-six** (6 ×11) books. According to Jewish tradition a council of **120** elders met under Ezra to decide the contents of the Old Testament scripture, which became **twenty-four** books under the Jewish canon.

In salvation history the number **six** and its multiples also plays a prominent role. For example, Noah was **six hundred** years old when he was saved from the flood. Isaac was **sixty** years old when his sons Esau and Jacob were born. **Sixty-six** descendants of Jacob came into Egypt (Gen. 46:26). **Six hundred thousand** were rescued out of Egypt (Ex. 12.37: Jewish families celebrate this great act of deliverance with **six** symbolic foods placed on the Passover Seder Plate). Aaron bore the names of **six** of the tribes of Israel on each shoulder as a memorial before the Lord (Ex. 28:9-12). And in Numbers 35:6 **six** cities of refuge were provided for those who committed unintentional manslaughter.

This pattern continues in the New Testament. As we saw in the previous section, Jesus experienced **six** final days in Jerusalem, where he went through **six** trials, and endured **six** hours on cross for our redemption.

Finally, in Revelation, it was the **sixth** of the seven churches in Revelation that is given an open door for its faithfulness (as opposed to the closed door of the seventh church) and receives a great commendation for its patient endurance:

> "'I know your works. Behold, I have set before you an open door, which no one is able to shut. ... The one who conquers, I will make him a pillar in the temple of my God. Never shall he go out of it, and I will write on him the name of my God, and the name of the city of my God, the new Jerusalem, which comes down from my God out of heaven, and my own new name. (Rev. 3:8,12)

Salt of the Earth

Recalling the cubic shape of the Holy of Holies in the temple, salt forms naturally into crystals with **six** equal sides.

Salt is a remarkable substance which accomplishes a dazzling variety of tasks, many of which have clear parallels in the spiritual realm. Among these extraordinary properties are:

- Dissolving completely in water
- Softening hard water
- Preventing freezing over
- Enhancing flavour in food
- Tenderising tough meat
- Preserving from decay
- Sustaining the functions of the human body
- Cleansing and disinfecting an open wound

Although we take salt for granted it provides a wonderful picture of how believers can season and enrich society around them, bringing the flavour of God's kingdom into a hurting world (Matt. 5:13).

You shall season all your grain offerings with salt. You shall not let the salt of the covenant with your God be missing from your grain offering; with all your offerings you shall offer salt. (Lev. 2:13)

SIX: THE NUMBER OF DOMINION

Above: Recalling the design of the Holy of Holies in the temple, salt forms naturally into crystals with **six** equal sides – a perfect cube, which can form the basis for still more remarkable structures (photos by Rob Lavinsky and Hans-Joachim Engelhardt).

Below: Tympanum from the south portal, Saint-Pierre, Moissac, c. 1115-30, depicting Christ surrounded by 24 elders (photo by Nick Thompson).

It is, however, in the number **twelve** that God's purposes for mankind are perhaps most fully expressed. Clearly the number plays a central role in the history of the Jewish people, evidenced for example in the **twelve** stones that Elijah uses to build the altar to challenge the prophets of Baal, the **twelve** yoke of oxen with which Elisha was ploughing when he was commissioned, the **twelve** minor prophets that are still grouped together in one book in Jewish Bibles, and so on.

But the significance of the number seems to extend beyond God's chosen people. Thus while Jacob becomes the father of the **twelve** tribes that make up the nation, so too does Ishmael, outside the covenant line (Gen. 25:16).

The number **twelve** and its multiples thus seems to play a role in the salvation of Gentiles as well as Jews. We should take note, for example, of the number of people saved in Nineveh, Israel's staunch enemy, after Jonah's preaching, even though God has to upbraid him for his hard heart:

> And should not I pity Nineveh, that great city, in which there are more than **120,000** persons who do not know their right hand from their left, and also much cattle?" (Jonah 4:11)

In the New Testament Jesus commissions **twelve** apostles to preach the gospel, and then sends out a further **seventy-two** to spread the message further afield **(6×12)**. **Twelve** baskets are left over after the feeding of the five thousand in Israel – a picture of how, like the 'crumbs under the table' left for the Syro-Phoenician woman shortly afterwards, divine provision has been made for Gentiles outside the covenant (Matt. 14:15-21; 15:21-28).

In Acts the number **120** marks the nucleus of the early church (1:15), mirroring the **120** priests who ministered in Solomon's temple before the glory fell (2 Chron. 5:12-14), and who at the day of Pentecost are led to speak in the languages of many of the surrounding nations (2:5-6).

In Revelation **twenty-four** elders seem to represent the fathers of both Israel and the church united together (compare Rev. 4:4 with 21:12-14), comprising the **twelve** sons of Jacob and the **twelve** apostles of Jesus.

If 12+12 plays a memorable role early in the book, 12×12 (144) plays a significant role in later chapters. In addition to being the square of **twelve**, 144 is the **twelfth** Fibonacci number, and the first Fibonacci number which is also a square number. When multiplied by 1,000, the cube of ten, it points to a state of God-given balance and perfection. When in Revelation 7:4, for example, **144,000** from all the tribes of Israel receive a protective seal, it portrays a completeness in God's plans.

SIX: THE NUMBER OF DOMINION

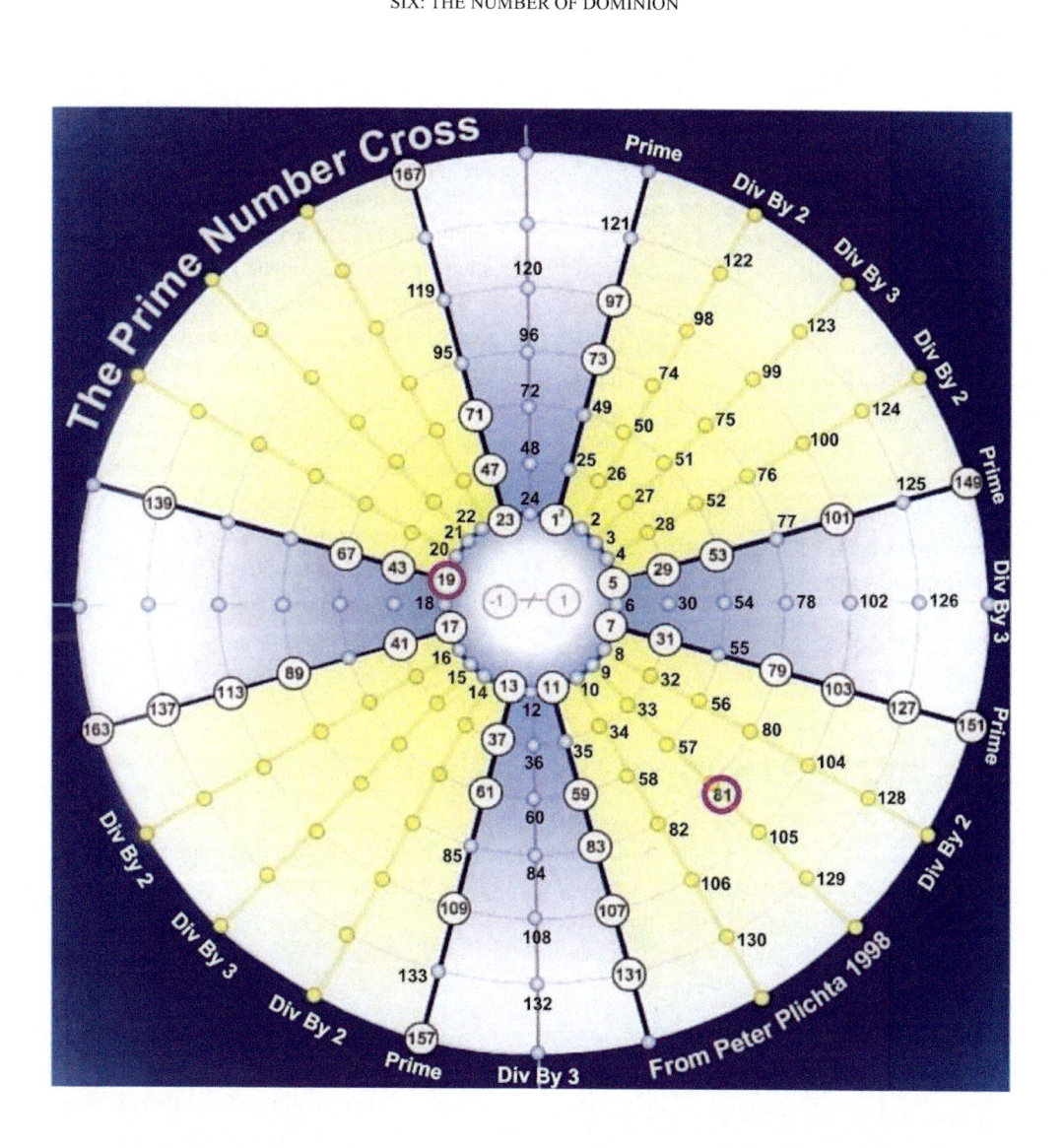

Prime numbers - numbers that cannot be broken down into equal units of more than one - appear to be scattered randomly through the number spectrum, but when the larger primes are arranged in rings of **twenty-four** and its multiples, they line up in a remarkable cross-shaped array (this image from *God's Secret Formula* by Peter Plichta). This provides an interesting numerical parallel with the arrangement of twenty-four elders around the throne in Revelation 4:4.

We later read:

> Then I looked, and behold, on Mount Zion stood the Lamb, and with him **144,000** who had his name and his Father's name written on their foreheads. And I heard a voice from heaven like the roar of many waters and like the sound of loud thunder. The voice I heard was like the sound of harpists playing on their harps, and they were singing a new song before the throne and before the four living creatures and before the elders. No one could learn that song except the **144,000** who had been redeemed from the earth. (Rev. 14:1-3)

The book culminates in the heavenly Jerusalem, now open to every nation of the world (21:24) which is **twelve** thousand stadia in length and breadth (thus **144,000,000** stadia square, enclosed by walls **144** cubits in thickness), with **twelve** gates made of **twelve** pearls, guarded by **twelve** angels, inscribed with the names of the **twelve** tribes of Israel; **twelve** foundation stones named after the **twelve** apostles, adorned with **twelve** jewels, and the tree of life bearing **twelve** crops of fruit. The promises made to the **twelve** tribes of Israel in the Old Testament and to the **twelve** apostles in the New Testament at last reach their final fulfilment.

4. **Six** and **twelve** as symbols of rulership

The numbers six and twelve symbolise not just a perfectly ordered society, but also point to dominion and rulership over the natural order. It is on the **sixth** day that man is given dominion over the created order:

> And God blessed them. And God said to them, "Be fruitful and multiply and fill the earth and subdue it and have dominion over the fish of the sea and over the birds of the heavens and over every living thing that moves on the earth." (Gen. 1:28)

Psalm 8 spells out that dominion over **six** aspects of the natural world:

> You have given him dominion over the works of your hands;
> you have put all things under his feet,
> all **sheep** and **oxen**,
> and also the **beasts of the field**,
> the **birds of the heavens**, and the **fish of the sea**,
> whatever passes along the paths of the seas. (Ps. 8:6-8)

SIX: THE NUMBER OF DOMINION

Standard Model of Elementary Particles

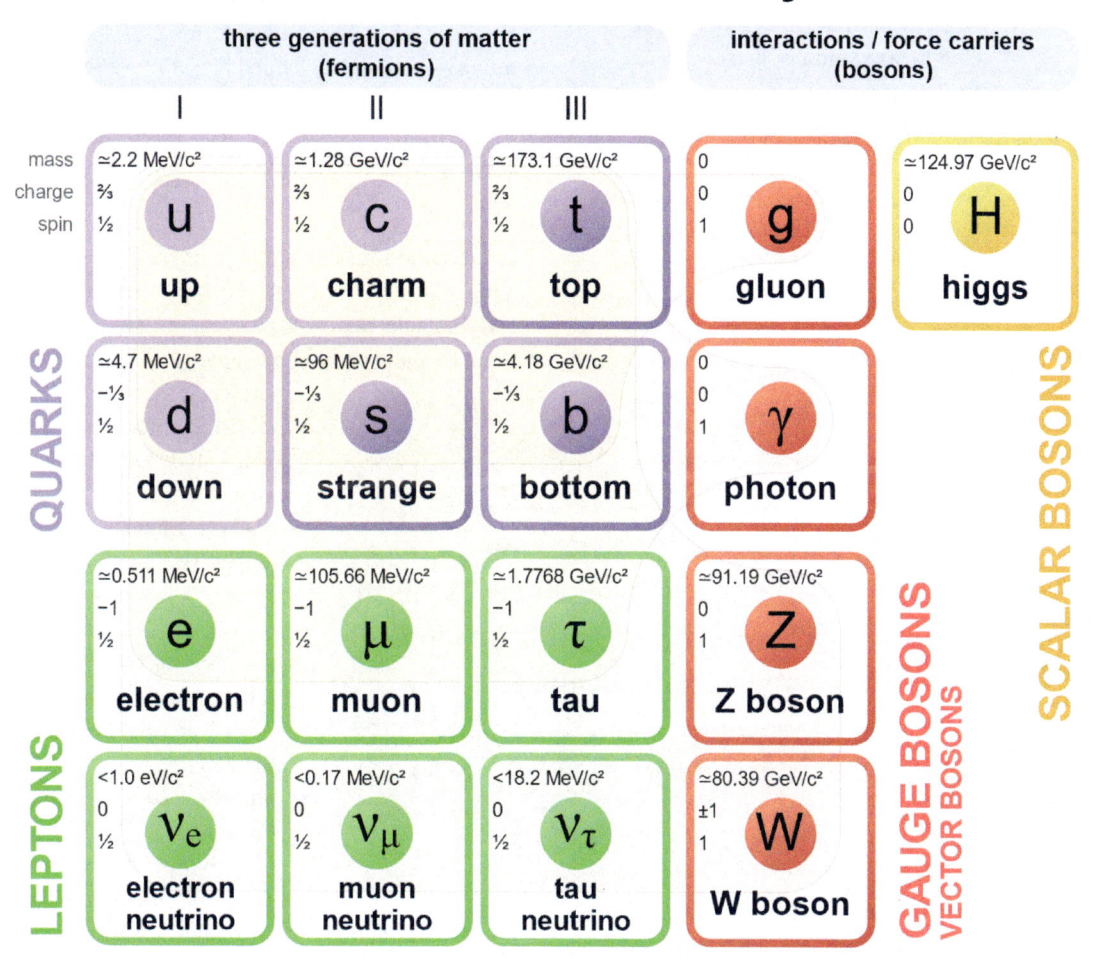

three generations of matter (fermions)

interactions / force carriers (bosons)

	I	II	III		
mass charge spin	≃2.2 MeV/c² ⅔ ½ **u** up	≃1.28 GeV/c² ⅔ ½ **c** charm	≃173.1 GeV/c² ⅔ ½ **t** top	0 0 1 **g** gluon	≃124.97 GeV/c² 0 0 **H** higgs
QUARKS	≃4.7 MeV/c² -⅓ ½ **d** down	≃96 MeV/c² -⅓ ½ **s** strange	≃4.18 GeV/c² -⅓ ½ **b** bottom	0 0 1 **γ** photon	
	≃0.511 MeV/c² -1 ½ **e** electron	≃105.66 MeV/c² -1 ½ **μ** muon	≃1.7768 GeV/c² -1 ½ **τ** tau	≃91.19 GeV/c² 0 1 **Z** Z boson	SCALAR BOSONS
LEPTONS	<1.0 eV/c² 0 ½ **νe** electron neutrino	<0.17 MeV/c² 0 ½ **νμ** muon neutrino	<18.2 MeV/c² 0 ½ **ντ** tau neutrino	≃80.39 GeV/c² ±1 1 **W** W boson	GAUGE BOSONS / VECTOR BOSONS

On the left of the table above we see **twelve** elementary particles (fermions) which are grouped into three 'generations' of matter, the normal matter around us being part of the first generation. These twelve elementary particles of matter are divided into **six** quarks (up, down, strange, charm, top, and bottom) and **six** leptons, of which half are electrons (electron, muon and tau) and half neutrinos (e, muon and tau). Each fermion has a corresponding antiparticle with an opposite charge, therefore making **24** possible fermions in total (diagram by M. J. Cush).

We see this theme of dominion worked out through the entire span of the Bible. Thus

- **twelve** tribes were commissioned by God to take land in Canaan
- **twelve** successive judges were appointed in the book of Judges to govern the land
- **twelve** apostles were given authority by Jesus over demons and sickness (Matt: 10:1).
- **twelve** legions of angels could have rescued Jesus (Matt. 26:53)
- **six** pieces of armour are described in Ephesians 6:14-18 for the believer to use against the powers of darkness.

These defensive images remind us how the principle of dominion also extends into the military sphere: an army of **twelve** thousand from Israel gained victory over the Midianites (Num. 31:3-12), while much later Joab struck down **twelve** thousand Edomites in the Valley of Salt (see preface to Psalm 60). Subsequently Ahithophel suggests to Absolom an army of **twelve** thousand men should rise up against David (2 Sam. 17:1).

Multiples of six are present in a number of military victories: **sixty** cities were taken from the kingdom of Og in Bashan (Deut. 3:4); an army of **six hundred** men defeated the Philistines at Gibeah under Saul (1 Sam. 14:2,16-23); while **six hundred** men under David defeated the Philistines at Keilah (1 Sam. 23:1-5, 13) and an elite force of **sixty** trained swordsmen guarded David's son Solomon (Song 3:7-8). **Six** prophetic arrow shots by King Joash would have been sufficient to overcome the armies of Aram completely (2 Kings 13:14-19).

Solomon in turn had a throne of **six** steps (1 Kings 10:19), received **six hundred and sixty-six** talents of gold in a year (10:14), and built a temple **sixty** cubits long (6:2). He set **twelve** officers over all Israel, who provided food for the king and his household (4:7) and he employed **twelve thousand** horsemen (4:26). At his accession as king **twenty-four** priestly divisions were given responsibility for priestly service (1 Chron. 24:7-18), **twenty-four** divisions of musicians given authority to lead worship (25:9-31), **twenty-four** thousand Levites given responsibility for maintenance and service in the temple (23:4), while **twenty-four** thousand troops were arranged in each of **twelve** army divisions (27:1-15).

Of course, six and its multiples can also be used to express the concept of unrighteous dominion. Thus Pharoah sends out **six hundred** chariots to pursue the Israelites as they

> Jesus said to them, "Truly, I say to you, in the new world, when the Son of Man will sit on his glorious throne, you who have followed me will also sit on **twelve** thrones, judging the **twelve tribes** of Israel. (Matt. 19.28)

escape from the country (Ex. 14:7) and the Philistines dispatch **six thousand** horsemen against Israel (1 Sam.13:5). Israel's arch-enemy Goliath was **six** cubits in height, had **six** pieces of armour, and had a spearhead weighing **six hundred** shekels of iron (1 Sam. 17:4-7), while we later hear of another man of great stature, who had **six** fingers on each hand, and **six** toes on each foot, who also fought against the nation (2 Sam. 21.20).

Later Nebuchadnezzar set up an image which was **sixty** cubits high and **six** cubits wide (Dan. 3:1), which was worshipped when music from **six** specified instruments was heard. Meanwhile Ezekiel has a vision of the glory of the LORD departing from the temple just before the **sixth** day of the **sixth** month of the **sixth** year of the exile in Babylon, because of the idolatry being practised there (Ezek. 8:1; 10:18; 11:23).

The ultimate example of unrighteous dominion, of course, appears in Revelation, associated the number **six hundred and sixty-six** (Rev. 13.18). But what exactly does this figure symbolise? Is it a numerical representation of the Emperor Nero? Or a total of all Roman numerals up to 500? Or an eclipse of a thousand by exactly one third (an important proportion in Revelation)? Or a falling short of the perfect 777, just as the name 'Jesus', at 888 (see page 96), exceeds that number?

Although all these explanations are possible, no single answer seems to completely satisfy. One thing is certain, however: the 'beast' who owns this number (or 'man of sin', as Paul calls him), will be completely defeated at the return of Jesus (2 Thess. 2:3-8; Rev. 19:20) who will then rule unopposed over a transformed earth (Ps. 2:6-9; Is. 11:1-10; Acts 3:19-21; 1 Cor. 15:24-28; Rev. 20:4-6).

5. **Six** as a picture of completeness

All single-digit numbers speak of different levels of completeness. As we observed earlier, six has often been felt to be incomplete because it is both less than seven, the perfect number, and only half of twelve. Yet it is striking that God offers his own completed work of creation in **six** days as a clear model for mankind to emulate (Ex. 20:9-11; 31:15-17). While the fifth church in Revelation is told that its deeds are incomplete, and those of the seventh church are effectively non-existent, it is the **sixth** church, in Philadelphia, which accomplishes the goals it has been set (Rev. 3:7-13).

This serves as a powerful reminder of the importance of completing assignments, and not having our lives littered with half-finished projects or unfinished business. Some of the greatest words in scripture are where Jesus cries out, after **six** final days in Jerusalem, **six** trials, and **six** hours on cross, the **sixth** of the seven utterances recorded in his final hours:

"It is finished". (John 19:30)

This was not a cry of dereliction but a great shout of accomplishment. The work of redemption was now complete and God's kingdom fully inaugurated. All this makes John's mention of a Sabbath rest immediately after this passage particularly meaningful.

Jesus' example of pushing through to the end, despite the enormous cost, serves as a powerful, if daunting, example for us to follow, as the writer to the Hebrews points out:

> Therefore, since we are surrounded by so great a cloud of witnesses, let us also lay aside every weight, and sin which clings so closely, and let us run with endurance the race that is set before us, looking to Jesus, the founder and perfecter of our faith, who for the joy that was set before him endured the cross, despising the shame, and is seated at the right hand of the throne of God. (Heb. 12:1-2)

Just as the twelve tribes of Israel never took all the land allotted to them by God, our own lives can be full of half-measures and weak compromises, leaving tragically unconquered territory for the enemy to exploit.

As Ecclesiastes reminds us:

> Something completed is better than something just begun; patience is better than too much pride. (Ecc. 7:8 CEV)

'It is Finished!'

In Hebrew the cry 'it is finished' (*m'shaalam* or *ze nigmar*) was the phrase used by the High Priest after the final Passover lamb had been sacrificed at 3pm. Jesus' use of these very words at the exact same moment, after **six** hours on the cross, reminds us that he is the final Passover lamb, the end to all sacrifice, and the ultimate victor over sin and death.

In the New Testament this cry is rendered by the Greek word TETELESTHAI. This was the word uttered by servants to say their mission was accomplished, by artists to declare their masterpiece was complete, or by merchants, written across a bill, to certify that the debt had been **paid in full**.

'Since the foundation of the world there never was a single word uttered, in which such diversified and important matter was contained. ... To do justice to it, is beyond the ability of men or angels: its height, and depth, and length, and breadth, are absolutely unsearchable." (Charles Simeon)

He has appeared **once and for all** at the climax of history to **abolish sin** by the sacrifice of himself (Heb. 9:26 NEB)

Six and its multiples also speak to us of a wider completeness at the level of church, community and society as a whole. As we have seen, **twenty-four** elders around the throne represent the fulness of redeemed humanity (Rev. 4:4), just as **twenty-four** divisions of priests in the Old Testament represent the completeness of the Old Testament priesthood (1 Chron. 24:7-18). **120** marks the fullness of the early church (Acts 1:15), and **144,000** the completeness of redeemed Israel (Rev. 7:4). This is not to devalue the role of the individual within this greater body, for each has their own unique and essential role to play, but all form part of a greater and harmonious order, such that if one part is missing, the fulness is incomplete (1 Cor. 12:14-26). It is striking that when one of the **twelve** took their own life, the place had to be filled by another (Acts 1:21-26).

> On each side of the river stood the tree of life, bearing **twelve** crops of fruit, yielding its fruit every month. And the leaves of the tree are for the healing of the nations. (Rev. 22.2)

Finally, we should note that the number six and its multiples speak of the balanced and proportioned use of time. In a world where **sixty** seconds make up a minute, **sixty** minutes make up an hour, **twenty-four** hours make up a day, **thirty** days make a lunar month and **twelve** months make a year, we need to remember that each moment is unique, precious and totally unrepeatable. Without God at the centre, the passage of time can so easily be cheapened and devalued. Living life in all its fulness means making every second count for God, and offering him the firstfruits of the harvest of time that rightfully belongs to him anyway. The challenge for us is to try and make each moment matter as if it were our last, and to allow every second, however inconsequential, to be filled with the glory and majesty of God.

Chapter Seven

Seven

The Number of Perfection

1. **Seven** as a fingerprint of creation

Each of the numbers we have considered so far reveal something unique and special about God's character and nature. But with seven we step up to a new level, drawing us into the innermost essence of the Godhead and ushering us into the very throne room of heaven. It is a number which points beyond itself, lifting us into a dimension where majesty, holiness and glory mingle together in the unfathomable mystery of deity.

Yet it also describes something very familiar. Billions of people across this planet, of every faith and none, now organise their lives around a seven-day week, a lingering echo of God's primordial act of creating the world in seven stages. At the very outset of Genesis we see how the number seven crowns the entire creation story to measure out a completed divine act, setting a rhythm that would sound out a regular drumbeat throughout human history:

> And on the **seventh** day God finished his work that he had done, and he rested on the seventh day from all his work that he had done. So God blessed the **seventh** day and made it holy, because on it God rested from all his work that he had done in creation.
> (Gen. 2:2-3)

However, the influence of this divine clock takes the significance of the number far beyond the limits of the human calendar. In fact, as we look throughout the natural world, **seven**-day circadian rhythms appear at every level of living organism, from the smallest unicellular sea algae up to plants, insects, fish, birds and mammals.

Above: *7 Days of Creation* by New York artist Jacob Mezrahi.
Below: The West Window of Truro Cathedral, also depicting the seven days of Genesis 1.

The Sabbath rest, therefore, provides a foundational template not just for human society but appears to be written into the very DNA of every living thing. But the scope of the number seven seems to go far beyond this.

In physics, for example, we find **seven** classes of electromagnetic waves, with the **seven** colours of the rainbow (following Newton's classification) in the very centre.

In chemistry we discover **seven** levels in the periodic table of elements, related to the number of electron shells that a particular element possesses.

In biology we find **seven** levels for living organisms: kingdom, phylum, class, order, family, genus and species.

In astronomy we see **seven** main types of star according to their spectral class.

In geology we find **seven** crystal systems and seven associated lattice systems.

As an engineering problem, **seven** is the maximum number of cylindrical objects that can be tied securely in a bundle.

In mathematics, the number **seven**, when expressed as a reciprocal, might be said to behave like a crystal, in that when written out in decimals it produces a regularly repeating pattern, as we see at the top of the next column:

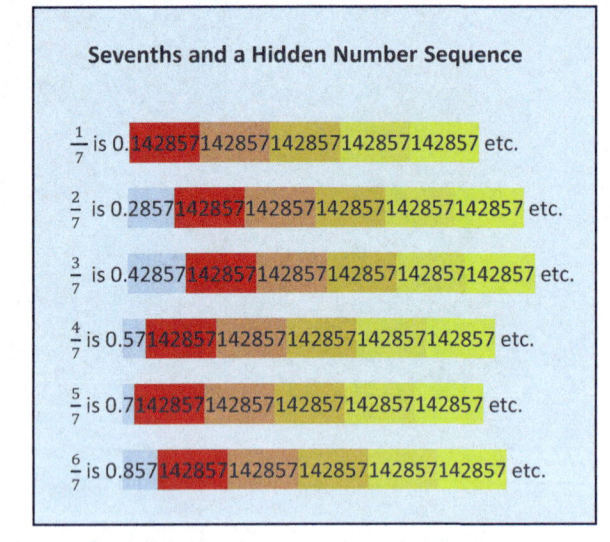

Sevenths and a Hidden Number Sequence

$\frac{1}{7}$ is 0.142857142857142857142857142857 etc.

$\frac{2}{7}$ is 0.285714285714285714285714285714 etc.

$\frac{3}{7}$ is 0.428571428571428571428571428571 etc.

$\frac{4}{7}$ is 0.571428571428571428571428571428 etc.

$\frac{5}{7}$ is 0.714285714285714285714285714285 etc.

$\frac{6}{7}$ is 0.857142857142857142857142857142 etc.

In music we find the number **seven** governs the number of different notes within a major or minor scale, from which a seemingly infinite array of artistic structures can be created.

Finally, in culture, folklore and tradition, seven has always exerted a fascination: thus we have **seven** seas, **seven** wonders of the world, **seven** deadly sins, and many similar groupings.

> **Seven** times a day I praise you for your righteous rules. (Ps. 119.164)

In summary, seven is truly a remarkable number, which displays many aspects of God's fingerprint on the natural world and the human cultures that arose within it. All this serves as a rich backdrop for the pervasive role it plays within scripture itself, as we shall see.

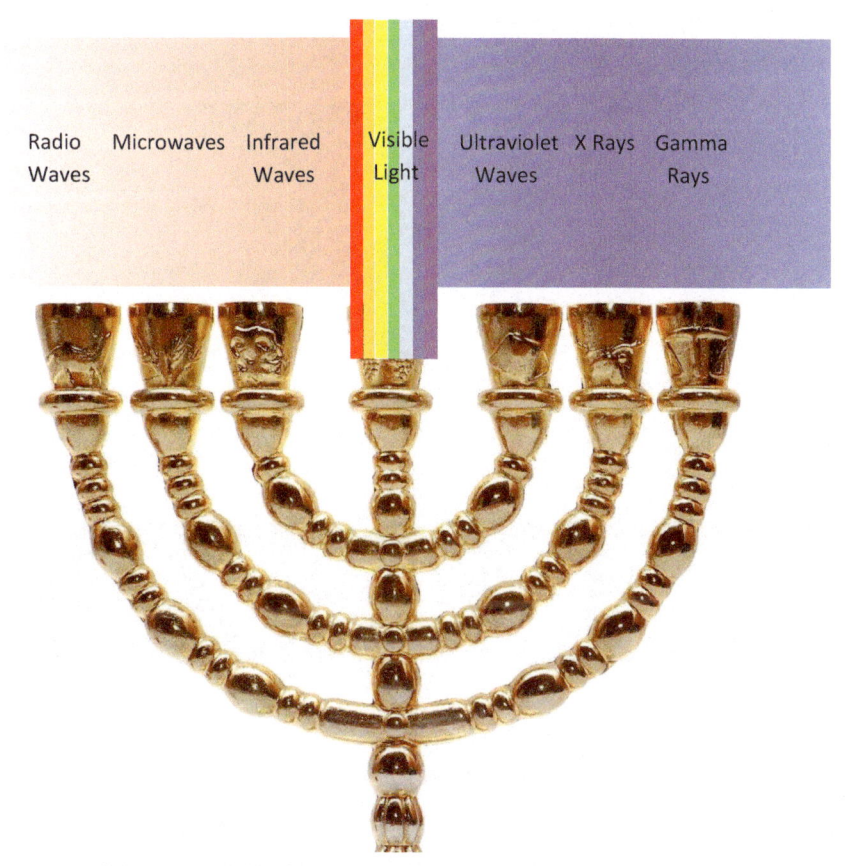

Above: The electromagnetic spectrum divides into **seven** different portions according to wavelength, with an intriguing relationship to the structure of the *Menorah* in the temple (about which we will discover more later).

Below: The Periodic Table of elements divides into **seven** levels according to the number of electron shells orbiting the nucleus of the atom (the two rows at the bottom being expansions of the sixth and seventh levels).

FINGERPRINT

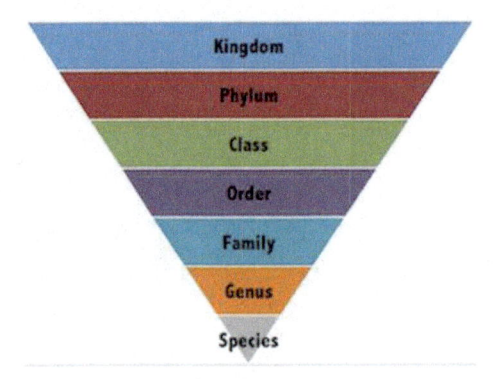

Top: The **seven** levels of classification in biology

Above: Stars fall into **seven** different categories according to their temperature, spectral type and brightness

Below: Crystals fall into **seven** different types according to their molecular structure and arrangement

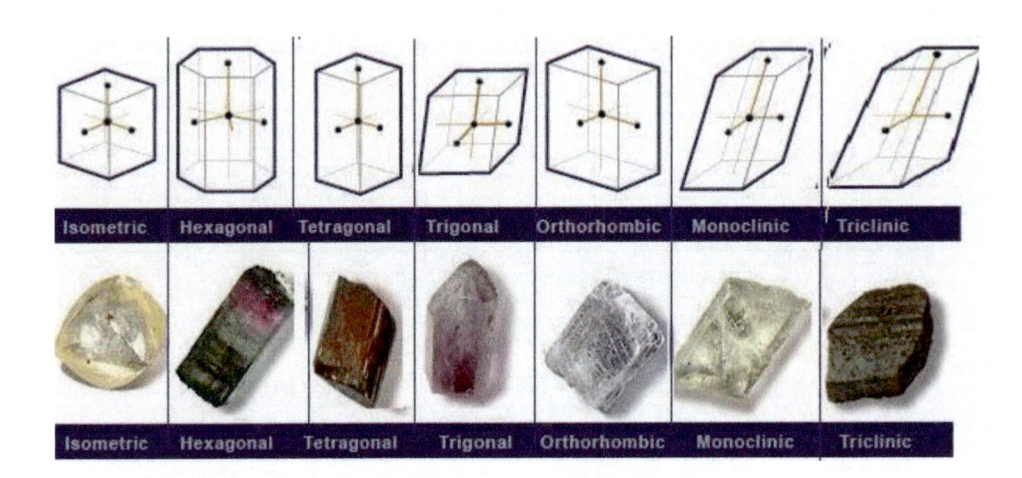

2. **Seven** as the number of covenant

Just as the number seven underlines a heavenly order, it also draws attention to God's unbreakable promises on earth.

The root of the Hebrew word for seven comes from שָׁבַע (*shaba*) which means to swear, or to make an oath. This sense of binding confirmation is clear from its first occurrence in Genesis 21:22-34, where Abraham makes an unbreakable covenant with Abimelech by setting **seven** ewe lambs apart from his flock:

> So Abraham took sheep and oxen and gave them to Abimelech, and the two men made a covenant. Abraham set seven ewe lambs of the flock apart. And Abimelech said to Abraham, "What is the meaning of these seven ewe lambs that you have set apart?" He said, "These seven ewe lambs you will take from my hand, that this may be a witness for me that I dug this well." Therefore that place was called Beersheba, because there both of them swore an oath. (Gen. 21:27-31)

Beersheba, 'the well of the oath', where the pact was made, still stands today (almost four thousand years later) as a mark of this agreement. It was also a critical location in the reestablishment of the modern state of Israel, as the town where Allied forces in 1917 made their first breakthrough into the Holy Land. This took place on the very same afternoon that the Balfour Declaration, which promised the establishment of a Jewish homeland after two thousand years of Gentile rule, just happened to be being signed in London.

In this sense from the very beginning of scripture the number might be said to provide a kind of combination lock on God's promises. God's setting aside the **seventh** day of creation as a day for work to cease paints a picture of the ultimate liberation of mankind (Gen. 2:2,3; Deut. 5:14-15; Luke 13:16); his **sevenfold** mark on Cain (Gen. 4:15) reminds us of his unrelenting provision of mercy to fallen man; his translation to heaven of Enoch, the **seventh** of Adam's line, powerfully looks ahead to the resurrection of the faithful (1 Thess. 4:13-17); while the **sevenfold** rainbow serves as a still-visible reminder of his covenant promises to Noah and his descendants.[8]

Later God's covenant of blessing on Abraham also appears in a **sevenfold** form:

> And I will **make of you a great nation**,
>
> and I will **bless you** and **make your name great**,
>
> so that **you will be a blessing**.
>
> I will **bless those who bless you**,
>
> and **him who dishonours you I will curse**,
>
> and **in you all the families of the earth shall be blessed**." (Gen 12:2-3)

FINGERPRINT

Above: The ancient ruins of Beersheba, where Abraham made a sevenfold covenant with Abimelech.

Below: The description of the Sabbath in Exodus 31 as a covenant sign for Israel is presented as a symmetrical structure with **seven** steps:

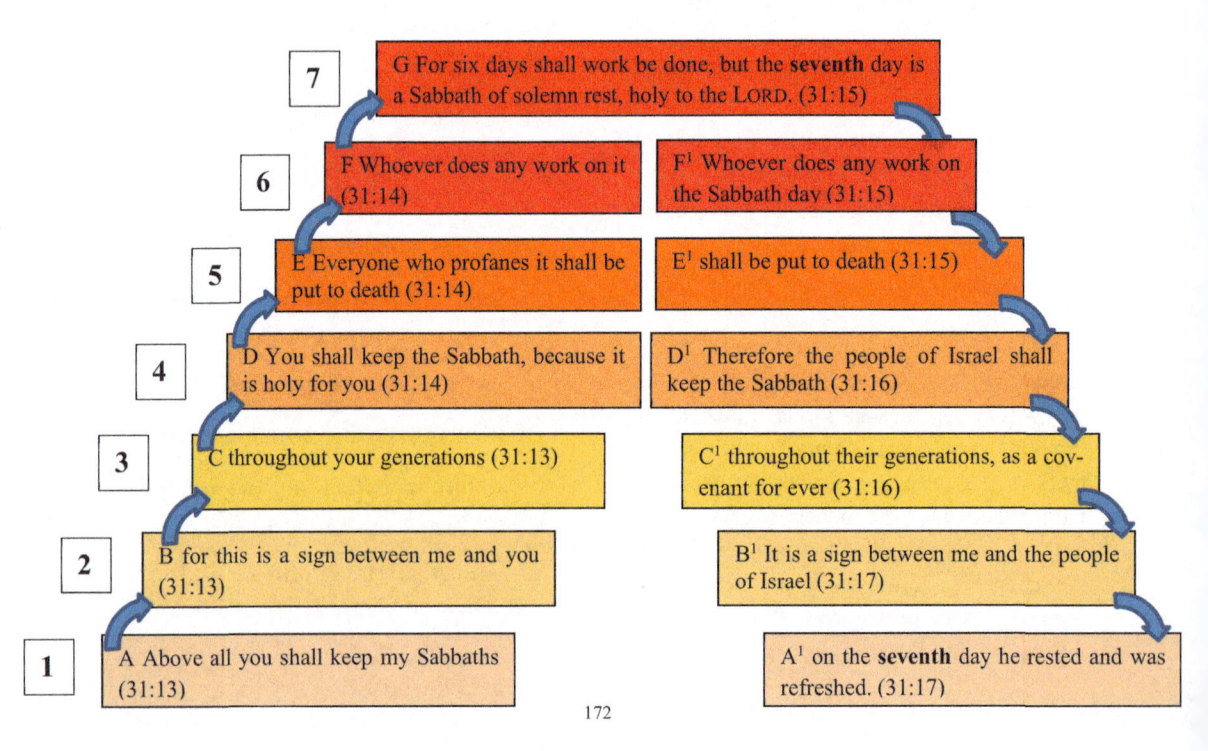

7 — G For six days shall work be done, but the **seventh** day is a Sabbath of solemn rest, holy to the LORD. (31:15)

6 — F Whoever does any work on it (31:14) / F¹ Whoever does any work on the Sabbath day (31:15)

5 — E Everyone who profanes it shall be put to death (31:14) / E¹ shall be put to death (31:15)

4 — D You shall keep the Sabbath, because it is holy for you (31:14) / D¹ Therefore the people of Israel shall keep the Sabbath (31:16)

3 — C throughout your generations (31:13) / C¹ throughout their generations, as a covenant for ever (31:16)

2 — B for this is a sign between me and you (31:13) / B¹ It is a sign between me and the people of Israel (31:17)

1 — A Above all you shall keep my Sabbaths (31:13) / A¹ on the **seventh** day he rested and was refreshed. (31:17)

A similar pattern appears in Exodus 6:6-8. **Seven** times God declares "I will" as a binding promise to Abraham's descendants:

> ☙❧
>
> **I will** bring you out from under the burdens of the Egyptians
>
> **I will** deliver you from slavery to them
>
> **I will** redeem you with an outstretched arm and with great acts of judgement.
>
> **I will** take you to be my people
>
> **I will** be your God, and you shall know that I am the LORD your God, who has brought you out from under the burdens of the Egyptians.
>
> **I will** bring you into the land that I swore to give to Abraham, to Isaac, and to Jacob.
>
> **I will** give it to you for a possession.
> (Ex. 6:6-8)
>
> ☙❧

This pattern of sevens continues unabated throughout the Old Testament. The land which God promised them here was to be a land of **seven** peoples (Deut. 7:1-2) who would flee in **seven** directions (Deut. 28:7). Even when Balaam offered **seven** bullocks and **seven** rams on **seven** altars to attempt to reverse this advantage, it simply released further waves of blessing (Num. 23:1, 14, 29).

Under God's covenant order time was to be structured in weekly cycles of **seven** days, annual cycles of **seven** feasts, and larger **seven-year** cycles, which provided rest for the land and restitution for those in debt. The laws underlying this covenant were to be read out every **seven** years at the Feast of Tabernacles (Deut. 31:9-11), the **seventh** feast of Israel -which took place in the **seventh** month and which lasted **seven** days.

The fingerprint of the number seven in God's developing promises can also be traced through the tabernacle and the sacrificial system. The priests, who acted as God's representatives, went through an ordination period of **seven** days; the instructions for their service are laid out in Leviticus, which as we saw in Chapter Five is made up of **seven** symmetrically arranged sections; and the Tabernacle, where they served, contained **seven** furnishings (the altar of sacrifice, the bronze basin, the golden lampstand or Menorah (which itself had **seven** branches), the table for the bread of the presence, the altar of incense, the ark of the covenant, and the mercy seat). The temple, which ultimately replaced the tabernacle, took **seven** years to build and Solomon kept the Feast for **seven** days.

The sacrifices underpinning the work of the priesthood also bore the fingerprint of the number **seven**, echoing the **seven** pairs of clean sacrificial animals Noah was instructed to take onto the ark. Under the Levitical system animals were able to be offered up in the tabernacle after they were **seven** days old (Exodus 22:30), and the **sevenfold** sprinkling of blood is mentioned again and again as a means of complete redemption and a restored relationship with God, enabling the complete forgiveness for the sinner, cleansing for the leper and consecration for the altar.

Ultimately this sevenfold pattern of atonement and consecration was fulfilled by Jesus, whose **seven** wounds and **seven** last words on the cross marked the perfect fulfilment of the sacrificial system and the institution of a new and eternal covenant in his own blood. This is heralded by the 'single stone with **seven** eyes' given to the High Priest in Zechariah's vision, where God promises to 'remove the iniquity of this land in a single day' (Zech. 3:9).

In the great vision of heaven in Revelation, John sees the glorified Jesus as a sacrificed lamb with **seven** horns and **seven** eyes, representing **seven** spirits of God, underpinning the completed work of atonement, opening the scroll of seven seals and receiving a **sevenfold** acclamation of praise:

The Seven Wounds of Jesus

- On his head (Matt. 27:30; Mark 15:17)
- On his back (Is. 50:6; Matt. 27:26)
- On both hands (Ps. 22:16; Luke 24:40; John 20:25)
- On both feet (Ps. 22:16; Luke 24:40)
- On his side (John 19:34; 20:25)

*But he was wounded for our transgressions;
he was crushed for our iniquities;
upon him was the chastisement that brought us peace, and with his stripes we are healed.
(Is. 53:5)*

The Seven Last Words of Jesus

- "Father, forgive them, for they know not what they do." (Luke 23:34)
- "Truly, I say to you, today you will be with me in Paradise." (Luke 23:43)
- He said to his mother, "Woman, behold, your son!" Then he said to the disciple, "Behold, your mother!" (John 19:26-27)
- "My God, my God, why have you forsaken me?" (Matt. 27:46; Mark 15:34)
- "I thirst" (John 19:28)
- "It is finished" (John 19:30)
- "Father, into your hands I commit my spirit!" (Luke 23:46)

"Truly this was the Son of God!". (Matt. 27:54)

And between the throne and the four living creatures and among the elders I saw a Lamb standing, as though it had been slain, with **seven** horns and with **seven** eyes, which are the **seven** spirits of God sent out into all the earth. And he went and took the scroll from the right hand of him who was seated on the throne …
Then I looked, and I heard around the throne and the living creatures and the elders the voice of many angels, numbering myriads of myriads and thousands of thousands, saying with a loud voice, "Worthy is the Lamb who was slain, to receive **power** and **wealth** and **wisdom** and **might** and **honour** and **glory** and **blessing!**"
(Rev. 5:6-7; 11-12)

SEVEN: THE NUMBER OF PERFECTION

At a higher level the successive stages in God's progressively unfolding plan of salvation have also led some (but by no means all) schools of Biblical interpretation to identify **seven** successive dispensations in Scripture, each linked with an associated covenant:

Dispensation:	Time Period:	Primary Commission:	Associated Covenant:	Covenant made with:	Covenant Sign:	Failure:	Judgement:
Innocence	Creation to Fall (Gen. 1:26 - 3:6)	Multiply, have dominion, tend the earth, avoid the forbidden fruit (Gen. 1:28-29, 2:16-17)	Edenic (Gen. 1:26-29, 2:15-17)	Mankind (Gen. 1:28-29, 2:16-17) (conditional)	Marriage (Gen. 2:21-25)	Disobedience (Gen. 3:6; Hos. 6:7; Rom. 5:12)	Curse on humanity; spiritual and physical death (Gen. 3:15-19)
Conscience	Fall to Flood (Gen. 3:7 - 7:24)	Do what is right; overcome evil (Gen. 3:15; 4:7)	Adamic (Gen. 3:15)	Mankind (Gen. 3:15) (unconditional)	Blood Covering (Gen. 3:21; 4:15)	Wickedness (Gen. 6:5; 2 Pet. 2:5)	Flood (Gen. 7:17-24)
Government	Flood to Call of Abraham (Gen. 8:1-Gen. 11:9)	Multiply, rule, protect innocent blood (Gen. 9:1-7; Rom 13:1-7)	Noahic (Gen. 8:20-9:17; Is. 54:9-10)	Mankind and all Creatures (Gen. 9:9-11) (unconditional)	Rainbow (Gen. 9:12-17)	Rebellion (Gen 11:3-4; Rev. 18:5, 24)	Scattering of humanity (Gen. 11:8-9)
Promise	Call of Abraham to Law of Moses (Gen. 11:10-Ex. 18:27; Gal. 3:17-19)	Believe in God's promises (Gen. 15:6; Rom. 4:1-25)	Abrahamic (Gen. 12:1-3, 13:14-17, 15:1-21; 17:4-21)	Abraham's offspring (Gen. 17:4-21) (unconditional)	Circumcision (Gen. 17:9-14)	Forced manipulation of events (Gen. 16:1-4; 27:5-29; Ex. 2:11-15)	Family division; exile (Gen. 21:8-21; 27:41-45; 37:3-4; Ex. 2:15)
Law	Law of Moses to Death of Christ (Ex.19:1-Matt. 27:51; John 19:30)	Obey the law; remain faithful to God (Deut. 5:1-6:25; Matt. 22:34-40)	Mosaic (Ex. 19:3-6, 20:1-31:18, Deut. 28:1-29:1)	Israel (Ex. 19:3-6; Deut. 28:1; Ps. 147:19-20) (conditional)	Revelation of Sabbath (Ex. 31:13,17; Ezek. 20:12, 20)	Unfaithfulness (2 Kings 17:7-23; 2 Chron. 36:14-21)	Exile from land (2 Kings 17:6; 2 Chron. 36:20-21; Neh. 9:30; Ezek. 36:19)
Grace	Death of Christ to his return (John 1:10-18; Rom. 5:1-21)	Trust in Jesus; make disciples (John 3:16; Matt. 28:19-20)	New (Mark 14:22-24; 1 Cor. 11:23-26; Heb. 13:20)	Jew and Gentile (Eph. 2:11-22) (unconditional)	Baptism (Rom. 6:3); Lord's Supper (Mark 14:22-24; 1 Cor. 11:23-26)	Falling Away; Deception (Matt. 24:10-12; 2 Thess. 2:9-12)	Trumpet and Bowl judgements (Heb. 10:26-31; Rev. 8:2-18:24)
Kingdom	Return of Christ to Final Judgement (1 Cor. 15:24-28; Rev. 20:1-15)	Reign with Christ (Rev. 20:4); Witness to nations (Is. 60:1-3)	New (Jer. 31:31-34; Acts 3:19-21; Rom. 11:25-32)	Israel outwards (Is. 11:10-12; 62:1-3; Ezek. 36:22-37:28) (unconditional)	Divine Glory (Is. 4:5-6; 60:1-21; 62:1-3; 66:18-19) Universal peace (Is. 2:2-4; 11:9)	Final rebellion (Rev. 20:7-9)	Fire and Final Judgement (Rev. 20:9-15)

3. Seven as the number of consummation

All the numbers we have considered in previous chapters seem to signify some measure of completeness and closure. However, the number seven seems to imply a deeper level of consummation and fulfilment, stamped with the very fingerprint of heaven itself.

This association between 'seven' and a wholly completed task is clear in the foundational verse we considered earlier:

> And on the **seventh** day God **finished** his work that he had **done** (Gen. 2:2)

As in Genesis, so also in Revelation:

> Then I saw another sign in heaven, great and amazing, **seven** angels with **seven** plagues, which are the last, for with them the wrath of God is **finished**. (Rev. 15:1)

And likewise in this passage:

> The **seventh** angel poured out his bowl into the air, and a loud voice came out of the temple, from the throne, saying, "It is **done**!" (Rev. 16:17)

Whether in the context of creation or judgement, therefore, we see 'seven' carrying the sense of consummation and completion, even when working against a background of adversity, sin, suffering and judgement.

It is striking, for example, that Enoch (the **seventh** generation in line from Adam) overcame death, the result of man's disobedience, just as Jesus (the **seventy-seventh** in the same line) did in a more absolute way thousands of years later (Gen. 5:24; Jude 14; Luke 3:23-38).

Enoch's grandson Lamech, who lived to **seven hundred and seventy-seven** years, was the father of Noah, who entered the ark with **seven** others, **seven** days before the flood came, taking **seven** pairs of each clean animal with him. After the flood he sent out a dove at **seven**-day intervals to check the waters had subsided (Gen. 5:31; 7:1-10; 8:8-12).

Jacob worked **seven** years for Leah and **seven** for Rachel, fled for **seven** days from his relative Laban and bowed before his estranged brother Esau **seven** times to be reconciled with him. Of his **seventy** descendants alive by the time of his death, his son Joseph foretold **seven** years of plenty and **seven** of famine in Egypt after Pharoah's dream about **seven** cows and **seven** ears of wheat (Gen. 29:18-30; 31:23; 33:3; 41:1-36; 46:27).

Job's friends, who had sat silent for **seven** days and **seven** nights, after he lost his **seven** sons, were told to make an offering of **seven** bullocks and **seven** rams after God turned his life around (Job 1:2, 18-19; 2:13; 42.8).

SEVEN: THE NUMBER OF PERFECTION

A depiction of the battle of Jericho by the French painter Jean Fouquet (c.1420-1481).

Israel under Joshua marched around Jericho **seven** times over the course of a week while **seven** priests blew **seven** trumpets, circling **seven** times on the **seventh** day, causing the walls to collapse (Joshua 6:3-21).

Elijah prayed **seven** times before the drought in Israel was broken (1 Kings 18.44). His successor Elisha told Naaman to bathe in the Jordan **seven** times before he would be healed of his leprosy (2 Kings 5:10).

These examples suggest that, in addition to signifying fulness and completion, the number seven can also sometimes imply an intensification or exponential increase. For instance, the word of God is likened to silver refined and made **seven** times purer (Ps. 12:6); the furnace in Daniel is made **seven** times hotter (Dan. 3:19); the sun in the millennial kingdom will shine **seven** times brighter (Is. 30:26).

The picture of marching round Jericho seven times, with a sevenfold circuit on the last day, may provide a particularly significant model for events in Revelation, where **seven** bowls arise from **seven** trumpets which in turn are concealed within **seven** seals. In Chapter One we saw how the whole book seems to portray 'wheels within wheels' (Ezek. 1:16) – both at a physical level with a concentric rainbow surrounding God's throne, and circles of creatures around it, but also in the spiralling out of events, tracing out the pattern of a scroll steadily unwound when its seals are broken (Rev. 5:1-8:2).

The number seven was already prominent in judgement earlier in scripture: Israel were warned that she would face her enemy in one direction but flee in **seven** if she rejected the LORD (Deut. 28:25); she is exiled for **seventy** years from the land for her idolatry (Jer. 25:11-12; 29:10; Dan. 9:2); while her arch-oppressor Nebuchadnezzar is reduced to madness for **seven** years for failing to acknowledge the ultimate sovereignty of God (Dan. 4:25-33). Jesus in turn issued **seven** stinging rebukes to the Pharisees and teachers of the law in Matthew 23.

A precedent for the escalating sevens in Revelation can also be seen in the book of Leviticus, in God's warning to Israel about the consequences of disobedience:

> "And if in spite of this you will not listen to me, then I will discipline you again **sevenfold** for your sins, ...
>
> "Then if you walk contrary to me and will not listen to me, I will continue striking you, **sevenfold** for your sins ...
>
> "And if by this discipline you are not turned to me but walk contrary to me, then I also will walk contrary to you, and I myself will strike you **sevenfold** for your sins. ...
>
> "But if in spite of this you will not listen to me, but walk contrary to me, then I will walk contrary to you in fury, and I myself will discipline you **sevenfold** for your sins."
> (Lev. 26:18, 21, 23-24, 27-28)

An even earlier example of such 'spirallng sevens' can be seen in Lamech's warning in Genesis (all quotations on page 180 from the New International Version of the Bible):

Above: Stained Glass made in 1862 depicting seven archangels at St Michael and All Angels Church, Brighton.
Below: Seven angels are given seven trumpets (from the Great East Window in York Minster).

> "I have killed a man for wounding me,
> a young man for injuring me.
> If Cain I's avenged **seven** times,
> then Lamech **seventy-seven** times."
> (Gen. 4:23-24)

This passage, of course, meets its remarkable mirror image in the words of Jesus:

> Then Peter came to Jesus and asked, "Lord, how many times shall I forgive my brother or sister who sins against me? Up to **seven** times?"
> Jesus answered, "I tell you, not **seven** times, but **seventy-seven** times."
> (Matt. 18:21-22)

This contrast between absolute judgement and exponential forgiveness leads us in turn to one of the most remarkable sequences of sevens in scripture, which culminates both in God's sovereign act of wiping away sin and his declaration of judgement against the powers of darkness. Praying about the **seventy** years set aside for the captivity of Israel in Babylon, the prophet Daniel receives an extraordinary vision of the future made up of **seventy** 'weeks' of **seven** years each, leading to the coming of a Messiah who would be God's remedy for the sin of the nation:

> '**Seventy "sevens"** are decreed for your people and your holy city to finish transgression, to put an end to sin, to atone for wickedness, to bring in everlasting righteousness, to seal up vision and prophecy and to anoint the Most Holy Place. ... from the time the word goes out to restore and rebuild Jerusalem until the Anointed One, the ruler, comes, there will be **seven "sevens"**, and sixty-two **"sevens"**. ... After the sixty-two **"sevens"**, the Anointed One will be put to death and will have nothing.'
> (Dan. 9:24-26)

Interpretations of the passage differ, as we can see from the contrasting diagrams on the facing page, and controversy remains over the interpretation of the final 'seven' that comes at the end of this period:

> He will confirm a covenant with many for one "seven". In the **middle of the "seven"** he will put an end to sacrifice and offering. (Dan. 9:27)

Whether this refers to Christ's atoning work on the cross, or to a future antichrist figure, as some hold, the division of this final 'seven' into two equal and balancing halves may highlight a significant underlying pattern in scripture, as we will see in the section which follows. Either way, God's purposes are completely accomplished, with the number seven playing a decisive role.

SEVEN: THE NUMBER OF PERFECTION

490 YEARS

"70 weeks (490 years) are determined for your people and for your holy city"
Daniel 9:24-27

7 + 62 weeks = 483 years   Final Week

3 ½ years   3 ½ years

457 B.C.
Command to rebuild Jerusalem

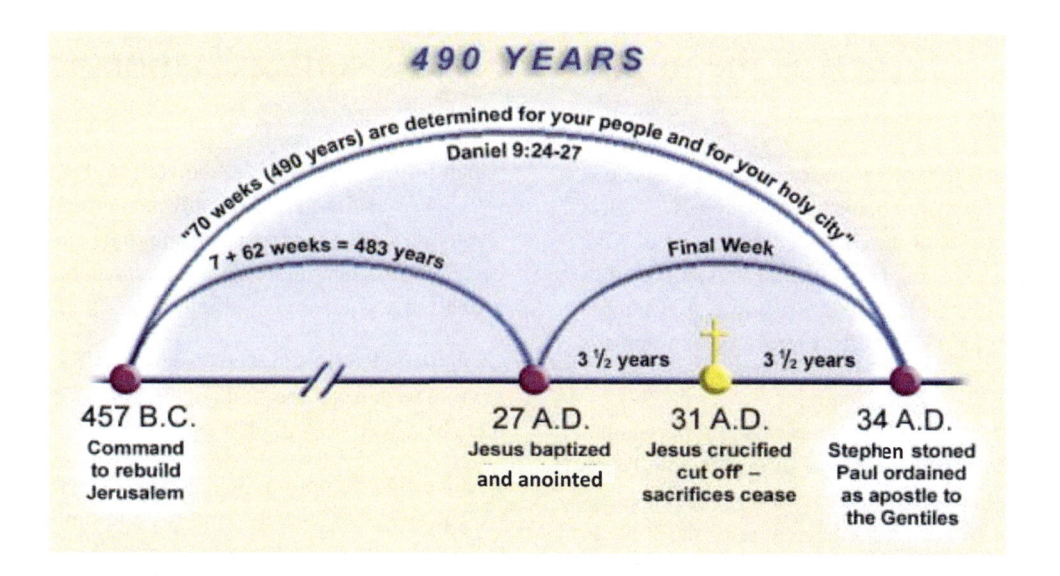

27 A.D.
Jesus baptized and anointed

31 A.D.
Jesus crucified 'cut off' – sacrifices cease

34 A.D.
Stephen stoned Paul ordained as apostle to the Gentiles

The prophet Daniel received a vision of **seventy** 'weeks' of **seven** years each, which would reach their climax in the coming of a Messiah to Israel. As we see from the diagrams above and below, calculating either in solar years from the decree to rebuild the temple in 457 BC, or in lunar years from the later decree given by Artaxerxes to rebuild Jerusalem in 444 BC, takes us exactly to either the baptism or death of Jesus. The second interpretation postpones the final 'week' to a future seven-year period of tribulation which takes place under the rule of the antichrist, to accommodate some passages in the book of Revelation. In both schemes the midpoint of the final seven-year period occupies a position of critical importance.

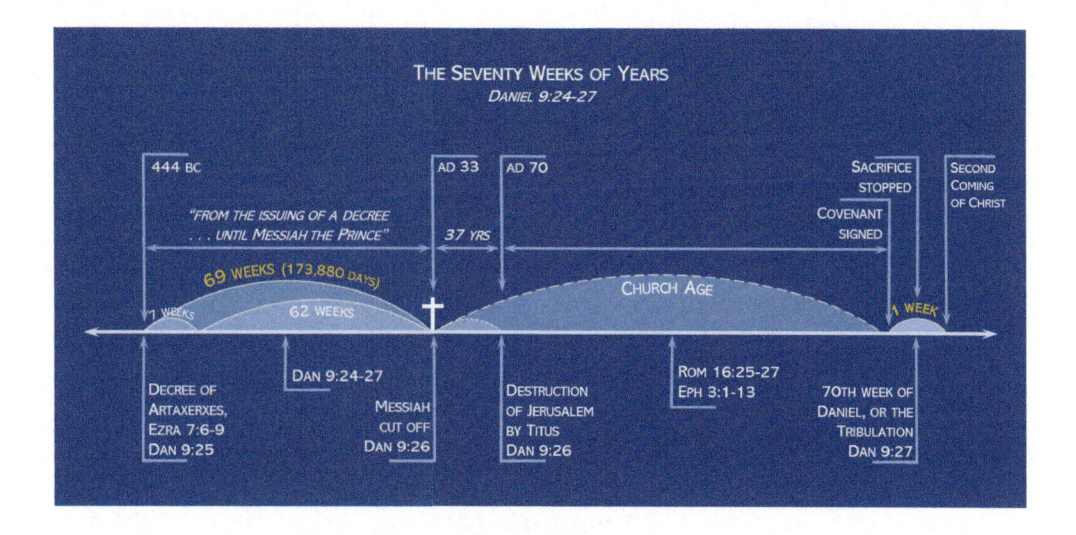

THE SEVENTY WEEKS OF YEARS
Daniel 9:24-27

444 BC — AD 33 — AD 70 — SACRIFICE STOPPED — SECOND COMING OF CHRIST

"FROM THE ISSUING OF A DECREE ... UNTIL MESSIAH THE PRINCE"   37 YRS   COVENANT SIGNED

69 WEEKS (173,880 DAYS)

7 WEEKS   62 WEEKS   CHURCH AGE   1 WEEK

DECREE OF ARTAXERXES, EZRA 7:6-9 DAN 9:25

DAN 9:24-27
MESSIAH CUT OFF
DAN 9:26

DESTRUCTION OF JERUSALEM BY TITUS
DAN 9:26

ROM 16:25-27
EPH 3:1-13

70TH WEEK OF DANIEL, OR THE TRIBULATION
DAN 9:27

4. **Seven** as the number of God's self-revelation

We have explored in some detail in this book how each number in scripture seems to reflect an aspect of the character and nature of God. Thus the number **one** reflects something of God as the source of true identity, the number **two** as the fountain of relationship and the number **three** as the basis for community.

But the number **seven** seems to reflect something still deeper about his inner being. To get a glimpse of this, we need to go back to original 'seven' at the beginning of the Bible in Genesis, where we see the intimate relationship between God's speech and its creative results.

The diagram at the top of the next page shows the close correspondence between the first three days in Genesis and the three days which follow. Remarkably, the verb 'to be', which lies at the very heart of human language, seems to share precisely the same underlying structure in its six corresponding forms and accompanying infinitive.

Given that God uses speech (specifically the verb 'to be') to call creation into being, could there be a deep-seated relationship here?

The question becomes more intriguing when we consider the gateways into the end-time temple shown in a vision to the prophet Ezekiel, a building whose very dimensions were intended to reveal the nature of God to Israel (Ezek. 43:10-11). Here the distinctive structure seems to express exactly the same pattern in spatial terms. We should note that this was the entrance to the place of God's glory:

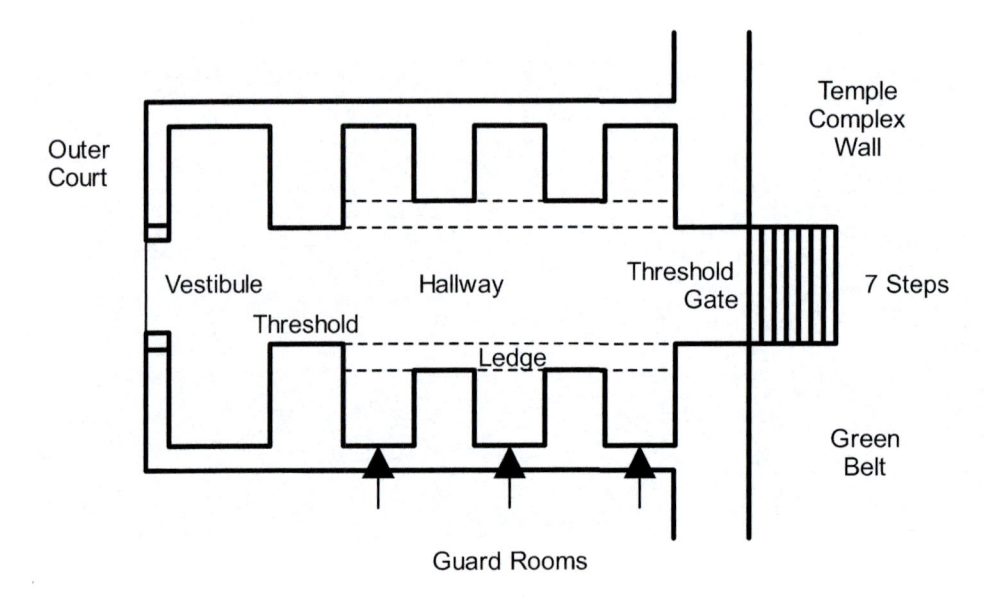

SEVEN: THE NUMBER OF PERFECTION

Top Right: The structure of Genesis 1 is best understood when arranged in two columns showing three successive stages, the second column fulfilling the blank canvas of the first.

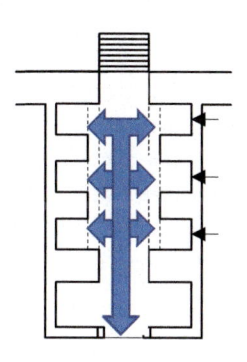

FORMING:
- DAY ONE: Light and Darkness
- DAY TWO: Waters and Sky
- DAY THREE: Land and Plants

FILLING:
- DAY FOUR: Lights for Day and Night
- DAY FIVE: Fish and Birds
- DAY SIX: Land Animals; Mankind

DAY SEVEN: Sabbath Rest

Bottom Right: The structure of a verb is best understood when arranged in two columns showing it relating to three successive persons, each with a singular and plural form. The Bible tells us that God *spoke* creation into being, with all three members of the Trinity involved. Both diagrams bear an uncanny resemblance to the entrance to the temple described in Ezekiel's vision (above).

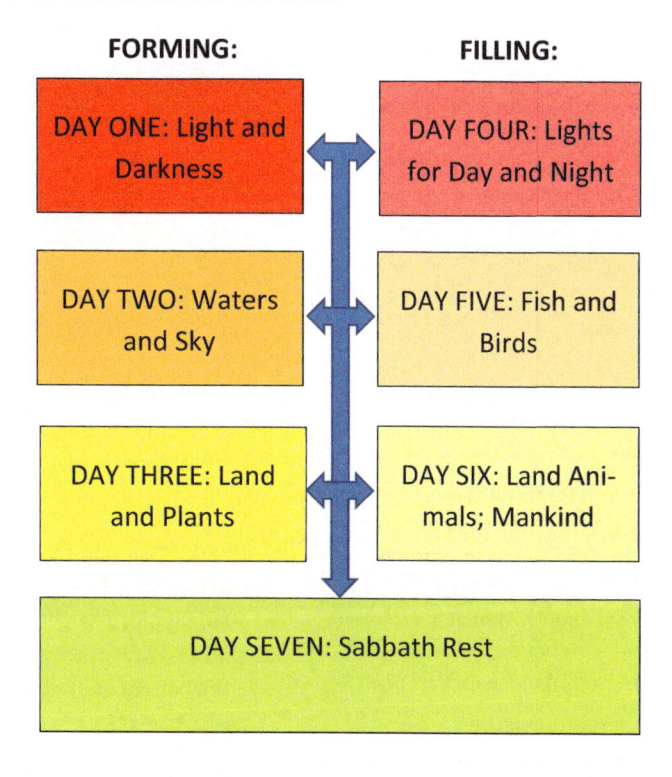

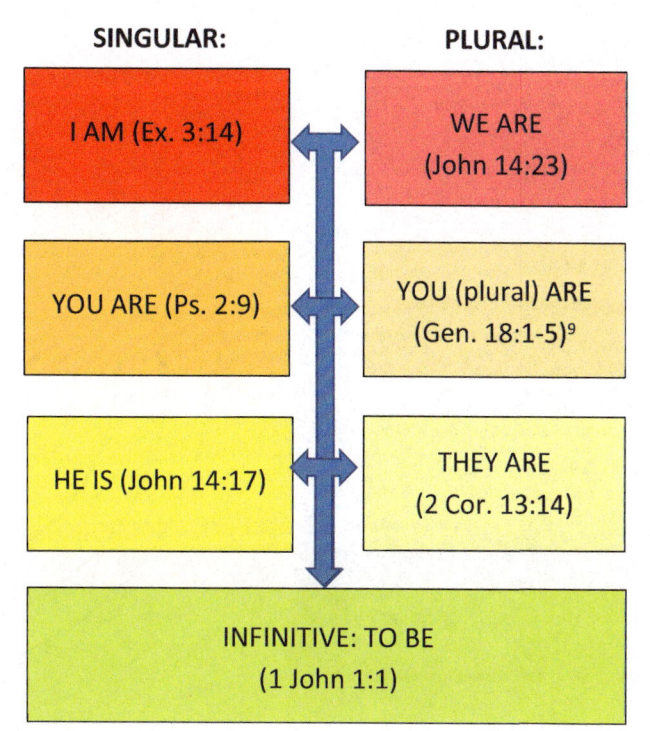

SINGULAR:
- I AM (Ex. 3:14)
- YOU ARE (Ps. 2:9)
- HE IS (John 14:17)

PLURAL:
- WE ARE (John 14:23)
- YOU (plural) ARE (Gen. 18:1-5)[9]
- THEY ARE (2 Cor. 13:14)

INFINITIVE: TO BE (1 John 1:1)

The Lampstand

The central candle of the Menorah or golden lampstand is known as the *shamash* candle. It is also referred to as the 'servant' or 'helper' candle. This candle is the one that is lit first, and is then used to light the other candles, so it 'serves' the other candles by enabling them to burn.

In the larger Menorah used in the Jewish celebration of Hannukah, the shamash candle is placed at a level higher than the other candles. Although it is lowered to serve the other candles, it is exalted to the highest place.

Jesus described himself as 'the light of the world' (John 8:12), but calls us to shine our own light together with his (Matt. 5:14). He came to serve, but calls us in turn to serve others (John 13:12-17). He was in very nature God, but emptied himself and became nothing that we might become the righteousness of God through him.

And being found in human form, he humbled himself by becoming obedient to the point of death, even death on a cross. Therefore God has highly exalted him and bestowed on him the name that is above every name, so that at the name of Jesus every knee should bow, in heaven and on earth and under the earth. (Phil. 2:8-10)

Indeed this 'deep structure' of glory seems to appear all over scripture, an example being the prophecy of the Messiah's coming in Isaiah 11:2:

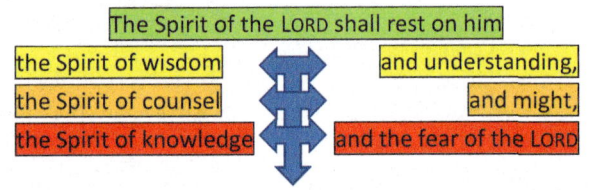

The Spirit of the LORD shall rest on him
the Spirit of wisdom and understanding,
the Spirit of counsel and might,
the Spirit of knowledge and the fear of the LORD

Could God be revealing something very profound about his identity here, as the true 'I am' from which everything else proceeds?

An answer to this question might be found in the shape of the Menorah, the sevenfold lampstand in the tabernacle, whose three concentric semicircles, moulded from a single piece of gold, seem to provide a veiled hint of God as Trinity (see page 71), following the same underlying pattern of branches that we have seen on the previous two pages.

As one example, the verse shown above could also be seen as a pictorial representation of a Menorah shape:

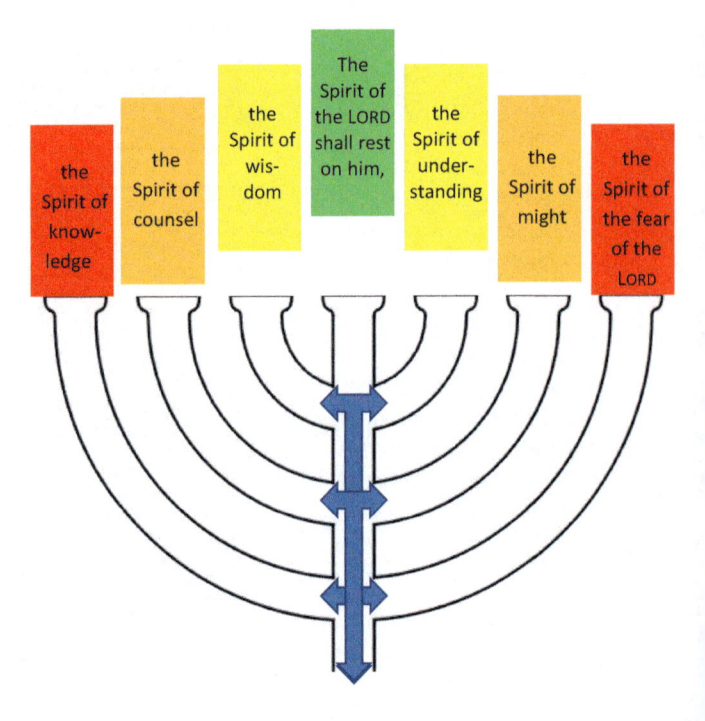

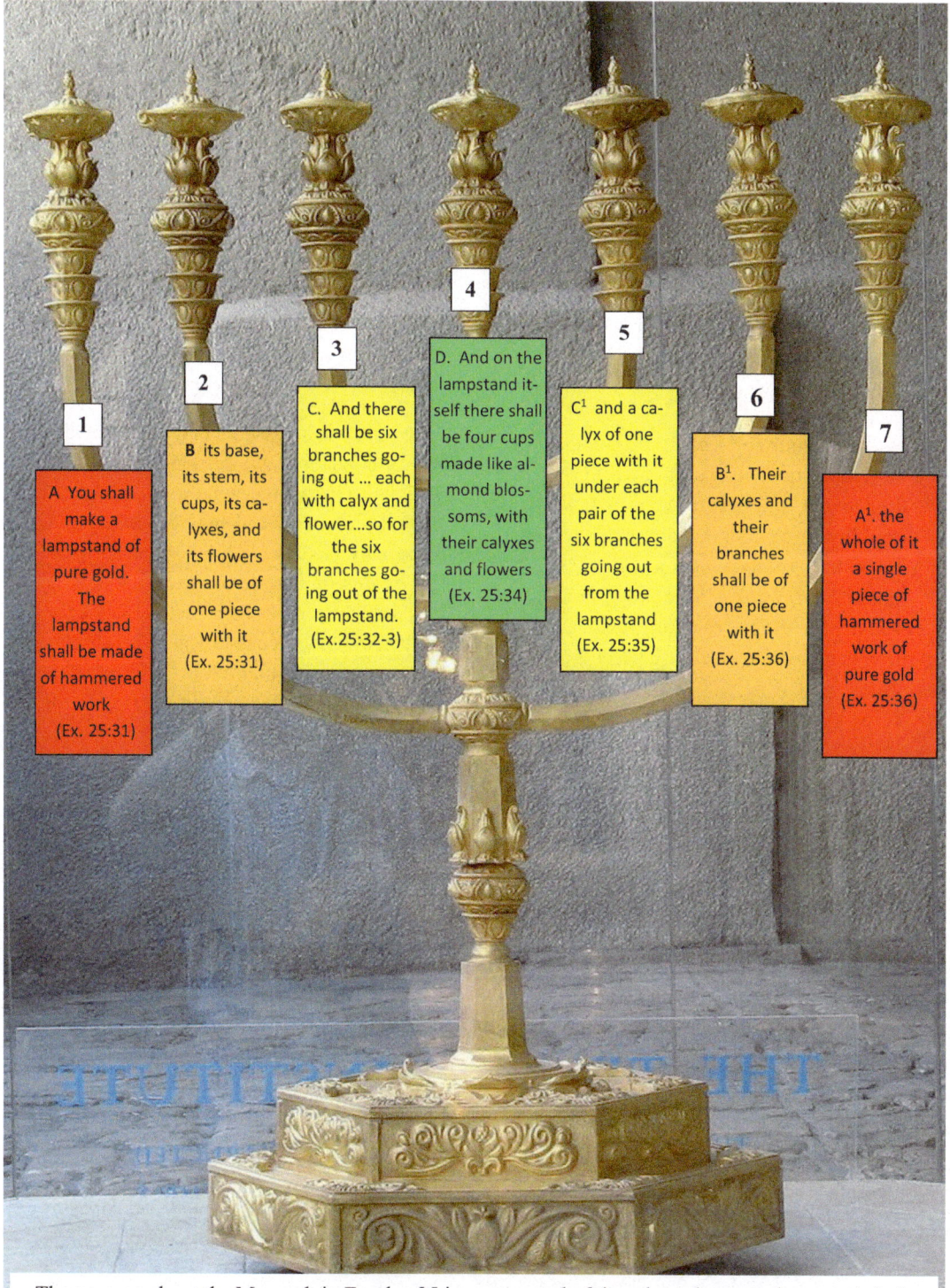

1 — A. You shall make a lampstand of pure gold. The lampstand shall be made of hammered work (Ex. 25:31)

2 — B. its base, its stem, its cups, its calyxes, and its flowers shall be of one piece with it (Ex. 25:31)

3 — C. And there shall be six branches going out ... each with calyx and flower...so for the six branches going out of the lampstand. (Ex.25:32-3)

4 — D. And on the lampstand itself there shall be four cups made like almond blossoms, with their calyxes and flowers (Ex. 25:34)

5 — C[1] and a calyx of one piece with it under each pair of the six branches going out from the lampstand (Ex. 25:35)

6 — B[1]. Their calyxes and their branches shall be of one piece with it (Ex. 25:36)

7 — A[1]. the whole of it a single piece of hammered work of pure gold (Ex. 25:36)

The passage about the Menorah in Exodus 25 is constructed of three branches round a central shaft, just like the object it is describing.

This sevenfold aspect of the Messiah's ministry might help to explain the later prophecy in Zechariah, where the coming deliverer is described as a 'stone with **seven** eyes' who, as we have seen, would cleanse the land of sin in a single day (Zech. 3.9). The link with the Menorah is strengthened in the next chapter, where Zechariah is shown the **seven** lamps illuminated on the Menorah and is asked:

> "What do you see?" I said, "I see, and behold, a lampstand all of gold, with a bowl on the top of it, and **seven** lamps on it, with **seven** lips on each of the lamps that are on the top of it. ... Then the angel who talked with me answered and said to me ..."These **seven** are the eyes of the LORD, which range through the whole earth." (Zech. 4:2,5,10)

The connection between these 'seven eyes' and the ministry of Jesus is further deepened in Revelation, where, as we noticed earlier, the exalted Lamb of God is also described as having seven eyes, which are 'the seven spirits of God sent out into the world'.

A further connection between the number seven and the coming ministry of Jesus can be seen in Proverbs 9, where we read the following statement:

> Wisdom has built her house; she has hewn her **seven** pillars. ... (Prov. 9.1)

We noted in Chapter One that the Old Testament figure of Wisdom seems to be a figure for the coming of Christ. The connection between Jesus and Wisdom is repeatedly emphasised in the New Testament (if we look at 1 Cor. 1:24 and Col. 2:3; or compare Prov. 1.28 with John 7:34), while the striking invitation from Wisdom to eat bread and wine following this verse in Proverbs might remind us of the sharing of the Lord's supper (Prov. 9:5; Mark 14:22-24).

These different passages may help provide a background for the way in which, particularly in John's Gospel, the number **seven** is used to underline the divine identity of Jesus. This is especially the case with the so-called 'I am' statements. In Chapter One we saw how Jesus used the phrase 'I am', central to the revelation of God's being, to declare his absolute identity with God himself. In the Greek of the New Testament this appears as two words, containing **seven** letters: *egō eimi*.

There are **seven** passages in John's Gospel where *egō eimi* is tied to a specific description of Christ:

> **I am** the bread of life (John 6:35/41)
> **I am** the light of the world (8:12)
> **I am** the door (10:7/9)
> **I am** the good shepherd (10:11/14)
> **I am** the resurrection and the life (11:25)
> **I am** the way, and the truth, and the life (14:6)
> **I am** the true vine (15:1/5)

There are **seven** other passages in John's Gospel where it is used by Jesus in absolute terms (translations from the Common English Bible and the New American Bible):

Jesus said to her, "**I Am**—the one who speaks with you." (4:26)

He said to them, "**I Am.** Don't be afraid." (6:20)

"If you don't believe that **I Am**, you will die in your sins." (8:24)

"When you lift up the Son of Man, then you will realize that **I AM**" (8:28)

"I assure you," Jesus replied, "before Abraham was, **I Am.**" (8:58)

"I'm telling you this now, before it happens, so that when it does happen you will believe that **I Am.**" (13:19)

He said to them, "**I Am.**" (18:5)

Jesus spoke unto them, saying, Trust *that* **I AM**; be not afraid. (Matt. 14:27)

Be of good cheer; **I AM**; be not afraid. (Mark 6:50)

Many will come in my name, proclaiming, '**I AM**,' and they will deceive many people. (Mark 13:6)

Jesus said, "**I AM**, and 'you will see the Son of Man seated at the right hand of the Power' and 'coming with the clouds of heaven.'" (Mark 14:62)

... many will come in my name, proclaiming, '**I AM**,' and, 'The time has come.' (Luke 21:8)

"Are you, then, the Son of God?" He answered them, "You said it—**I AM**." (Luke 22:70)

See my hands and my feet, that **I AM** he (Luke 24:39)

There are also **seven** absolute uses linked to Jesus in the three other gospels (translations from the International Standard Version, Jubilee Bible and *Young's Literal Translation*):

We are faced with a choice, therefore: either we have a remarkable coincidence, a suspicious level of collusion between the Biblical authors - or a divine signature!

FINGERPRINT

Finally, on a much larger scale, the Menorah provides a picture of the seven annual feasts of Israel laid down in Leviticus, and how they, too, are fulfilled in the coming of Jesus. The three spring feasts, which come in close succession, seem to point ahead towards the first coming of Christ, just as the three autumn feasts announce his return. Between these, at some distance, comes the Feast of Weeks (later known as Pentecost) which, within such a larger scheme, would represent the church age in which we now live:

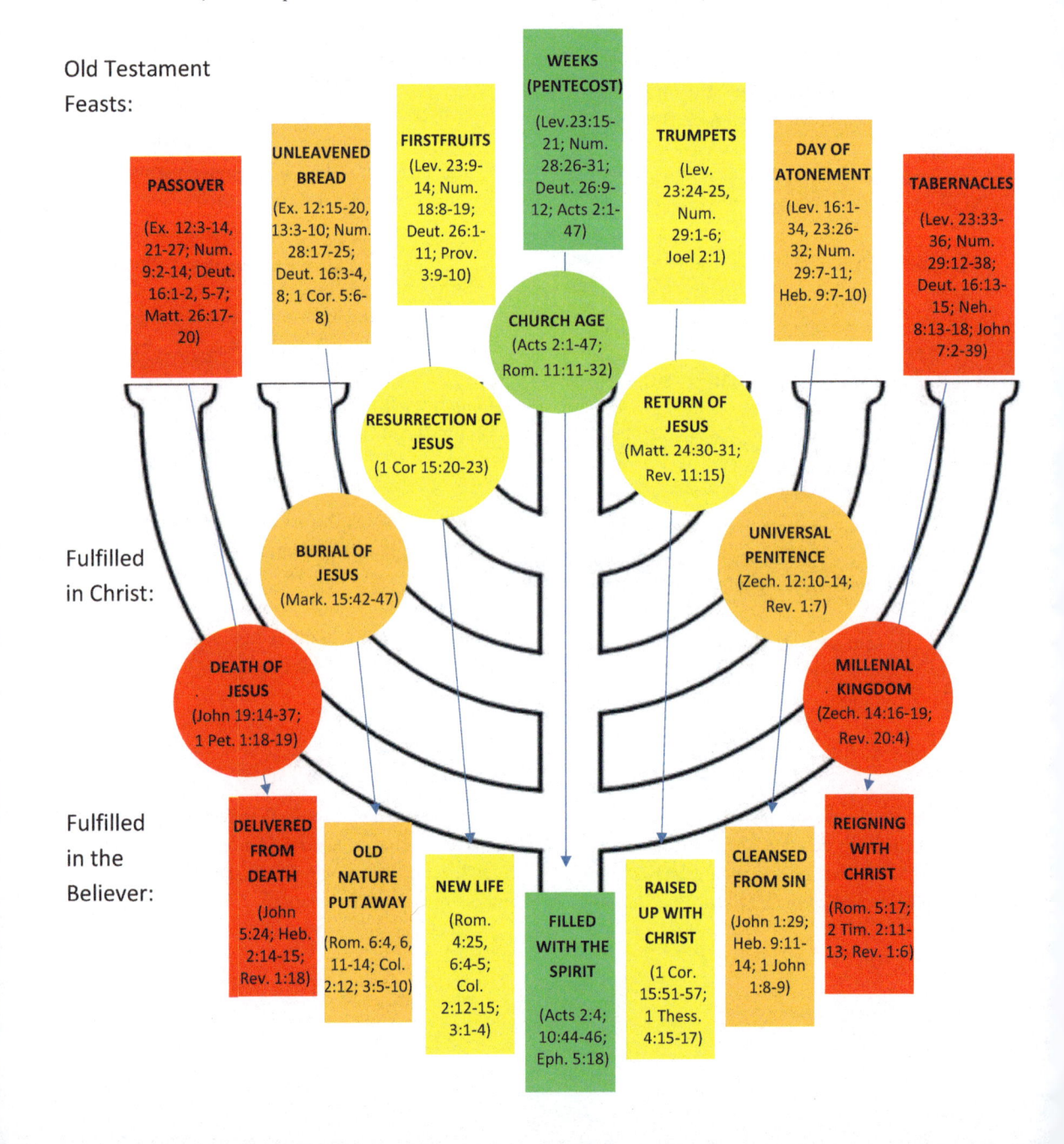

Old Testament Feasts:

- **PASSOVER** (Ex. 12:3-14, 21-27; Num. 9:2-14; Deut. 16:1-2, 5-7; Matt. 26:17-20)
- **UNLEAVENED BREAD** (Ex. 12:15-20, 13:3-10; Num. 18:8-19; Num. 28:17-25; Deut. 16:3-4, 8; 1 Cor. 5:6-8)
- **FIRSTFRUITS** (Lev. 23:9-14; Num. 18:8-19; Deut. 26:1-11; Prov. 3:9-10)
- **WEEKS (PENTECOST)** (Lev. 23:15-21; Num. 28:26-31; Deut. 26:9-12; Acts 2:1-47)
- **TRUMPETS** (Lev. 23:24-25, Num. 29:1-6; Joel 2:1)
- **DAY OF ATONEMENT** (Lev. 16:1-34, 23:26-32; Num. 29:7-11; Heb. 9:7-10)
- **TABERNACLES** (Lev. 23:33-36; Num. 29:12-38; Deut. 16:13-15; Neh. 8:13-18; John 7:2-39)

Fulfilled in Christ:

- **DEATH OF JESUS** (John 19:14-37; 1 Pet. 1:18-19)
- **BURIAL OF JESUS** (Mark. 15:42-47)
- **RESURRECTION OF JESUS** (1 Cor 15:20-23)
- **CHURCH AGE** (Acts 2:1-47; Rom. 11:11-32)
- **RETURN OF JESUS** (Matt. 24:30-31; Rev. 11:15)
- **UNIVERSAL PENITENCE** (Zech. 12:10-14; Rev. 1:7)
- **MILLENIAL KINGDOM** (Zech. 14:16-19; Rev. 20:4)

Fulfilled in the Believer:

- **DELIVERED FROM DEATH** (John 5:24; Heb. 2:14-15; Rev. 1:18)
- **OLD NATURE PUT AWAY** (Rom. 4:25, 6:4, 6, 11-14; Col. 2:12; 3:5-10)
- **NEW LIFE** (Rom. 4:25, 6:4-5; Col. 2:12-15; 3:1-4)
- **FILLED WITH THE SPIRIT** (Acts 2:4; 10:44-46; Eph. 5:18)
- **RAISED UP WITH CHRIST** (1 Cor. 15:51-57; 1 Thess. 4:15-17)
- **CLEANSED FROM SIN** (John 1:29; Heb. 9:11-14; 1 John 1:8-9)
- **REIGNING WITH CHRIST** (Rom. 5:17; 2 Tim. 2:11-13; Rev. 1:6)

Seven as a Divine Watermark

Ivan Panin was a literary critic and agnostic in the late nineteenth century who after converting to Christianity discovered thousands of extraordinary numeric patterns in the Bible, many constructed around the number seven.

In the very first verse of the Old Testament, for example, he pointed out:

- There are 7 Hebrew words in total containing 28 Hebrew letters (7×4).
- The first three Hebrew words (translated 'In the beginning God created') consist of 14 letters (7×2), and the remaining four words (translated 'the heavens and the earth') also consist of 14 letters (7×2).
- The fourth and fifth words combined consist of 7 letters, as do the sixth and seventh words together.
- The Hebrew letters in the three nouns (God, heaven and earth) add up to 14 (7×2), as do the Hebrew letters in the four other words.
- The numeric value in Hebrew of the first, middle and last letters in the verse is 133 (7×19).

Turning to the first eleven verses of the New Testament (the first part of Matthew's genealogy of Jesus), Panin found even more elaborate sevenfold patterns. For example, he observed that

- The passage has a vocabulary of 49 different words (7×7), 28 of which (7×4) begin with a vowel and 21 (7×3) begin with a consonant.
- In total these 49 vocabulary words contain 266 letters (7×38), the sum of whose factors is 28 (7×4) while the sum of its figures is 14 (7×2).
- Of these 266 letters, 140 (7×20), are vowels, and 126 (18×7) are consonants.
- 14 (7×2) of the words occur only once in the passage, while 35 (7×5) occur more than once.
- 42 (7×6) of these words occur in only one grammatical form, while 7 appear in more than one form.
- 42 (7×6) of the words are nouns, and of these 35 (7×5) are proper nouns, which, allowing for repetition, appear 63 (7×3) times in all.
- 28 (7×4) of these proper nouns are male ancestors of Jesus, which, allowing for repetition, appear 63 (7×3) times in all.
- The number of compound nouns is 7, containing a total of 49 letters (7×7)

While these are both taken from highly patterned and structured passages, Panin also found wide-ranging mathematical patterns across scripture, including the disputed final chapter of Mark's Gospel. The conclusion he came to was that no mere human being could have constructed such elaborately coded texts. Rather, they point us inevitably to an infinitely wise and loving Creator.

It does seem extraordinary that, in an age when we scour the universe in a desperate search for intelligent life, the answer may actually have been staring us in the face for thousands of years!

The words of the LORD are pure words,
like silver refined in a furnace on the ground,
*purified **seven** times.*
(Psalm 12:6)

Seven Disciples Named in John's Gospel

1. Andrew (1:40)
2. Peter (1:42)
3. Philip (1:43)
4. Nathanael (1:45)
5. Thomas (11:16)
6. Judas Iscariot (12:4)
7. The other Judas (14:22)

Seven Other Men Named in John's Gospel

1. John the Baptist (1:6)
2. Nicodemus (3:1)
3. Lazarus (11:1)
4. Annas (18:13)
5. Caiaphas (18:24)
6. Pontius Pilate (18:29)
7. Joseph of Arimathea (19:38)

The Seven Women in John's Gospel

1. Mary, mother of Jesus (2:3-5)
2. Samaritan woman (4:7)
3. Woman caught in adultery (8:3)
4. Mary, the sister of Lazarus (11:1)
5. Martha (11:1)
6. Mary, wife of Clopas (19:25)
7. Mary Magdalene (19:25)

The Seven Signs in John's Gospel

1. Turning water into wine (2:1-11)
2. Healing the nobleman's son (4:46-54)
3. Healing the man at Bethesda (5:1-14)
4. Feeding of the five thousand (6:1-14)
5. Walking on water (6:16-21)
6. Healing the man born blind (9:1-7)
7. Raising of Lazarus (11:1-44)

Seven Sabbath Miracles across the Gospels

1. The withered hand (Matt. 12:10-13)
2. The unclean spirit (Mark 1:21-26)
3. Peter's mother-in-law (Mark 1:29-31)
4. The crippled woman (Luke 13:10-16)
5. The man with dropsy (Luke 14:2-4)
6. The paralysed man (John 5:2-9)
7. The man born blind (John 9:1-14)

Seven Church Gifts in Romans 12

1. Prophecy (12:6)
2. Service (12:7)
3. Teaching (12:7)
4. Exhortation (12:8)
5. Generosity (12:8)
6. Leadership (12:8)
7. Mercy (12:8)

Seven Foundations in Ephesians 4

1. One body (4:4)
2. One Spirit (4:4)
3. One hope (4:4)
4. One Lord (4:5)
5. One faith (4:5)
6. One baptism (4:5)
7. One God and Father of all (4:6)

Seven Facets of Wisdom in James

1. Pure (3:17)
2. Peaceable (3:17)
3. Gentle (3:17)
4. Open to reason (3:17)
5. Full of mercy and good fruits (3:17)
6. Impartial (3:17)
7. Sincere (3:17)

Seven Churches in Revelation 2-3

1. Ephesus (2:1-7)
2. Smyrna (2:8-11)
3. Pergamum (2:12-17)
4. Thyatira (2:18-29)
5. Sardis (3:1-6)
6. Philadelphia (3:7-13)
7. Laodicea (3:14-22)

Seven Titles of Jesus in Revelation 2-3

1. The one who holds **seven** stars and walks among **seven** golden lampstands (2:1)
2. The first and the last, who died and came to life (2:8)
3. The one with the sharp two-edged sword (2:12)
4. The Son of God, with eyes like a flame of fire, and feet like burnished bronze (2:18)
5. The one who has the **seven** spirits of God and the **seven** stars (3:1)
6. The holy one, the true one, who has the key of David (3:7)
7. The Amen, the faithful and true witness, the beginning of God's creation (3:14)

Seven Gifts of Christ in Revelation 2-3

1. The tree of life in the paradise of God (2:7)
2. The crown of life (2:10)
3. Hidden manna, and a white stone with a new name written on (2:17)
4. Authority over the nations, and the morning star (2:26-28)
5. White garments (3:5)
6. Sharing Christ's name (3:12)
7. Sharing Christ's throne (3:21)

Seven Blessings in Revelation

1. Blessed is the one who reads aloud the words of this prophecy (1:3)
2. Blessed are the dead who die in the Lord (14:13)
3. Blessed is the one who stays awake, keeping his garments on (16:15)
4. Blessed are those who are invited to the marriage supper of the Lamb (19:9)
5. Blessed and holy is the one who shares in the first resurrection (20:6)
6. Blessed is the one who keeps the words of the prophecy of this book (22:7)
7. Blessed are those who wash their robes (22:14)

The Sabbath Day by William Teulon Blandford Fletcher (1858–1936), displayed in Worcester City Art Gallery and Museum

5. **Seven** as God's gift to mankind

This chapter has opened up in a very small way the wonders of the number seven. To do the number full justice (together with its multiples such as 14, 42 and 70) would require a whole book in its own right. It is sufficient here to underline, as we have already shown, that the coming of Jesus represents its ultimate embodiment.

We saw at the beginning of this chapter how God had already communicated the saving power symbolised by the number seven through the revelation of the Sabbath. For Israel, this was to be kept as a sign of God's special covenant relationship with them:

> "Therefore the people of Israel shall keep the Sabbath, observing the Sabbath throughout their generations, as a covenant for ever. It is a sign for ever between me and the people of Israel that in six days the Lord made heaven and earth, and on the **seventh** day he rested and was refreshed.'".
> (Ex. 31:16-17)

It applied not just as a rhythm for days, but for weeks (a cycle of **seven** weeks marked the transition from Firstfruits to the Feast of Weeks in the Old Testament, just as it now does from Easter to Pentecost in the Christian calendar).

Beyond this it applied to years (after **seven** years a slave had to go free) and 'weeks' of years (after **seven** of these **seven-**year cycles, at the Year of Jubilee, all property had to be restored to its original owner:

> "You shall count **seven** weeks of years, **seven** times **seven** years, so that the time of the **seven** weeks of years shall give you **forty-nine** years. Then you shall sound the loud trumpet on the tenth day of the **seventh** month. On the Day of Atonement you shall sound the trumpet throughout all your land. And you shall consecrate the fiftieth year, and proclaim liberty throughout the land to all its inhabitants. It shall be a jubilee for you, when each of you shall return to his property and each of you shall return to his clan. (Lev. 25:8-10)

It therefore became a sign of rest, renewal and restoration, and ultimately a sign of the coming Messianic age (Is. 61:1-9; Luke 4:16-21; Acts 3:19-21).

Taken together, this represents the most wonderful news for the believer. In traditional religion, including much of what masquerades as 'Christianity', the road to salvation is charted by keeping to a set of rules.

The Revolutionary Power of the Sabbath

Observance of the Sabbath is the only one of the ten commandments not specifically taught in the New Testament. Yet the message behind it seems to underpin the revolutionary nature of the gospel itself, God's free gift of salvation to all people.

By the time of Jesus, the Sabbath seems to have degenerated into an observance aimed primarily at earning God's favour. Indeed, we hear about it in the gospels mainly because Jesus is considered by the religious leaders to have broken it.

However, the Sabbath, a day where no work of any kind was to be done, pictures in its original context the unconditional grace of God in liberating his people:

> You shall remember that you were a slave in the land of Egypt, and the LORD your God brought you out from there **with a mighty hand and an outstretched arm**. Therefore the LORD your God commanded you to keep the Sabbath day (Deut. 5:15).

If creation can be understood as a temple, the Sabbath rest might be said to represent the Holy of Holies. It provided a picture of the Promised Land (Deut. 12:10-12); of universal redemption (Ex. 23.12); of the millenium to come (Is. 66:18-23); a picture, indeed, of heaven itself (Neh. 9:14; Rev. 14:13).

Above all, it emphasises what God has unilaterally **DONE FOR US,** not the things **DONE BY US**.

The Sabbath is reminder that we cannot make ourselves righteous or holy through our own actions: it is only God who can do this. For instance, God tells Ezekiel that '**I gave them my Sabbaths** as a sign between us, so they would know that **I the LORD made them holy**.' (Ezek. 20:12 NIV: see also Ex. 31.13)

Rather, the Sabbath points ultimately to Jesus' finished work on the cross, through which alone we can enter into God's eternal rest:

> 'So then, there remains a Sabbath rest for the people of God, for whoever has entered God's rest has also rested from his works as God did from his ... Let us then with confidence draw near to the throne of grace, that we may receive mercy and find grace to help in time of need'. (Heb. 4:9-10, 16)

By trusting in Christ we no longer need to work for our salvation. Paul writes:

> For by grace you have been saved through faith. And this is not your own doing; it is the gift of God, not a result of works, so that no one may boast. (Eph. 2:8-9)

The wonderful news is that Jesus has entered into that Holy Place on our behalf as our representative, having completed his work for us (Heb. 4:9; 10:11-13). By trusting fully in this, rather than the tyranny of relying on our own works, we can take to heart Jesus' wonderful invitation to each one of us:

> "Come to me, all who labour and are heavy laden, and I will give you rest. Take my yoke upon you, and learn from me, for I am gentle and lowly in heart, and you will find rest for your souls. For my yoke is easy, and my burden is light." (Matt. 11:28-30)

Then the Lord answered him, "You hypocrites! Does not each of you on the Sabbath untie his ox or his donkey from the manger and lead it away to water it? And ought not this woman, a daughter of Abraham whom Satan bound for eighteen years, be loosed from this bond on the Sabbath day?" As he said these things, all his adversaries were put to shame, and all the people rejoiced at all the glorious things that were done by him. (Luke 13:15-17)

The amazing news of the gospel is that, by contrast, Jesus has completely obeyed these rules *on our behalf* (Rom. 8:1-4; Col. 2:10-15). Rather than trying to earn anything through our own merits, which the Bible describes as 'filthy rags' before God (Is. 64:6), we can simply trust in the completed work of Jesus on the cross for us.

All the good works God calls us to do flow out as a *consequence* of this, rather than being a *precondition* that we can never fully meet. That is why the **seven**-day principle of restoration (see the box opposite) is such an amazing revelation. Not only does it offer the possibility of much-needed refreshment and recuperation, but it enshrines at a deeper level the principle that we can rest in Christ's completed work.

While people in history with a religious mindset have tried to enforce the Sabbath principle as a set of rules, it is, in fact, a wonderful charter of liberation. Forsaking our own efforts, we can enjoy the riches of God's free gift to us, and discover the peace that alone flows out of that. It is not just about a day in the week, but an entire way of life.

The **seventh** 'I am' statement that Jesus makes in John's Gospel is a beautiful invitation to abide in him:

> "I am the vine, you are the branches. He who abides in Me, and I in him, bears much fruit; for without Me you can do nothing.
> (John. 15:5 NKJV)

This is not simply an invitation, however, to be passive recipients of the peace that he gives: God calls us to carry it into the world and to pass it on to others (2 Cor. 5:19-20). It is not a call for us to withdraw, but an empowerment to advance!

Indeed, just as the vine is a picture both of Christ himself, and the sum total of all believers who abide in him as branches, so too is the Menorah, the sevenfold golden lampstand which has featured heavily in this chapter. Resembling the vine in its multiple buds and branches, it points both to the person of Christ himself (Rev. 5:6), and to the church, which is his body (Eph. 1:22-23; Rev. 1:20).

Each of us, then, is called to shine out for him. Jesus is the light of the world (John 8:12), but so, too, are we (Matt. 5:14). When we radiate that light together in unity, the darkness has to retreat, a lesson we can learn from the Old Testament:

> The LORD said to Moses ... "When you set up the lamps, see that **all seven** light up the area in front of the lampstand.'"
> (Num. 8:1-2 NIV)

Let us be bold and fearless, then, in being his lights in a dark place (Phil. 2:15), standing together in love (Phil. 2:1-4), and carrying his life-changing message of salvation and peace to a bruised a hurting world.

Chapter Eight

Infinity and Beyond

The Voyage Beyond Number

1. Beyond Counting

So much of our lives today is dominated by numbers. They control our finances and time, and the way we organise and plan our lives. We become a statistic when we are born, and another statistic when we die.

Yet those who have accepted the new life that Jesus offers are being prepared for a realm in which the tyranny of human numbers will become a thing of the past. We will instead be overwhelmed by the glory and greatness of God beyond anything we have ever experienced on earth.

God, the author of mathematics, transcends number as he transcends space and time. The book of Job hints at this this when it declares:

This contrast between what can and cannot be counted is apparent in Chapter 7 of Revelation. At the beginning of the chapter we see clear numerical totals for the servants of God remaining on earth, but in heaven there is a great multitude that 'no one could number' (7:9).

Time, too, will be changed. At the end of Revelation 'the old order of things has passed away' (Rev. 21:4 NIV) suggesting a new way of thinking about time. Although days and months will continue to exist in some form (21:25; 22:2) the nature of time becomes open-ended (22:5), as the last verse of 'Amazing Grace' reminds us:

> ಸಿಂಧ
> "He is wise in heart and mighty in strength ... who does great things beyond searching out, and marvellous things **beyond number**."
> (Job 9:4, 10)
> ಸಿಂಧ

> ಸಿಂಧ
> When we've been there ten thousand years,
> Bright shining as the sun,
> We've no less days to sing God's praise
> Than when we first begun.
> ಸಿಂಧ

The Baptistry Window of Coventry Cathedral, designed by Patrick Reyntiens and Basil Spence. The absence of clear geometric shapes or pictorial images typical of more traditional stained glass points us to a higher level of reality, where time and space are understood in different terms.

With their receding perspective, domes have been used traditionally to convey the idea of heaven and eternity, with God at the centre. Above: the Dome of the Monastery of the New Jerusalem in Istria, Russia. Below: Cupola of St Steven's Basilica, Budapest (photo by Carlos Delgado).

This is not to deny the huge importance that numbers still hold in heaven: their symbolism plays out unceasingly throughout Revelation. But there they exist primarily as patterns and pointers to the glory of God, rather than as ends in themselves. The day will come when our lives will no longer be driven by targets or schedules, but by the undiluted life of God himself.

So often human arithmetic limits God because we treat it as a closed system which shuts him out. This may be what provoked God to anger when David counted the fighting men in 1 Chronicles 21, trusting in his own natural resources rather than God's. Likewise, faced with the challenge to feed five thousand people, the disciples responded with purely mathematical rather than divine reasoning (John 6:7), missing the heart of what Jesus wanted them to learn.

Christ's response in this situation, by contrast, was to turn mathematics on its head. In his hands five loaves and two fish were imbued with life-like properties of multiplication. The final result was that there was far more *left over* at the end than had existed at the beginning.

The life of God is boundless and never-ending. And it appears that he has left an imprint of this even within mathematics itself. We can see this in the one value, which when added to any finite number will always produce the *same* end result, irrespective of what we started with.

This mysterious quantity is infinity. It is often represented as a figure 8 on its side, as follows: ∞

It may be difficult to get our head round the idea of infinity. It literally means something that never ends. It occupies a completely different order to countable things. Even multiplying unimaginably large numbers cannot get us remotely close to it. It lies completely outside the realm of our everyday experience.

Something of a taste of infinity can, however, be gained from the end of John's gospel. Here we read the following:

> ೫೦೦೩
> Now there are also many other things that Jesus did. Were every one of them to be written, I suppose that the world itself could not contain the books that would be written. (John 21:25)
> ೫೦೦೩

To get a sense of perspective here, the complete list of all the things that the most active human being accomplishes might fill an average-sized public library at most. But it pales into insignificance in contrast with the limitless activity of Christ, who has been working continuously since the beginning of time (Col. 1:17; Heb. 1:3). The Greek says, literally, 'the *cosmos* itself could not contain the books that would be written'.

In fact, because we can't attach a precise value to it, infinity isn't strictly speaking a number at all, and therefore can't be dealt with by normal arithmetic. However, a special branch of maths using the 'extended real number line' has been set up which is able to explore it. It tells us that, for example:

Complex Numbers

The natural number sequence containing the series of numbers we are familiar with (-2, -1, 0, +1, +2 and so on) can be thought of as a one-dimensional line. But mathematicians have conceived of a two-dimensional plane of numbers on either side of this which makes new kinds of arithmetic possible. These numbers are called *complex numbers*. These numbers seem to defy common sense, and yet much of the technology we use today relies upon them.

In the same way, the supernatural realm, about which many people scarcely have any awareness, exerts a huge impact upon us every day. It might be thought of as another dimension which intersects the linear timeline of our normal lives. This is the dimension in which we can encounter God, but we can only gain access to it through simple, child-like faith, which lets us harness unlimited possibilities.

At that time Jesus declared, "I thank you, Father, Lord of heaven and earth, that you have hidden these things from the wise and understanding and revealed them to little children; yes, Father, for such was your gracious will." (Matt. 11:25-26)

$$0 + \infty = \infty$$
$$½ + \infty = \infty$$
$$22 + \infty = \infty$$
$$595 + \infty = \infty$$
$$27{,}001 + \infty = \infty$$
$$585{,}796 + \infty = \infty$$
$$4{,}678{,}420{,}168{,}783 + \infty = \infty$$
$$574{,}356{,}908{,}274{,}152{,}437{,}481 + \infty = \infty$$
$$792{,}714{,}692{,}223{,}956{,}174{,}562{,}083{,}296{,}513 + \infty = \infty$$

Infinity added to a number changes it into its own likeness but cannot itself be changed. Its value is unaffected by the number it touches. For this reason, the apparently huge differences between the values in the left hand column in the above list are totally deceptive, in that they have absolutely no impact on the final result. From this perspective every natural number is equally far away from infinity, no matter how large it is.

There is a clear lesson here when we are considering humanity in relation to the infinite being of God. There is no level of greatness or goodness that we can achieve on our own that would make us able to survive intact for a split second in God's presence, or to cope with the dazzling glory of heaven. In comparison with the absolute and infinite goodness of God, the difference between the world's greatest hero and a common criminal, though huge in our eyes, may prove to be negligible on the scale of eternity. Isaiah reminds us that:

ಶಿಧ
We have all become like one who is unclean,
and all our righteous deeds are like a polluted garment.
We all fade like a leaf,
and our iniquities, like the wind, take us away. (Is. 64:6)
ಶಿಧ

As a result, the gulf between our sinfulness and God's total goodness remains an unbridgeable chasm. We have no hope whatsoever of reconnecting to the one who alone could give our lives value, meaning or purpose.

Dictionaries testify that the original root of the word 'sin' comes, extraordinarily enough, from the verb 'to be'. It is intrinsic to our very nature: we are sinful through and through, facing completely in the opposite direction from God's purposes.

Yet fellowship with God is the very purpose for which we have been brought into existence! God longs for us to be reunited with him and for his original plans and purposes for us to be accomplished. His passionate desire is for an unbroken relationship with each one of us.

However, since our sin is infinite in God's sight (Job 22:5), it requires an infinite sacrifice to atone for it. Only God himself, bearing his own punishment for our sins, could bridge that immeasurable gulf to restore us back to fellowship with him.

This is the background to the Lord of glory stepping into his own creation and appearing on the earth in his Son Jesus. On the cross the one who was infinitely powerful became infinitely powerless.

We know from the everyday experience of cleaning how powerfully a vacuum works, drawing particles of dirt into itself. In the same way Paul tells us that Jesus emptied himself of everything but love, to draw the sin of the world into himself on the cross. In doing so he reunited the broken dimensions of finite and infinite, natural and supernatural, earthly and heavenly. This provided us with a way back into relationship the Father:

> ꙮꙮ
>
> For in him all the fullness of God was pleased to dwell, and through him to reconcile to himself all things, whether on earth or in heaven, making peace by the blood of his cross. (Col. 1:19-20)
>
> ꙮꙮ

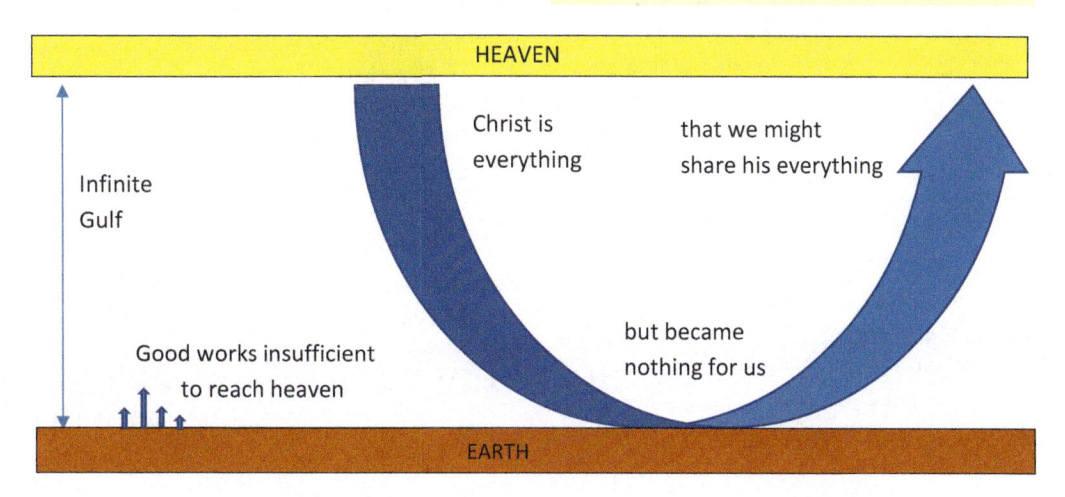

2. Beyond Proportion

If infinity might seem inconceivably large to us, it can also encompass the indescribably small. A fractional quantity might get smaller and smaller, acquiring more and more zeros after its decimal point without ever actually reaching zero.

Three hundred years ago the writer Jonathan Swift summed up the idea rather deftly in a neat little poem:

> So, naturalists observe, a flea
> Hath smaller fleas that on him prey
> And these have smaller fleas to bite 'em
> And so proceed *ad infinitum*.

In earlier chapters we have seen the importance that God attaches to simple ratios between whole numbers. This governs many realms from the proportions in the temple to the way chemicals bond together.

It seems puzzling, therefore, that the ratio between the distance across a circle and the distance around its edge produces a number of never-ending complexity. It is given the symbol π, which is the Greek letter pi. It is something that is simple to understand, but its exact value is completely unknowable and we can never reach a precise answer.

This might not be obvious reading the Bible where, on two occasions, the text implies that that π is equivalent to three:

> Then he made the sea of cast metal. It was round, ten cubits from brim to brim, and five cubits high, and a line of thirty cubits measured its circumference. (1 Kings 7:23)

However, in the 18th century a Jewish scholar known as the Vilna Gaon noticed a discrepancy between the spelling of the Hebrew word for 'circumference' in this account and the related passage in 2 Chronicles 4:2. Using the numerical values of the Hebrew letters in both words as a ratio (111/106) results in the number 1.0472; and multiplying this by the actual number three implied by the text gives the answer 3.1415, more accurate than any estimate of π known until the second century AD.

In fact, the pursuit of this elusive number has been a prized goal for mathematicians throughout the ages. Below are some estimations from different people in different times in different parts of the world:

The Quest for π

3.125 Babylonian tablet (c 1800 BC)

3.1605 Egyptian Rhind Papyrus (1650 BC)

3.142 Archimedes (250 BC)

3.1416 Ptolemy (150 AD)

3.141592926 Zu Chongzhi (480 AD)

3.14159265359
　　　Madhava of Sangamagrama (c. 1400)

3.14159265358979324
　　　Jamshīd Al-Kāshī (1424)

3.1415926535897932384626433832795 0288
　　　Ludolph van Ceulen (1596)

3.14159265358979323846264338327950 2884199
　　　Christoph Grienberger (1630)

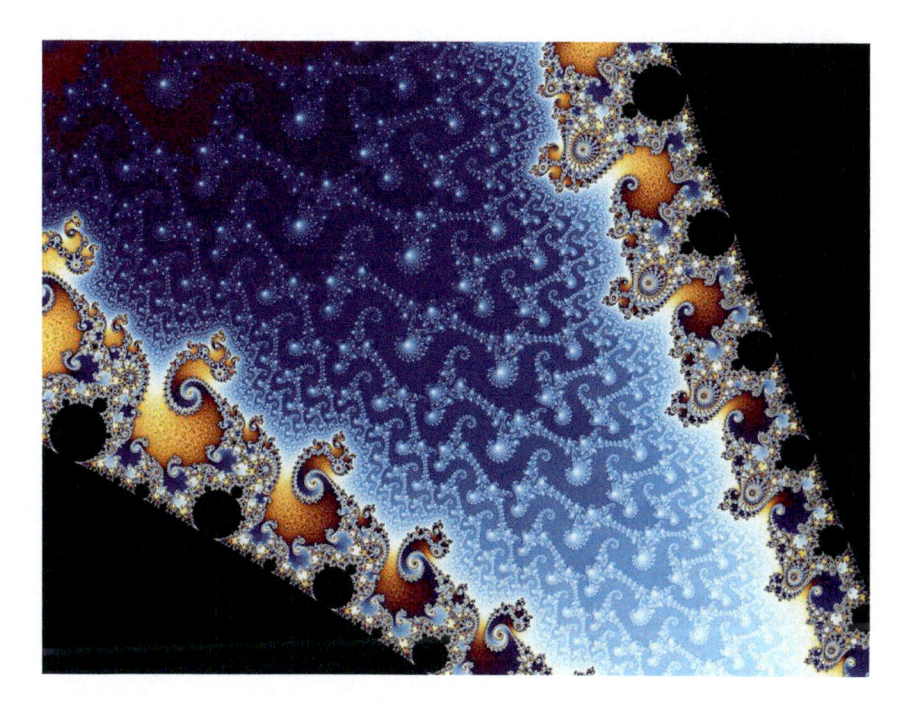

Fractals are infinite patterns based on complex numbers that repeat at smaller and smaller levels. They are created by repeating a simple mathematical process over and over in an ongoing loop to produce strikingly beautiful and intricate patterns which literally go on forever, with endless variation. These patterns have been created by Wolfgang Beyer using the program *Ultra Fractal 3*.

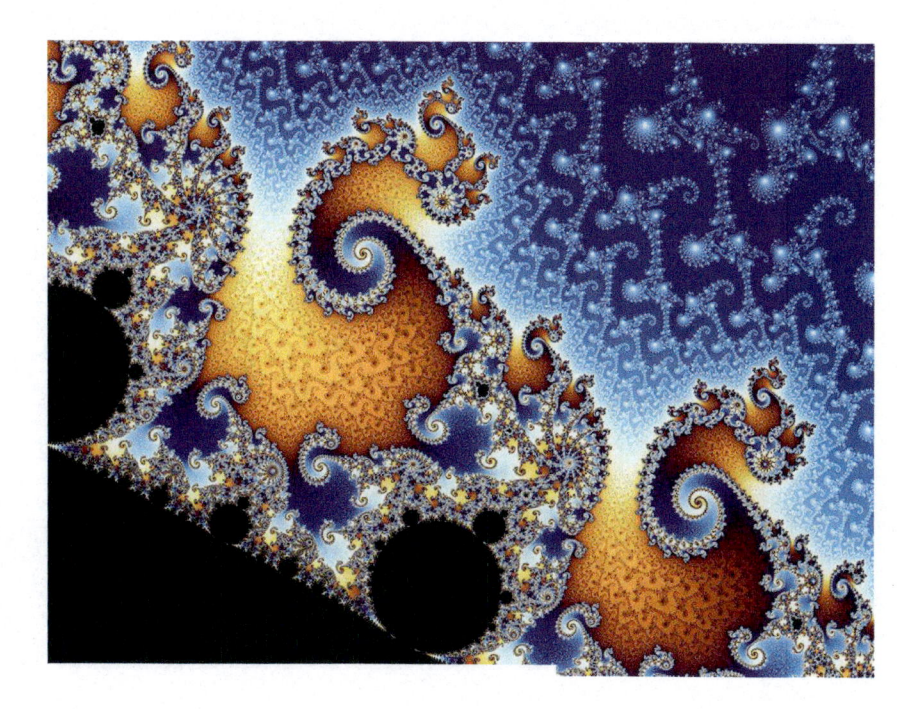

Clouds, coastlines, and plants all provide natural examples of fractals. Fractals can be used to analyse unpredictable systems such as financial markets or weather patterns. The computer-generated island shown above and the designs on the previous page are both generated mathematically by a particular fractal system called the Mandelbrot Set.

Below: the real island of Sark shows remarkable natural parallels (photo by Phillip Capper).

But the answers don't look very elegant or tidy. And as humans we generally like to have things boxed up in neat little packages. It is interesting, therefore, to discover that in 1897, a bill was put before the Indiana State Legislature in America which attempted to kill the controversy once and for all by proposing to set a statutory value for π at 3.2 exactly!

In fact, this ill-conceived bill was already swimming against the tide. Twenty years earlier, the English mathematician William Shanks had calculated the number to no less than 527 decimal places. He did in fact make a mistake on the last digit, although nobody spotted it for another seventy years:

3.14159265358979323846264338327950288419716939937510582097494459230781640628620899862803482534211706798214808651328230664709384460955058223172535940812848111745028410270193852110555964462294895493038196442881097566593344612847564823378678316527120190914564856692346034861045432664821339360726024914127372458700660631558817488152092096282925409171536436789259036001133053054882046652138414695194151160943305727036575959195309218611738193261179310511854807446237996274956735188575272489122793818301194912983367336244065664308602139501609244807723094362855309662027556939798695022247499620607497030412366886199511008920238377021314169411902988582544681639799904659700081700296312377381342084130791451183980570985

William Shanks (1873)

But that wasn't the final answer. The number just kept getting longer and longer and longer. After World War Two computers began to step in. In 1949 an early computer took 70 hours to work out π to the first 2,037 decimal places. By 1958, the first 10,000 digits had been cracked. The current record, at the time of writing, calculates the number to over **100 trillion** digits.[10]

To give a better idea of how large a hundred trillion would be, if you started writing it on a piece of paper, it would need to stretch from Earth to Mars!

And the extraordinary thing is that, even when we got through writing all those digits, we would still be no nearer to reaching the true end of π than when we first began. It simply goes on spiralling on and on for ever and ever, without any sense of pattern or rhythm.

If we were able to carry on writing the full number out, we would eventually encircle the entire universe. And then do so again, and again, and again, and again.

So maybe it is like that with our understanding of Jesus. At one level he is so simple and straightforward that even a child can take him in. And yet, at another, he is so far beyond anything we can ever conceive that it would simply blow our minds even to try. As we encounter Jesus as Saviour and Lord, in other words, we are stepping out on a journey that never ends:

I have come in order that you might have life—life in all its fullness.
(John 10:10 GNB)

3. Beyond Nature

Like the ill-conceived attempt to give a 'doctored' value to π, scientists sometimes prematurely give the impression that they have all the answers. Indeed, the great discoveries of Newton and Leibniz in the 17th and 18th centuries, which pointed to universal laws governing everything, led many to believe that the mysteries of the universe had been solved. It led increasingly to a philosophy called 'Deism', the idea of God as a kind of 'absentee landlord' who sets everything in motion and then stands back, and later to out-and-out atheism.

In 1900 Lord Kelvin is reputed to have addressed the British Association for the Advancement of Science with these words: "There is nothing new to be discovered in physics now. All that remains is more and more precise measurement."[11]

Yet physics was about to be delivered a seismic jolt. Within a few years, Einstein, Bohr and others overturned many fundamental assumptions about the nature of reality and the way the universe works.

Even Newton himself had sensed an incompleteness in his ideas. He is said to have declared, shortly before his death, "I do not know what I may appear to the world, but to myself seem to have been only like a boy playing on the seashore, and diverting myself now and then finding a smoother pebble or a prettier shell than ordinary, whilst the great ocean of truth lay all undiscovered before me."[12]

If Einstein's discovery of relativity was extraordinary enough, challenging many existing preconceptions about space and time, the breakthrough in quantum mechanics was even more mind-boggling. It opened up a world that appears to defy the laws of common sense.

In this shadowy new realm things can appear to exist and yet not exist at the same time, and sub-atomic particles can spontaneously come into being and self-destruct. At first sight, such particles may appear to travel along every possible path and exist in every possible state simultaneously. And yet, as soon as we attempt to pin down their exact position or momentum, the measurement itself instantly forces them into just one fixed value.

More intriguingly, it is possible for particles to be 'entangled' such that whatever happens to one happens to the other at the same instant, even if they are at opposite sides of the universe. With two such 'entangled' particles, when one particle of the pair is

> It is the glory of God to conceal things,
> but the glory of kings is to search things out.
> (Prov. 25:2)

measured, its twin instantly settles into the same state, without any physical communication between them. Einstein, borrowing deliberately 'supernatural' language, once famously dismissed this as 'spooky action at a distance'.[13]

And yet this seems to be the tip of the iceberg. It appears that the more we discover, the less we really know. Current calculations suggest that between two thirds and three quarters of the mass of the universe consists of undetectable 'dark energy', and just under a quarter of equally mysterious 'dark matter', neither of which physicists yet know anything about. Less than a twentieth of the total is normal matter, and even this is mostly spread out as diffuse interstellar particles. Just below half of one per cent of the matter in the universe makes up the stars and planets we can see with our eyes:

Makeup of the Universe

- Dark Energy — 68.3%
- Dark Matter — 26.8%
- Interstellar Gas — 4.42%
- Visible Matter — 0.48%

Looking from the Bible's perspective, the existence of this vast unseen realm is no surprise. Two thousand years earlier Jesus had drawn attention to the elusive nature of the invisible world around us:

> The wind blows where it wishes, and you hear its sound, but you do not know where it comes from or where it goes. (John 3:8)

Paul also described the universe as divided into 'visible' and 'invisible' dimensions (Col. 1:16), and contrasts these temporal and eternal realms in 2 Corinthians:

> We look not to the things that are seen but to the things that are unseen. For the things that are seen are transient, but the things that are unseen are eternal.
> (2 Cor. 4:18)

It is interesting in this regard that the pioneer of quantum mechanics Niels Bohr once concluded: 'Everything we call real is made up of things that cannot be regarded as real.'

In doing so he seems to have been echoing words used (with slightly different import) in the letter to the Hebrews:

> It is by faith that we understand that the universe was created by God's word, so that what *can be seen* was made out of *what cannot be seen*. (Heb. 11:3 GNB)

Moreover, some verses in scripture seem to behave very much in the manner of a quantum particle, defying human logic, by appearing to point in two directions at once. A famous example is John 1:1 which, as we saw in Chapter 2, hints at the mystery of a being who is both 'God' and yet also 'other than God':

> In the beginning was the Word, and the Word was *with* God, and the Word *was* God. (John 1:1)

The same enigma reappears elsewhere in scripture, where two beings are both apparently described as 'God', as the following examples suggest:

> "Listen to me, O Jacob, and Israel, whom I called! I am he; I am the first, and I am the last. ...from the beginning I have not spoken in secret, from the time it came to be I have been there." And now the LORD God has sent me, and his Spirit. (Is. 48:12, 16)
>
> For the LORD of Hosts says this: "He has sent Me for His glory against the nations who are plundering you ... Then you will know that the LORD of Hosts has sent Me." (Zech. 2:8-9 HCSB)

Other verses seem to imply the same person being in two places at the same time:

> Then the LORD rained on Sodom and Gomorrah sulphur and fire from the LORD out of heaven. (Gen. 19:24)
>
> Jesus answered and said to him ... "No one has ascended to heaven but He who came down from heaven, *that is,* the Son of Man *who is in heaven."* (John 3:10, 13 NKJV)

Elsewhere we see opposite qualities merging in the face of something still greater:

> If I say, "Surely the darkness shall cover me,
> and the light about me be night",
> even the darkness is not dark to you;
> the night is bright as the day,
> for *darkness is as light with you.*
> (Ps. 139:11-12)

It appears, then, to use the language of quantum physics, that many Bible truths that we think might require either/or answers actually exist in a state of 'superposition' with each other. These questions include not just the 'oneness', 'twoness' and 'threeness' of God, but other issues such as predestination versus free will, 'already' versus 'not yet', and the deity and humanity of Christ.

These may be difficult ideas for us to grasp, but as John 4:24 tells us, 'God is spirit' and therefore unlimited by human logic or spatial dimensions. There is no reason to assume we can ever fully make sense of them with our limited human minds.

In Isaiah God reminds us:

> ℬ⃝
> "For my thoughts are not your thoughts, neither are your ways my ways, declares the LORD.
> For as the heavens are higher than the earth, so are my ways higher than your ways and my thoughts than your thoughts."
> (Is. 55:8-9)
> ℬ⃝

Likewise Solomon declares:

> ℬ⃝
> He has also set eternity in the human heart; yet no one can fathom what God has done from beginning to end.
> (Ecc. 3:11 NIV)
> ℬ⃝

Psalm 119, meanwhile, tells us that

> ℬ⃝
> To all perfection I see a limit, but your commands are boundless.
> (Psalm 119:96)
> ℬ⃝

Despite these limitations to what we *can* know about God, the convergence between scripture and some of the discoveries of modern physics is often remarkable.

For example, physicists speculate about 'quantum foam' with bubbles quadrillions of times smaller than an atomic nucleus, in which particles momentarily flit in and out of existence. The Bible says that in the beginning the Spirit of God was hovering over the face of the waters (Gen. 1:2).

Physics tells that the universe underwent a period of rapid expansion in the early moments of its existence. The Bible tells us that God stretched out the heavens like a tent (Ps. 104:2).

Physics describes a division between matter and antimatter, with the existence of stars or even entire galaxies made up of antimatter as one possible suggestion. The Bible says that God separated the light from the darkness (Gen. 1:4).

Physicists talk about the four fundamental forces (strong, weak, electromagnetic and gravitational) that keep things from flying apart. The Bible says that in Christ all things hold together (Col. 1:17).

Physics demonstrates the First Law of Thermodynamics, which tells us that matter and energy can never be created or destroyed. The Bible says that:

> ℬ⃝
> What has been is what will be, and what has been done is what will be done, and there is nothing new under the sun.
> (Ecc. 1:9)
> ℬ⃝

Physics has also revealed a Second Law of Thermodynamics, which states that everything proceeds from an ordered to a disordered state. The Bible declares that:

> For the creation was subjected to frustration, not by its own choice, but by the will of the one who subjected it, in hope that the creation itself will be liberated from its bondage to decay and brought into the freedom and glory of the children of God. (Rom. 8:20-21 NIV)

Around us, then, we see vast unexplained mysteries, but also an incredible signature of order imprinted throughout. This reflection of God's being in the natural realm around us makes it possible for Paul conclude as follows:

> For his invisible attributes, namely, his eternal power and divine nature, have been clearly perceived, ever since the creation of the world, in the things that have been made. (Rom. 1:20)

4. Beyond Space

Since the dawn of history human beings have looked up at the stars with awe and wonder. Job testifies to this when he declares,

> [He] alone stretched out the heavens and trampled the waves of the sea; who made the Bear and Orion, the Pleiades and the chambers of the south. (Job 9:8-9)

Stories of the constellations that Job names have traversed continents: the tale of the hunter (Orion) chasing the seven sisters (Pleiades) reappears the world over, from the ancient Greeks to the Australian Aborigines. Similarly, labelling the stars around the 'Plough' as a 'Great Bear' links swathes of peoples across northern Europe, and Russia with several native North American tribes and may consequently date from the earliest reaches of history, before man had spread across the earth.

Another verse reflecting awe and wonder at the cosmos appears in the Psalms:

> When I look at your heavens, the work of your fingers,
> the moon and the stars, which you have set in place,
> what is man that you are mindful of him, and the son of man that you care for him? (Psalm 8:3-4)

INFINITY: THE VOYAGE BEYOND NUMBER

Above: 'The Pillars of Creation' in the Eagle Nebula, taken by the Hubble Space Telescope. In choosing its name NASA scientists purposefully borrowed from an 1857 sermon by the Victorian preacher Charles Haddon Spurgeon entitled 'The Condescension of Christ'. In it Spurgeon declares: 'And now wonder, ye angels, the Infinite has become an infant; he, upon whose shoulders the universe doth hang, hangs at his mother's breast; He who created all things, and bears up *the pillars of creation*, hath now become so weak, that He must be carried by a woman!' The paradox of infinite power allied to infinite weakness is one of the great mysteries of the Incarnation, and is the only way we can truly understand the nature of the universe.

Yet the incredible thing is that we occupy a central place in this divine architecture. We mentioned in Chapter One that after Abraham was ready to surrender to God his most precious possession, his beloved son Isaac, God made him an extraordinary promise:

> ಯಲ
> I will surely multiply your offspring as the stars of heaven and as the sand that is on the seashore. (Gen. 22:17).
> ಯಲ

How would Abraham have understood this? The number of stars visible to him on a really clear night would at best have been a few thousand. In fact, the greatest astronomer of the ancient world, Hipparchus, listed just 850 stars in his catalogue. This was expanded by Ptolemy of Alexandria in the second century AD to 1,022.

By contrast, the number of grains of sand in all the beaches in the world is mind-boggling - the Australian scientist Chris Flynn has suggested as a very crude estimate 10^{24} - that is, a ten with twenty-four zeros after it![14] How do we solve this apparent disparity, then, between a mere scattering of stars and an almost endless quantity of sand?

Here modern astronomy comes to the rescue. The universe as we now know it is indescribably more vast than anything that could have been known in Abraham's day. The remarkable thing is that Flynn's calculation for the number of grains of sand on the earth's beaches actually matches with remarkable agreement one estimate for the number of stars in the universe recently given by the European Space Agency![15]

Whilst the accuracy of the Bible thousands of years before the advent of the telescope may amaze us, it could also leave us feeling completely dwarfed.

In our galaxy alone there are 100 billion stars and beyond this maybe 100 billion other galaxies, many much larger than our own. And this figure assumes that our universe is finite; some experiments suggest that it may extend forever, like the extraordinary number π that we examined earlier.

We may on the one hand feel a vast sense of awe at this. For some, however, it may also produce a tremendous sense of loneliness and insignificance.

In his book *The Mysterious Universe* Sir James Jeans wrote:

> We find the universe terrifying because of its vast meaningless distances, terrifying because of its inconceivably long vistas of time which dwarf human history to the twinkling of an eye, terrifying because of our extreme loneliness, and because of the material insignificance of that home in space – a millionth part of a grain of sand out of all the sea-sand in the world.[16]

He was echoing the French philosopher and mathematician Blaise Pascal, who, even as a passionate believer in Christ, had written likewise several centuries earlier that 'the eternal silence of these infinite spaces frightens me.'[17]

This sense of cosmic isolation is particularly apparent if we consider the minute size of the earth in comparison to the universe as a whole. If we shrink the earth to the size of a drawing pin as shown below, for example, the sun would be just under 12 metres from us, but our nearest star beyond our own solar system would still be 2,000 miles away. Yet even at this tiny scale we would need to take a journey of twelve million miles to get to the centre of our galaxy, and more than a billion to get our nearest large galactic neighbour, Andromeda.

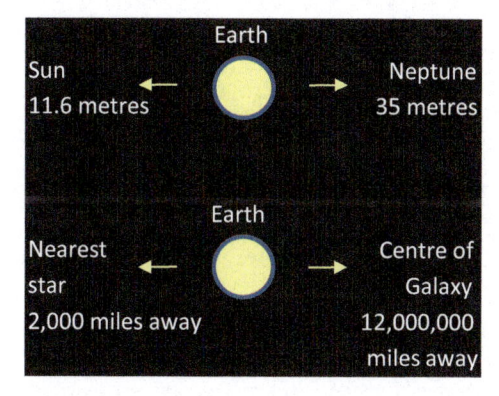

	Earth	
Sun 11.6 metres ←	●	→ Neptune 35 metres
	Earth	
Nearest star 2,000 miles away ←	●	→ Centre of Galaxy 12,000,000 miles away

Strangely enough, this sense of staggering distance and unbounded vastness also seems to characterise the microscopic world which exists at the other end of the scale inside of each one of us. For instance, we have as many as 7,000,000,000,000,000,000,000,000,000 (7×10^{27}) atoms in our bodies, ninety-eight per cent of which are replaced every year. To get some sense of perspective here, there are more atoms in a single glass of water than glasses of water in all the oceans in the world. Truly each one of us is a 'man of dust' (1 Cor. 15:47).

And yet, scaled down, the distances that exist within these atoms seem as vast as the cavernous reaches of outer space around us. If the central proton of the smallest atom (hydrogen) were blown up to the size of a drawing pin, for instance, it would be two thirds of a mile wide between its farthest points, while if we scaled up the quarks inside it to the same size, the atom would grow to become a staggering 1,000 miles across:

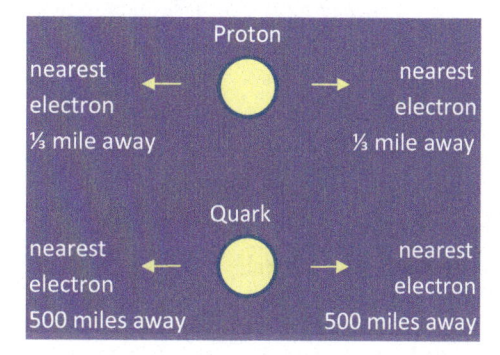

	Proton	
nearest electron ⅓ mile away ←	●	→ nearest electron ⅓ mile away
	Quark	
nearest electron 500 miles away ←	●	→ nearest electron 500 miles away

As a result, both the largest and smallest levels of matter just seem to be tiny pinpricks in a vast sea of nothingness. And we may feel the same thing about ourselves.

But this is very far from the way God thinks about us. In fact, each one of us has immense significance in his eyes. He calls the stars by name and yet he counts the number of hairs on our heads. He hangs the earth on nothing (Job 26:7) and yet our names are inscribed on the palms of his hands (Is. 49:16). He causes empires to collapse and yet he counts our tears in his bottle (Ps. 56:8).

In fact, God's kingdom works in such a way that even the tiniest and most insignificant detail can be of earth-shattering significance. It has often been stated that even if you or I had been the only person in the entire universe, Jesus would still have been willing to step in and die for us (Gal. 2:20). We can only bow down in awe and wonder in response to this extraordinary truth

5. Beyond Time

Staring up at the stars, as Abraham was called to do four thousand years ago, reveals not just the hugeness of space but the vastness of time. One of the most familiar sights to him would have been the constellation of Orion ('the Hunter'). It has inspired awe and wonder for thousands of years (see Job 9:9; Amos 5:8).

Yet a glimpse at its distinctive pattern of stars does not reveal an instant of time but something far bigger. Because of the different lengths of time it takes for light to cross the immense distances of space, we only see the stars as they *were*, not as they *are*. For instance, the light from Bellatrix, situated on Orion's right shoulder (from our vantage-point) began its journey around the time James Cook discovered Australia; Rigel, on Orion's right foot, appears as it did when the Plantaganet Henry III was king of England, while the sight of Alnilam in the middle of Orion's belt (a massive star 10,000 times brighter than our sun) takes us back to the time when the Anglo-Saxons first converted to Christianity.

In just one small segment of the night's sky, therefore, history seems to open up before our very eyes!

If the night sky seems to open many different windows of time simultaneously, the opposite is true of lightning and thunder, which are two primary symbols of God in the Bible (Ex. 19:16; Ps. 77:18). Here two signs mark the same event, but the passage of time sets them apart. Because of the difference between the speed of light and the speed of sound, one single event 'splits' into two separate moments in our perception.

Time is, therefore, not a totally straightforward subject. For many centuries it was regarded as an absolute and unvarying property. However, there are various passages in the Bible which suggest that the flow of time actually depends on the conscious observer.

Informally, most of us have an awareness of the relative nature of time. Experience tells us that some days seem to creep by very slowly, while others appear to shoot past. Jacob spent seven years working to win the hand of Rachel, but they seemed like a few days because of his love for her (Gen. 29:20). A similar sentiment is expressed in the Psalms:

> ෴ඏ
> Better is one day in your courts than a thousand elsewhere (Psalm 84:10 NIV)
> ෴ඏ

Studies on creatures of different sizes suggests that perceived time seems to flow at different speeds depending on their metabolic rate and the number of different tasks they accomplish. An hour, for example, might seem a much shorter timespan for a tortoise than it would be for an ant.[18]

However, the Bible seems to be saying something more fundamental than this. Peter declares that:

> But do not overlook this one fact, beloved, that with the Lord one day is as a thousand years, and a thousand years as one day. (2 Peter 3:8)

Wayne Grudem makes the following comment on this verse:

> It is as if that day never ends, but is always being experienced ... we can say from this verse that any one day seems to God to be present to his consciousness forever. These two statements together show an amazing way of viewing time: The whole span of history is as vivid as if it were a brief event that had just happened, but any brief event is as if it is going on forever![19]

In other words, in God's hands time has the ability to bud and enlarge within itself. It is as if every moment contains an infinity of new moments.

A concrete example of this appears in Joshua, where God appears to cause time to stand still, giving Israel an advantage over her adversaries:

> The sun stopped in the midst of heaven and did not hurry to set for about a whole day. There has been no day like it before or since, when the LORD heeded the voice of a man, for the LORD fought for Israel. (Josh. 10:13-14)

At the other extreme we see events that would normally be spread out across time being squeezed into an instant: water that becomes wine in a split second (John 2:6-9), or a boat that is miraculously 'teleported' to the shore of the lake (6:21).

Another instance of this appears in Acts, after Philip baptises the Ethiopian eunuch, where he suddenly finds himself miles away in Azotus:

> When they came up out of the water, the Spirit of the Lord *carried Philip away*, and the eunuch saw him no more, and went on his way rejoicing. (Acts 8:39)

Finally, we should note that there is at least one example in the Bible where time appears to run *backwards*. When Hezekiah is looking to be reassured that he will recover from his near-fatal illness, God causes the shadow of sun to go back ten steps, effectively sending time into reverse. This is accompanied by the strange phenomenon of the middle of the story appearing after the end of it, creating a oddly dislocated effect (Is. 38:1-8; 21-22).

Is the Future Predetermined?

Some verses in the Bible seem to imply that God determines the future in advance. Isaiah 46:9-10, for example, says that:

'I am God, and there is none like me,
  declaring the end from the beginning
  and from ancient times things not yet done.'

This poses interesting questions as to whether or not human beings can have genuine free will. Has God decided our individual destiny already? Psalm 139:16, for instance, declares that

Your eyes saw my unformed substance;
in your book were written, every one of them,
  the days that were formed for me,
  when as yet there was none of them.

In addition, a number of verses in the New Testament clearly teach that those believing in Christ have been prepared *in advance* for glory (Matt. 25:34; Rom. 9:22-23) and chosen *before* creation (Eph. 1:4). In Acts we discover that certain people were marked out for salvation even before they heard the gospel (Acts 13:48; Acts 18:9-10). Similarly, Revelation states that our names were written in the Book of Life *before* the foundation of the world (Rev 17:8).

These verses imply that a) each of us had some kind of potential existence in the mind of God in the remote past (Ps. 139:15-16; Jer. 1:5; 2 Tim. 1:9); b) he already sees what choices we will make, even hypothetical ones, in any situation (1 Sam. 23:10-12); and c) he *sometimes* dictates those choices (2 Kings 19:25-28).

But does that mean we have no choices at all? It is the Bible's way to sometimes speak about events that God has permitted as if he himself is the originator, where he has merely allowed them. For instance, God gets the blame in 2 Samuel 24:1 for an idea that 1 Chronicles 21:1 tells us was actually instigated by Satan.

Moreover, our most important choices do appear to be real ones. Jesus' wilderness temptations make no sense if Jesus was not genuinely tempted. Similarly, the agony in Gethsemane makes no sense if Jesus did not have a real choice as to whether or not to go through with the cross.

On top of this, the importance of making our *own* right choices is taught clearly in Scripture (Deut. 30:19-20; Josh. 24:15; Prov.1:29-31). To be meaningful to God and to us these must be *genuine* choices.

Furthermore, prayer appears capable of changing God's revealed will. Even though Job 14:5 teaches that God determines the time of our passing from this world, Hezekiah's prayer seems to be able to change what God has previously decreed (Is. 38:1-5).

Our human way of thinking reduces tends this to an either/or alternative. From God's perspective *both* our free will and his total sovereignty may be possible. It may well be, for example, that God hardening Pharoah's heart (Ex. 4:21) and Pharoah hardening his own heart (8:15) are two sides of the same coin.

As believers, our choices *are* important and prayer really *does* make a difference. Outside Christ our freedom may be an illusion, but in relationship with him a real freedom to choose is restored to us all.

*Jesus answered them, "Truly, truly, I say to you, everyone who commits sin is a slave to sin. The slave does not remain in the house for ever; the son remains for ever. So **if the Son sets you free, you will be free indeed.**"* (John 8:34-36)

The same is true in Revelation, where events and images such as the Beast, Babylon, and Armageddon seem to be 'remembered' before they are introduced and explained to the reader (11:7; 14:8; 16:16). Furthermore, it is never totally clear whether time is running sequentially, or running in circles or spirals; like the fractal patterns we saw earlier, the same pattern of events seems to recur in different forms over and over again.

How do we make sense of all these things? Firstly we need to remember that God, as Father, Son and Holy Spirit, stands outside time. His name, as we saw in Chapter One, is 'I AM'. In other words, he doesn't have a past or a future: he just *is*. This is as much true of Jesus in the New Testament as it is of the Father in the Old Testament. It helps to explain the strange mixture of tenses that Jesus uses in John 8:58 ('Before Abraham *was*, I *am*'), which is itself an echo of verse 2 from Psalm 90:

> Before the mountains *were* brought forth,
> or ever you *had* formed the earth and the world,
> from everlasting to everlasting you *are* God.

Everything in history is laid out before God's eyes just as we might view the horizon from left to right. He sees the end from the beginning and from that perspective past, present and future together form a single instant (Is 46:10). Every moment that has been or ever will be is part of God's 'now', as Jesus explains:

> 'But in the account of the burning bush, even Moses showed that the dead rise, for he calls the Lord "the God of Abraham, and the God of Isaac, and the God of Jacob". He is not the God of the dead, but of the living, *for to him all are alive*.' (Luke 20:37-38 NIV)

That means we can completely trust God with our lives: he knows what will happen to us tomorrow, next day, and next year (Ps. 139:16). He knows our every thought and action (Ps. 139:1-4; 2 Kings 19:27) and the outcome of every choice before it is made (1 Sam. 23:10-13).

On our own we are doomed to make the same mistakes over and over again; hand in hand with him we can achieve things beyond our understanding that we never thought were possible. The *Passion Translation* puts it beautifully like this:

> You are so intimately aware of me, Lord.
> You read my heart like an open book
> and you know all the words I'm about to speak
> before I even start a sentence!
> You know every step I will take before my journey even begins.
> You've gone into my future to prepare the way,
> and in kindness you follow behind me to spare me from the harm of my past.
> (Ps. 139:3-5)

6. Beyond Ourselves

One of the most powerful stories in the gospels is that of Jesus walking on the water. In the midst of this unprecedented event Peter is challenged to grapple with the unknowable and the impossible. Unlike all his companions he chooses to stand up against every known physical law and to overcome the limitations of the natural realm. In doing so, he is never going to be the same again. For all his later failures and retreats, it changes him forever.

God is wanting to change us, too, so that we can also navigate the realms of the impossible, the unknowable, and the limitless. But the means he has given us to harness the infinite is not human intellect or ingenuity. Rather, it is a radically simple gift that can turn the world upside-down. That gift is *faith*.

In many significant ways, the principle of faith runs against the tide of our normal thought processes, for a variety of reasons:

1 Faith challenges our existing notions of *self*. It involves abandoning any trust in our own human ability to overcome and throwing all our trust onto God. When we look in at ourselves and the limited resources we have, our doubts can only increase; but when we turn our gaze towards Jesus, they disappear. For this reason, as we saw in Chapter One, faith has often been spelt with the acronym:

>**F**orsaking
>**A**ll
>**I**
>**T**rust
>**H**im.

2 Faith challenges our inbuilt sense of *logic*. The walk of faith is not something we can comprehend with our natural minds. It has to be *revealed* to us supernaturally. That is why Jesus told us that we have to

---

Nothing can Separate Us

Einstein showed that the closer we approach the speed of light the more perceived time 'shrinks'. Since the photons which transmit light to us actually travel at that absolute speed, time is effectively at a standstill for them. *From the photons' point of view* the eight minute journey from the sun or the 2.5 million-year journey from the Andromeda galaxy to Earth are both instantaneous: they arrive at the same time that they leave!

Jesus' description of himself as 'the light of the world' (John 8:12) might lead us to an extraordinary conclusion here. From his perspective both distance and time are utterly meaningless. There is *no barrier* in all creation that can separate us from his love or the love of the Father (Rom. 8:39).

When Jesus said, "I am with you always, to the end of the age" (Matt. 28:20), therefore, we need to accept it as a fact, and not simply as a figure of speech.

If I take the wings of the morning
  and dwell in the uttermost parts of the sea,
even there *your hand shall lead me,*
  and your right hand shall hold me. (Ps.139:9-10)

become like a child to enter the kingdom of heaven. In this realm human reason is of no avail: so often it kills fragile flower of faith on the spot! The secret to a victorious Christian life is not so much increasing faith, therefore, as decreasing unbelief. James tells us that those who doubt will receive nothing:

> If any of you lacks wisdom, let him ask God, who gives generously to all without reproach, and it will be given him. But let him ask in faith, with no doubting, for the one who doubts is like a wave of the sea that is driven and tossed by the wind. For that person must not suppose that he will receive anything from the Lord.
> (James 1:5-7)

3 Faith challenges where we *focus*. In every problem, we have a choice: are we going to let ourselves be overwhelmed by the challenge, or are we going to let God have the last word?

We can take inspiration from David's battle with Goliath here. David's attention was not on the physical giant towering over him, but on the spiritual giant towering over them both! In putting his whole trust in God, the scale of the problem shrank. God is keen for us to face down the Goliaths in our own lives by fixing our eyes on *him*.

4 Faith challenges our view of *reality*. Abraham had been given a promise by God that his wife would bear a child at the age of 100 – but every fact of biology and common sense stood against him. Yet he was not discouraged. As Paul tells us,

> In hope *he believed against hope*, that he should become the father of many nations, as he had been told, "So shall your offspring be." He *did not weaken in faith* when he considered his own body, which was as good as dead (since he was about a hundred years old), or when he considered the barrenness of Sarah's womb. *No distrust made him waver* concerning the promise of God, but he grew strong in his faith as he gave glory to God, *fully convinced* that God was able to do what he had promised.
> (Rom. 4:18-21)

The question at stake here is whose reality are we going to believe – our reality or God's?

The book of Hebrews reminds us that faith is literally the *title deed* of things hoped for (11:1). In this case Abraham held on to the fact that God's word is 'Deep Truth': an ultimate reality that has power to change the temporary reality of the physical realm. We either let the facts overwhelm us or allow God's Truth to change the facts.

In the same way, Peter did not *stop* believing in the law of gravity at the moment he stepped out on the water. Rather, his faith rose above the circumstances by invoking a higher law, just as the laws of aerodynamics overcome the restrictions of gravity for an aircraft. It was only when he took his eyes *off* Jesus that he started sinking.

Left: There is NO spiral in this picture, but only concentric circles. Our eyes are very easily deceived, and in this case obstinately refuse to see the truth, even after it has been shown to us (picture by Mysid, based on the Fraser spiral illusion).

Below: *Convex and Concave*, by Maurits Cornelis Escher (1898-1972). At a casual glance the picture seems normal enough, but on closer inspection not all is at it seems. Stepping into the realm of faith involves a similar 'flip' of perspectives so that we see things from a different angle.

5 Faith challenges our existing notions of *time*. It transfers from the future tense to the past tense. It doesn't say 'I am going to receive' but 'I have already received'. It takes hold of what God has already given and can therefore rest on the basis of a fully completed action. Over and over again in the book of Joshua we see how Israel steps into a destiny *already prepared* by God (1:3; 2:24; 6:2).

The following passages from the Old Testament also suggest the same pattern, with the dice being fully loaded beforehand:

'Do not be afraid. Stand firm and you will see the deliverance the LORD will bring you today. ... The LORD will fight for you; you need only to be still.' (Ex. 14:13-14 NIV)

"Now therefore stand still and see this great thing that the LORD will do before your eyes." (1 Sam. 12:16)

"In returning and rest you shall be saved; in quietness and in trust shall be your strength." (Is. 30:15)

"You will not need to fight in this battle. Stand firm, hold your position, and see the salvation of the LORD on your behalf, O Judah and Jerusalem." (2 Chron. 20:17)

In this regard we should remember that God does not bring provisions into existence to meet our problems. Rather, he allows *our problems* to meet *his provisions* (John 9:3; 11:3).

So many of the needs in our life God has already met in advance through his grace. It might even be said that even salvation itself was in the world before sin: Revelation 13:8 talks about the Lamb slain *from the foundation of the world (*(NKJV translation).

Similarly, Isaiah 53 is written in past tense as if referring back to something that has *already taken place*, even though it is referring to something that would happen in physical time 500 years later, while Hebrews declares the following:

For by one sacrifice **he has made perfect** for ever those who are **being made holy**. (Heb. 10.14 NIV)

It appears, therefore, that when we pray to God in faith we are transferring the 'not yet' unseen realm into the 'already' visible realm. In the first recorded example of a formal prayer in the Bible, for example, the answer appears while the prayer is not yet finished (Gen. 24:12-15): it is as if the prayer has worked *backwards*. In fact, Jesus reminds us that God knows what we ask for even before we start praying (Matt. 6h :8).

Several passages in the New Testament show the power of the 'already' over the 'not yet' in our prayers:

> ❧☙
> "Truly I say to you, whatever you bind on earth **shall have been** bound in heaven; and whatever you loose on earth **shall have been** loosed in heaven." (Matt. 18:18 NASB)
>
> "Have faith in God. Truly, I say to you, whoever says to this mountain, 'Be taken up and thrown into the sea', and does not doubt in his heart, but believes that what he says will come to pass, it will be done for him. Therefore I tell you, whatever you ask in prayer, **believe that you have received it**, and it will be yours. " (Mark 11:22-24)
> ❧☙

> ❧☙
> For consider your calling, brothers: not many of you were wise according to worldly standards, not many were powerful, not many were of noble birth. But God chose what is foolish in the world to shame the wise; God chose what is weak in the world to shame the strong; God chose what is low and despised in the world, even things that are not, to bring to nothing things that are, so that no human being might boast in the presence of God.
> (1 Cor. 1:26-29)
> ❧☙

6 Faith challenges our existing notions of *power*. As Jesus reminds us, faith is like a mustard seed (Matt. 13:31; 17:20). It may be the tiniest of all seeds, but with a small, concentrated germ of life inside it is capable of moving mountains!

So often God likes to starts with small, insignificant things, which may appear laughable on the outside, but are infinitely powerful within. Within an acorn, for example, lies the blueprint to cover an entire continent with oak trees.

There are clear spiritual lessons to be learnt here. What appears to be of no import may actually contain colossal strength hidden inside. When Elijah's servant sees a tiny cloud the size of a man's hand, he knows that the drought is over and that a deluge is on its way (1 Kings 18:44).

God's kingdom works in the opposite way from human kingdoms. As Paul writes:

We see this principle expressed supremely at Bethlehem, where God steps into the world as a tiny helpless baby. Within a few centuries, the entire might of the Roman empire had been brought to its knees.

Such inauspicious beginnings are in God's hands potential interfaces for heaven to invade earth, and the infinite to invade the finite. Indeed, the whole Bible can be described as the germination of a seed, starting from its first, insignificant appearance after the fall of man in Genesis, when God places a curse on the serpent:

> ❧☙
> "And I will put enmity
> Between you and the woman,
> And between your seed and her seed;
> He shall bruise you on the head,
> And you shall bruise him on the heel."
> (Gen. 3:15 NASB)
> ❧☙

Over time this divine seed becomes a shoot (Is. 11:1), and then a branch (Jer. 23:5-6), and then a fully-formed plant (John 15:1). Like the sequence of whole numbers we have considered earlier in this book, each stage of revelation contains the next within itself, unfolding by progressive subdivision of the whole.

The abundant life in the seed overcomes the power of death around it, and every obstacle that comes in its way. God's infinite life is branching and begetting by nature. Joseph is likened in Genesis 49:22 to branches that climb over a wall, while a picture of God's inner life was displayed inside the ark of the covenant in the form of Aaron's rod, upon which miraculous buds had appeared (Num. 17:5, 8; Heb. 9:4). The Messiah is on several occasions described as the 'branch of the LORD' (Is. 4:2; Jer. 23:6; Zech 3:8), while the Nicene Creed talks about the Son as 'eternally begotten' of the Father.

This sense that seeds are much bigger on the inside than on the outside is also true of us. God places an H from his own name, YHWH, into Abram and he becomes Abraham, the Father of a multitude (Gen. 17:5). Likewise, the Spirit breathes on a valley of dry bones and they become a mighty army (Ezek. 37:4-10), while Jesus' breathing on his disciples is the first step towards changing them into a force which ultimately turns the world upside down (John 20:22). John reminds us that 'he who is in you is greater than he who is in the world' (1 John 4:4).

In fact, we were created as vessels to carry the glory of God. The word for 'glory' literally means weight, density and heaviness. Therefore, when God puts his glory upon and in a person, it is like squeezing an uncontainable force into a tiny space. Amazing things start happening when the dammed up life of God is released. David talks of how God 'burst through my enemies before me like a bursting flood' (2 Sam. 5:20) and describes elsewhere how his cup 'overflows' (Psalm 23:5). In the same way Jesus made the same promises of overflowing life:

> ೫೦೧೩
> "Good measure, pressed down, shaken together, running over, will be put into your lap. For with the measure you use it will be measured back to you." (Luke 6:38)
>
> "Whoever believes in me, as the Scripture has said, 'Out of his heart will flow rivers of living water.'" (John 7:38)
> ೫೦೧೩

There is one relevant picture here that crops up a number of times in the book of Ephesians. That is the Greek word *pleroma* or fullness. It implies life in concentrated abundance. Paul prays that we may be '*filled* with all the *fullness* of God' (3:19) and exhorts us to be '*filled* with the Spirit' (5:18). Jesus ascended higher than all the heavens to *fill* the whole universe (4:10), his goal being that we, too, might attain to the *fullness* of Christ (4:13). The church is therefore 'the *fullness* of him who *fills* all in all' (1:23).

These verses link us mysteriously to the cosmic grandeur which surrounds us. We saw in Chapter 1 the deep connection between the universal laws of nature and God's personal commitments to his chosen people; and how, in particular, God ties the very basis of the laws governing the universe to his covenant with Israel in chapter 31 of Jeremiah.

Likewise, our ever-expanding universe, which physicists have only recognised over the last hundred years, is linked in Isaiah to the calling of the Messiah and the spreading out of God's covenant to the Gentiles, and all who live in darkness:

> ഇരു
>
> Thus says God, the LORD,
> who **created the heavens and stretched them out**,
> who spread out the earth and what comes from it,
> who gives breath to the people on it
> and spirit to those who walk in it:
> "I am the LORD; I have called you in righteousness;
> I will take you by the hand and keep you;
> **I will give you as a covenant for the people**,
> **a light for the nations**,
> to open the eyes that are blind,
> to bring out the prisoners from the dungeon,
> from the prison those who sit in darkness."
> (Is. 42:5-7)
>
> ഇരു

We also saw how Abraham's offspring are compared to stars in the sky. This thought comes back in the final prophecy in Daniel:

> ഇരു
>
> "And those who are wise shall *shine like the brightness of the sky above*; and those who turn many to righteousness, *like the stars for ever and ever.*" (Dan. 12:3)
>
> ഇരു

Paul, likewise, uses the same imagery:

> ഇരു
>
> Then you will shine among them like *stars in the sky* as you hold firmly to the word of life. (Phil. 2:15-16 NIV)
>
> ഇരു

But if our citizenship is rooted in that remote past, we are also citizens of the future. Jesus taught about the kingdom of God, a future state, as already here in the present. We transfer it backwards by grasping it by faith and making it real in our everyday world. Paul talks about us being, from God's perspective, *already* raised up and seated in the heavenly places in Christ (Eph. 2:6) and *already* glorified in his eyes (Rom. 8:30).

Such verses point towards an extraordinary destiny. As Paul writes elsewhere:

> ഇരു
>
> For I consider that the sufferings of this present time are not worth comparing with the glory that is to be revealed to us. For the creation waits with eager longing for the revealing of the sons of God. For the creation was subjected to futility, not willingly, but because of him who subjected it, in hope that the creation itself will be set free from its bondage to corruption and obtain the freedom of the glory of the children of God.
> (Rom. 8:18-21)
>
> ഇരു

INFINITY: THE VOYAGE BEYOND NUMBER

Above: Stars provide a picture of saved humanity living in relationship with God. The Lagoon Nebula, where many stars are born, was discovered by the Italian astronomer Giovanni Hodierna before 1654 and is one of only two star-forming nebulae faintly visible to the eye from northern latitudes.

If stars begin their lives in spectacular fashion, they also end their lives in a blaze of glory. Above is the Crab Nebula in the constellation Taurus, the remnant of a supernova explosion observed by Chinese astronomers in 1054. Below is the Veil Nebula in the constellation Cygnus, the remnant of a supernova explosion of a star twenty times the size of our sun many thousands of years ago.

What we are now nothing like what we will become. To the Corinthians Paul writes the following:

> ❧❦❧
>
> Behold! I tell you a mystery. We shall not all sleep, but we shall all be changed, in a moment, in the twinkling of an eye, at the last trumpet. For the trumpet will sound, and the dead will be raised imperishable, and we shall be changed. For this perishable body must put on the imperishable, and this mortal body must put on immortality.
> (1 Cor. 15:51-53)
>
> ❧❦❧

Similarly John writes as follows:

> ❧❦❧
>
> Beloved, we are God's children now, and what we will be has not yet appeared; but we know that when he appears we shall be like him, because we shall see him as he is. And everyone who thus hopes in him purifies himself as he is pure.
> (1 John 3:2-3)
>
> ❧❦❧

As we wait in joyful anticipation of meeting Jesus again, in other words, we are stepping out on a journey that leads to a destination beyond our wildest dreams. It will be like *nothing* we have ever encountered before.

In this study we have taken a journey through numbers, starting very small, until they fill the entire universe. We have seen an organic connection between the different steps: how *Identity* gives rise to *Relationship*; how *Relationship* gives rise to *Fulfilment*, and how *Fulfilment* in turn gives rise to the expanding spheres of *Life*, *Order* and *Dominion*. We also saw how the ultimate goal of encountering God's *Holiness* and *Perfection* transcends these other qualities.

However, none of these are the defining qualities of the universe. The simple and most basic truth which far outstrips them all is that of *Love*, which is the essence of God's nature and underpins the whole created order, fallen and imperfect though it is. Love is the entire and only reason that the universe exists, and no 'explanation' or scientific rationale will ever be complete without it. It is the root from which every other aspect of reality branches off, and 'objective' descriptions will always fall far short of its all-consuming power.

But that Love demands a response from us. We cannot simply pass it by. It is knocking at the door of our hearts right now. Infinity without Love at the centre is a truly terrifying prospect that should make us quake at the knees. However, with Christ as its driving force, it opens up limitless vistas of possibility beyond anything we could ask or imagine.

And that is what makes the need for a response from us so urgent. The window of opportunity is open now, but it will not remain open forever. One day it will be too late. The doors of heaven will be closed, and there will be 'weeping and gnashing of teeth' outside.

ಶಲ

Behold I stand at the door and knock. If anyone hears my voice and opens the door, I will come in to eat with him, and he with me. (Rev 3:20)

ಶಲ

Without knowing Jesus as our Lord and Saviour, the true purpose of our lives is lost and the gates of eternal destiny are shut to us forever. What we decide about Jesus is the most critical question we will ever face.

Eugene Peterson's translation of Colossians 2, verses 8 and 9 spells it out very clearly:

> ಸಿಂಘ
> 'You don't need a telescope, a microscope, or a horoscope to realize the fullness of Christ, and the emptiness of the universe without him.' (*The Message*).
> ಸಿಂಘ

However big the mountain looming over our lives right now, Jesus is billions and billions and billions and billions times bigger. We have enormous grounds to trust him. He wants to be *our* shepherd and guide in *every* situation.

God has given us a choice the most important choice we can ever make. We can either receive Jesus as our Saviour or reject him. Whatever choice we make has eternal consequences.

If your heart is beating as you read this, please do not hesitate the pray the prayer below with all your heart. All of heaven is awaiting your decision!

ಸಿಂಘ

Lord Jesus,
Without you I realise I am lost for eternity;
I need you as my Saviour to take away my sin.
Thank you that you loved me so much
you were willing to die in my place.
Thank you for bearing my guilt in your own body on the cross.
Please cleanse me from all my sin
and come into my life as my Saviour, Lord and King.
I surrender myself completely to you now,
and ask you to flood my whole being with your everlasting presence.
Take me as I am, Lord, that I may be yours alone for evermore.
Amen.

ಸಿಂಘ

If you have prayed through these words from the depths of your being, and offered your life to Jesus unconditionally, you need be in no doubt that God has heard you! Let his Spirit transform you and give you a new hope and purpose for living.

We can trust completely in these words of the Lord Jesus: 'Anyone who comes to me I will *never* cast away'. May God bless you in every conceivable way, and may you grow each day in deeper and deeper love for Him.

ENDNOTES

1. See R. A. McGough, the BibleWheel.com. Although the author has since repudiated many of his findings, his initial insights are still worthy of study.

2. https://www.edge.org/conversation/lawrence_m_krauss-the-energy-of-empty-space-that-isnt-zero

3. David Pawson, *Unlocking the Bible* (London: Collins, 2003), p. 497-498.

4. Pawson, *Unlocking the Bible*, p. 177.

5. Alan Segal, *Two Powers in Heaven: Early Rabbinic Reports about Christianity and Gnosticism* (Leiden: Brill, 1977), p. 42.

6. https://www.livescience.com/2493-mind-limit-4.html

7. https://www.thenakedscientists.com/articles/science-news/bees-can-count-4

8. Strictly speaking, there is no generally accepted scientific basis for the identification of seven colours in a rainbow. Isaac Newton, who introduced the idea, may himself have been influenced by Biblical data on this matter (compare verses 3 and 5 of Revelation Chapter 4), as well as by the arrangement of musical notes in a scale. A possible science-based argument for the sevenfold division of a rainbow can however be found at https://www.bbvaopenmind.com/en/science/physics/why-does-the-rainbow-have-7-colors/.

9. While there can be little doubt that two of the figures are angels (see Genesis 19:1), it can be strongly argued that this was a *representation* of the Trinity. Augustine seemed convinced of this (*On the Trinity*, Book 2, Chapter 10), and the Jewish writer Philo seems to go even further (see page 75). It is otherwise difficult to see why 'the LORD' (18:1) should be described as appearing as 'three men' (18:2), a mode of appearance unrepeated elsewhere in scripture. See also the comments on page 72 regarding the use of pronouns in the Hebrew text.

10. https://cloud.google.com/blog/products/compute/calculating-100-trillion-digits-of-pi-on-google-cloud

11. There is some dispute as to whether Lord Kelvin actually made this remark. It may actually be a paraphrase of an earlier comment by the American physicist Albert A. Michelson.

12. David Brewster, *Memoirs of the Life, Writings, and Discoveries of Sir Isaac Newton*, vol. 2 (Edinburgh: 1855), p. 407-408. Again, there is some dispute about whether these are actually Newton's own words: they may simply be a verbatim record of remarks he made.

13. Letter to physicist Max Born on 3 March 1947.

14. http://www.astro.utu.fi/~cflynn/sand.html

15. http://www.esa.int/Our_Activities/Space_Science/Herschel/How_many_stars_are_there_in_the_Universe.

16. James Jeans, *The Mysterious Universe*, Cambridge University Press (1930), p.3.

17. René Descartes, *Pensées* (1670, ed. L. Brunschvieg, 1909) section. 2, no. 206.

18. https://www.sciencefocus.com/science/animal-time-perception/

19. Wayne Grudem, abridged by Jeff Purswell, *Bible Doctrine: Essential teachings of the Christian Faith* (Leicester: IVP, 1999), p. 77.

PICTURE ACKNOWLEDGEMENTS

Page 2: https://thefibonaccisequence.weebly.com/index.html, created by Eric Keller

Page 12: Circular Rainbow in Thailand:
https://i.pinimg.com/originals/7e/d1/bb/7ed1bb4ebec7efc13daa53f3b8b542aa.jpg

Page 12: Rainbow over Victoria Falls https://i2-prod.mirror.co.uk/incoming/article1566933.ece

Page 14 and 80: Bible Wheel by R.A McGough at BibleWheel.com

Page 51 By Christina Kekka from Athens, Greece. Light correction by Basile Morin - this file was derived from: Gregory of Nazianzus (4919335562).jpg

Page 51: Font at St Martin's: Andrewrabbott - Own work

Page 65: Monarch Butterfly Doug Wechsler/Minden pictures

Page 71: Menorah https://hoshanarabbah.org/blog/wp-content/uploads/2019/06/Menorah-AdobeStock_57218762-2-1024x1024.jpeg

Page 97 Ricardo André Frantz (User:Tetraktys) - taken by Ricardo André Frantz

Page 110: Map by Tataryn - Own work

Page 147: Photo by Enric Moreu on UnSplash

Page 152: Window from Abbey of St. Denis Photograph by T. Taylor

Page 152: Window from Basilica of Santa Maria in l'Aquila - By Aquilanus - Own work

Page 157: Salt crystal photograph (left) - Rob Lavinsky, iRocks.com

Page 157: Salt crystal photograph (right) - Hans-Joachim Engelhardt - Own work,

Page 157: Tympanum from St. Pierre - Photo by Nick Thompson

Page 161: MJ Cush - Own work by uploader, PBS NOVA, Fermilab, Office of Science, United States Department of Energy, Particle Data Group, Public Domain.

Page 192: St Steven's Basilica, Budapest, taken by Carlos Delgado

Page 197: Created by Wolfgang Beyer with the program Ultra Fractal 3. - Own work

Page 198: Sark photograph By Phillip Capper - Sark, Channel Islands, 17 September 2005.

Page 214: The Fraser spiral illusion, named for Sir James Fraser who discovered it in 1908. Mysid - Self-made in Inkscape; based on en:Image:Frasers.gif.

Page 220: Crab Nebula
NASA, ESA, J. Hester and A. Loll (Arizona State University)

Page 220: Veil Nebula: ESA/Hubble & NASA, Z. Levay

ABOUT THE AUTHOR

David Lambourn studied at Bristol University and Churchill College, Cambridge. His other publications include *But is he God?*, a study of the deity of Christ published by Authentic Media in 2014 with commendations from George Carey and R.T. Kendall, *The Forgotten Bride*, an exploration of God's purposes for the Jewish people, and *Babel versus Bible: the Battle for the Heart of Mankind*, which investigates the fault-line between two parallel kingdoms running from Genesis to Revelation. He is a freelance teacher and writer and is a member of Hope Community Church, Basingstoke.

Printed in Great Britain
by Amazon